Aunt Flossie
Uncle Jerry

MARKET BEATERS

What happened to
this guy? How did
he get so gray?

ART COLLINS

My prayers and best
wishes are with you
always.
(Ditto
for
Pat
and
Maggi.)

Traders Press, Inc.®
PO Box 6206
Greenville, SC 29606

Serving Traders since 1975
http://www.traderspress.com

Copyright© June 2004 by Art Collins

Published by Traders Press, Inc.®

All rights reserved. Printed in the United States of America. No part of this publication may be reproduced, stored in a retrieval system, or transmitted, in any form or by any means, electronic, mechanical, photocopying, recording, or otherwise, without the prior written permission of the publisher.

ISBN: 0-934380-95-3

This publication is designed to provide accurate and authoritative information with regard to the subject matter covered. It is sold with the understanding that the publisher is not engaged in rendering legal, accounting, or other professional advice. If legal advice or other expert assistance is required, the services of a competent professional person should be sought.

Editing by: Roger Reimer
&
Teresa Darty Alligood
Layout and Cover Design by: Teresa Alligood
Traders Press, Inc.®

Traders Press, Inc.®
PO Box 6206
Greenville, SC 29606

Books and Gifts
for Investors and Traders

With love,
To Pat and Maggie.
My sanctuaries amidst
the uncertainties.

Yes, they spelled maggi
wrong - one of 2 typos
I've found so far.

ACKNOWLEDGEMENTS

Thanks to my publisher, Edward Dobson, who deserves his sterling reputation.

To Teresa Alligood, a great editor and fun person to know.

Thanks to my parents, Noman and Norma, and my sister Kimberly Kline, for their support.

To my band, the Cleaning Ladys, for keeping me off the street at least one night every week or two. (Check them out www.cleaningladys.com)

Thanks to Landis Holdorf and Tom Schlosser, for your market insights (correct and otherwise), and for your willingness to break up my otherwise monotonous trading-writing isolation.

To Jack Schwager, who had no reason to assist me, but graciously supplied contacts anyway.

Finally, thanks to all 14 participants of my book. You went out of your way for me, over and above your fine interviews.

TABLE OF CONTENTS

**BASIC TERMINOLOGY OF MECHANICAL
SYSTEM TRADING**

Introduction 1
What is A Mechanical System?

A mechanical trading system is a methodology where every decision is determined mathematically. Sometimes the program can be automated, and sometimes the trader still enters all of the entry and exit orders, but all actions stem from research that uncovered a positive expectancy in past performance data. If the system was devised correctly, (and that's one of the big rubs, as the experts to follow will explain), then the idea becomes, follow the plan as mandated because the future figures to play out something like the past.

This approach solves many problems. It also opens several cans of worms that can only be fully appreciated as one lives through the actual wins and losses. Any system is going to experience drawdown periods; i.e. times when account equity is decreasing. There is no magical way to achieve nothing but winning trades. Sometimes even good, highly profitable systems will rack up many net losses over a distressingly long period of time. On such occasions, the trader may actually begin doubting the validity of the system. Scrupulous research may have produced a very encouraging performance table, but sometimes, faulty analysis or mere chance will do the same thing.

Was it just a fluky data run that created the impressive blueprint? Sometimes mistakes or omissions can loom large. Perhaps the five historic years that you analyzed represented nothing but a raging bull market, and you're about to find out how much of a mirror-image anti-system you get once the bear or stagnant market hits. Maybe you have an artist's eye for detail, but unfortunately, all you've painted is a perfect portrait of the past.

There are no definitive answers in the mechanical research universe— no undeniable blueprint. It's not like assembling a car engine, where someone could impart to you exactly which parts go where. It's not like a diet, in which if you took in the exact calories as mandated with no cheating, your body would not be able to avoid shedding pounds.

i

Even if one had trustworthy mentors, the nature of the mechanical beast is to not heed that which can't be demonstrated in a personal fashion. System developers tend to work alone, or within a closely regulated proprietary team. They won't blindly accept what someone else developed. Again, a main idea of the approach is to thoroughly understand what you're doing and why, based on the cold numbers in front of you. This will give you your best chance of staying fortified—of maintaining the faith necessary for profitability.

A key to this is consistency. You must take all signals. You must not pick and choose. Your approach must be steadfast and unshakeable, even when the signal seems horribly wrong. (*Especially* when the signal seems horribly wrong)! Many people affirm an interesting thing about investing psychology—the trades we fear the most are the ones that tend to be the biggest winners. The trouble source will be the moves we figure to breeze through.

There are all kinds of other psychological glitches that trading can precipitate. That's another key to mechanical methodology. Most people, (except for a very few instinctually blessed) will sabotage their trading—sometimes in spectacular fashion. System trading removes the human element with its two attendant components—fear and greed. Systems don't care if you're buying too high or selling too low. They don't care if you're afraid because this thing hasn't worked in the last half dozen attempts. Systems won't plunge, and systems won't flinch. Only the person behind them can stumble in such a fashion. Like the dieter with his diet, the whole key is *following* the thing. If nothing outside of 'x' contaminates your mix, nothing outside of 'x' can spit back at you.

Despite the less-than-definitive nature of mechanical research, there are both prudent and foolhardy approaches to it. It is certainly possible to get very good at this art (or is it a science?...or both?—that's one of the questions I seemed to keep re-asking). It's also possible to engage in self-deception and wish fulfillment. Hopefully, this book will nudge you in the right direction.

INTRODUCTION 2
"MAKE A THOUSAND DOLLARS A DAY"
—A SYSTEM CHALLENGE.

They present it so casually. "You can make a thousand dollars a day!" I hear it all the time. "I trade small. I don't get greedy. I'm happy making a thousand dollars a day." And that sounds great to me. I would like to trade modestly—to not be greedy—to settle for finite yet consistent profits. Terrific. Tell me—show me how. Better yet, direct me to it in my data; it's always better for system traders to discover something for themselves from the ground floor up.

That's where the great divide between mechanical and gut traders really manifests itself. "Stop nitpicking!" cry the armchair philosophers—you don't need your data field for this one! Pick your spot, run up your target amount and grab it! Take the rest of the day off.

A thousand dollars a day. Simple. There's only one problem with the thousand dollars a day idea. To average a thousand, you obviously have to be shooting for a somewhat higher best-case return. If you quit at 9'oclock to go to the golf course every day that you're up a grand, you're going to average less profit per day as the inevitable losing days hit.

So the question becomes, are these people really telling me that they're making $500, $300 or $200 a day overall? Or are they, on the other hand, saying that they're actually shooting for $1500 or $2000 a day in order to average $1000? No and no, apparently. The touters are maintaining they are making $1000 a day, while at the same time pulling up stakes just after hitting $1000.

Consistent with the disinclination they have toward viewing all trades together as a conceptual whole, discretionary traders don't regard the runaway losing day as a threat to the overall thousand-a-day performance because...because...I'm not exactly sure why 'because.' The little gray fudging area seems to vary from trader to trader, although in general, their lack of concern about the issue seems to dovetail with their belief that bad situations can be recognized and dealt with quickly. Similarly, especially good ones can be milked a little here and there. I think what the advocates are saying is, you go for the thousand but you will have some opportunities to ride it for a little extra. On the day where the thousand profit isn't possible, you just monitor closely to make sure the day doesn't get away from you.

And maybe that doesn't seem unreasonable. Some people are blessed with intangible abilities. You ask them why they abruptly changed their mind about a trade, and they'll say something like "it was obviously about to turn."

Obvious to whom? Certainly not to the majority of traders. A common gateway into the mechanical trading world is one of survival; the average person cannot succeed in markets by relying on his or her judgment. Fact: Trading is overwhelmingly at odds with human nature. Many very prominent people in this book concur with that.

I approach the thousand-a-day issue mathematically. There are several theoretical pathways out there, which, if doable, would assuredly produce a thousand dollars a day. Some examples:
1. In a five-day week, make $3000 one day, make $1500-a-day for two days, and lose $500 a day for the remaining two. (Bigger and more plentiful winning days than losers).
2. In a five-day week, make $2000 a day for four days and lose $3000 on one. (Smaller wins, but more of them).
3. Plus $9000 one day, minus $1000 for each of the remaining four days. (Bigger profit on less wins).

The same thought strikes me every time I churn through this series of examples. None of the scenarios appear likely. Could you count on having one runaway day every week worth nine times the normal return? (3). Are you likely to come up with anything that makes money four out of five days? (2).

We can maybe get it a little more realistic.
4. Plus $2500, plus $2500, plus $2000, minus $1500, minus $500.

Not quite so outlandish perhaps, although it still says that we need both bigger wins and more of them to pull it off. This is somewhat troubling.

Maybe we can blow up all the numbers so that the thousand becomes incidental by comparison.
   5. Make $11,000 each day for two days, lose $8000 each day for two days, lose $1000 on the last day.

Then, of course, you're faced with the reality of generating such large returns. Again, there are finite possibilities available.
   1. Step up your trading size—many more contracts.
   2. Invent a super system that swings widely in the course of a day. How far we can tweak that, of course, is going to be determined by how much the market offers you between the highs and lows of its given swings. My bet is it's going to turn out to be less than we think.

We keep pushing up against an invisible yet insistent wall. So much of what we wish to be true just doesn't pan out, which is typical of what you find in the world of research. Questions, problems, logistical realities...

Happily, some favorable physical market characteristics do exit. Momentum does persist, for example, validating even the most basic systems. On a daily chart, you can buy the highest high and short sell the lowest low of the last x number of days and produce a profit in most markets. Twenty day, 40 day—all kinds of numbers will work for "x".

This may produce drawdowns bigger than most individuals can stomach, (barrier) and overnight exposure (another barrier). People compensate by going into other realms—intra-day trading, for example. No overnight gap risks. But then you're dealing with much smaller trading arcs. The slippage and commission you can expect on every trade becomes a much bigger percentage of your return per trade. One hundred dollars per trade is regarded as a reasonable projected penalty in most cases. That's two-fifths of a full-sized S&P point or just over three bond ticks. The potential profit range might shrink from 150 ticks to 24 between daily and intra-day, but again, your costs of trading won't—they will remain constant. If there's not enough give in a market to overcome the edges—well, too bad. That's what we're stuck with.

Obstacles—again the omni-present challenge of mechanical research. You can always compensate for one problem area, but generally another problem is created. It's like trying to work a Rubik's cube.

Obviously, somebody is making a thousand dollars a day. Somebody's making many times that—a thousand a day isn't really the issue. What is really being ballyhooed here is, let's make a *smooth, consistent* thousand dollars a day.

To which every technician might well say "amen." This is well-traveled terrain for the mechanical researcher. Impressive total net return figures are mere piece of the total mechanical puzzle. Just as important is the evenness of the profit distribution.

As system traders, we're all looking for smoother equity curves. We've all thought of consistently getting on base by bunting. Unlike other traders, though, if we can't confirm it, we're not going to proclaim it to be a done deal.

Mechanical trading is the one approach that determines what is actually real and what isn't. That presents a two-edged sword. On the one hand, to implement it, you have to be ready to jettison so many feel-good axioms and widely held beliefs that don't work. Suddenly, you're accountable. You can determine, in cold black and white numbers, why you can't afford to keep going down a comfortable familiar pathway that research proves to be a dead end. You can no longer cling to those half-baked notions that you cannot quantify.

Conversely, through mechanical trading, you can determine with near certainty what a winning course is. You can know that, given a big enough account, given a willingness to endure drawdowns that you've actually accounted for in theory, given that you've set up your program correctly—you can now trade without fear or greed. You can trade without your guts providing the fuel—you can avoid panic, despair, and burnout. Given the proper setup, you can theoretically do so without enduring the usual costly learning curve.

I doubt that the thousand dollars a day scenario will ever be realized as it is commonly fantasized. By that I mean people imagine trading one system in one market with a small startup and that such nuisances as changing markets won't diminish the ample returns. I indulge in this whimsy, too, lest anyone think I'm being condescending here.

I will say, though, that my years of research experience have made me better at anticipating what is and isn't going to be doable. I think the perfect thousand-a-day machine is not, although I'm sure other individuals have gotten closer to the ideal than I have.

But maybe we can also gain some ground. To do so, I think we'll have to concede the following.

1. The necessity of a very large trading account. (Many, many multiples of the projected
    daily bounty).

2. A cooperative market—liquid and volatile.

3. A de-emphasis of the "smooth, consistent" qualifier. Chances are, the pathway will be irregular, rocky and at times, harrowing.

Again, there are no free rides once the pipedreams give way to cold, hard number crunching.

ROBERT PARDO

"THE BASIC GOAL OF EVERYBODY TRADING FUTURES SHOULD
BE TO MAKE THE MOST AMOUNT OF MONEY WITH THE
LEAST AMOUNT OF RISK."

As the author of "Design, Testing and Optimization of Trading Systems," *Robert Pardo has written one of the foremost expositions on how to realistically approach mechanical system development. He helped pioneer many early commercial system testing programs including Swing Trader—the first software to enable the construction and testing of customized trading models, and Advanced Trader, which incorporated graphic representation. His burgeoning system and software reputation led to money management positions for large traders and corporate firms including Goldman Sachs and Daiwa Securities of Japan.*

For both companies, Robert developed proprietary in-house trading platforms that featured significantly broader applications than today's popular commercial programs. Via their specialized features and in-depth allocation capabilities, Robert and his assistants were able to create trading models that exceeded all initial expectations.

One of the Daiwa projects led Robert and his team to assist in the development of what is now known as the Chase Physical Commodity Index. Like its competitor, the Goldman Sachs Physical Commodity Index, the Chase Index tracks a basket of futures markets the way the S&P Index keys off given stocks.

1

Robert has also endured some disappointing business developments in his career. Notably, Daiwa had an abrupt management change just as he was preparing to become involved in managing proprietary money. This may be part of the reason that in recent years, he has backed away from writing software for other individuals and institutions.

"Now if I do anything for anybody, it's more the testing of individual ideas," he said. "It would not be of any real interest to me to have someone come up and say 'build me a trading system.' If I build an original system that works, why would I want to sell it to someone? I'd just use it for my own trading."

This wouldn't necessarily preclude bringing others along for the ride, however. Robert has recently been managing money under Pardo Capital Limited. It has been documented in **Futures Magazine** *and* **The Barclay Managed Funds Report** *as having a return in excess of 300 percent since its June 1999 inception. It was listed six times as one of the yearly top five performers in* **Futures Magazine**, *attaining the number one spot in 2001.*

The interview took place in Robert's Kenilworth, Illinois home. One obvious facet of the conversation was how uninterrupted it was by market activity. There were no trading screens or other market paraphernalia anywhere in sight. If they existed elsewhere on the premises, Robert was not anxious about checking up on them or his trading progress. He had the serenity of one possessed of total faith in his system's ability to hum along just fine without him.

GIVE US THE SIMPLE ANSWER - HOW DOES ONE MAKE MONEY TRADING?

If you're going to get involved with this business, you've really got to do your homework. You've got to realize that a lot of really smart people have spent a lot of money and time on it. It doesn't mean that you have to be smarter or better. It just means you have to find something that you know works—something you're comfortable with. Once you have that, you're fine.

Anyone who makes money in this business has got some angle, some niche. You have to find your niche, one that will survive and work for you. Systems are a great way to do that.

HOW DID YOU ARRIVE AT THAT CONCLUSION?

It may sound odd considering that I trade for a living, but I'm rather risk-averse. I don't take unnecessary risks. I take calculated risks. I can afford the risks that I take.

I have seen the whole gamut of traders. I have had clients who have done extremely well trading on the floor. I started out working for guys who made millions trading cattle. I had seen traders driving the nice cars with the big houses, so I knew, yeah, somebody does it. Then I saw a lot of people trading marginally and they'd make a little bit, lose a little, and I saw a lot of guys who just lost. So I asked, "How does this work?" A lot of smart people lose money trading futures, and I decided that I wasn't going to be one of them. I was determined to be in this for the long haul, not for two or three years. I was not interested in going into something half-baked.

When I first started getting into systems, I was persistent, objective and analytical. I've always been willing to say what it is that I do know, and what it is that I don't know. If somebody said to me, "This will work." I'd say, "Well, *why* will it work? What's the proof?"

3

A thoroughly researched trading system will tell you *that* something works, where it works, when it works, how it works, what your rate of return is, and what your risk is, among other things. It allows you to trade a bunch of markets simultaneously, which wouldn't be possible if you had to analyze them manually and in real-time. Once a trading system has been perfected, it's really no work to trade it. It strikes me as the lazy man's solution to a hard problem. It can quantify how much money you need to trade with, and what to expect in the future. To a risk-averse person, that's all very appealing.

HOW EASY WAS IT FOR YOU TO GET INTO THE ACTUAL MECHANICS OF PROGRAMMING?

Even in the early days, I could use BASIC. I had the elements that would read the data, write the reports and analyze the trades. I could type in a new trading idea in a couple of hours and test it on a bunch of markets on an Apple II. I figured if you could do that, why *wouldn't* you do it? Why wouldn't you want to know if a trading idea is going to work?

IT SEEMS SO LOGICAL, AND YET PEOPLE ARE SO RESISTANT TO THE CONCEPT. THEY AVOID DOING THE TESTING WORK AT ALL OR THEY DO IT IN INCOMPLETE OR FOOLHARDY WAYS.

I had a customer in the early 1980s who had my software and who had a system he thought was brilliant. I include some of this dialogue in my book where I have a fictitious dialogue of the programmer talking to the trader. He told me the idea as best he could and I asked him all the questions that would ensure it was working as he said it was supposed to work; that it was consistent and there were no errors. And it just lost money in all these markets.

So what did he do? He got really angry and said "You must be doing something wrong!" So I said, "OK, maybe I did" and so we went over it again with a fine-toothed comb two or three times. It was what he said it was supposed to be, but it just didn't make money.

They call this sort of thing cherry picking now. So many people, when they're looking at an idea by hand will say, "Oh, it worked here, it worked here, it worked there, and boy, did it work great!" They ignore the fact that it had seven losers before this big win, and three more losers before that big win. They may be small, but they do add up. They need to be included in the equation.

WHAT OTHER BAD BEHAVIORS DO PEOPLE TEND TO BRING TO THE TABLE?

A lot of people come to trading because they're interested in gambling or the excitement. They come for all the wrong reasons, and then they lose money.

They're unprepared and unrealistic. They think trading is something they can just jump into. (W.D.) Gann had a great statement in one of his many books. He said, "A doctor goes to school for four years, then he's an intern for four more years. A lawyer goes to college and then four more years. Why does somebody think that just because they have $10,000, they're an expert in trading commodities?"

IT SEEMS THAT MANY PEOPLE LOOK TO FUTURES AS A WAY OF PROPELLING THEMSELVES QUICKLY INTO A SIGNIFICANTLY HIGHER FINANCIAL ECHELON, WHICH IS SELDOM POSSIBLE. WHAT IS A REALISTIC SCENARIO FOR SOMEONE THAT HOPES TO MAKE $50,000 A YEAR? HOW MUCH DO THEY NEED FOR START-UP GIVEN WHAT KIND OF RETURN RATE, ETC.?

If you had a decent system and you wanted to make 50 grand a year, you probably need to trade with between 250 and 500 thousand dollars. If you're going to make 10 percent a year, you're doing pretty good. Fifty thousand dollars off $250,000 is 20 percent a year. My compound rate of return for the last three years is 40 percent, which makes me the fourth highest performing advisor for the past three years.

People hear stories about a floor trader who makes $300,000 a year trading with maybe $100,000. They figure, "Well, if he can do it, so can I." It's not the same thing. Floor traders can leverage their clearinghouses in a way that isn't possible for the average person trading as an outside retail customer.

I have a friend who does marketing for the software application, *Advanced GET*. He teaches classes in how to use the program, and he's a good trader in his own right. He says guys are trading with $10,000 and they want to make $50,000 a year. Well who wouldn't? You'd have to be unbelievably good and probably pretty lucky, too. I suspect most professional traders would just laugh at the notion. The kind of skills required to make that kind of return are far in excess of what it takes just to make respectable money trading futures.

Anyone trading futures should have a realistic expectation of what they can make. You need to make sure that the trading capital you're going to trade with is adequate to handle the most extreme risk that may and eventually will come your way.

PLEASE GIVE US A ROUGH IDEA OF WHAT YOUR PROGRAM IS AND HOW IT TRADES.

It's similar to the volatility breakout and range breakout ideas, but it's used and formulated in a unique way. Then, we have a proprietary weighting mechanism that determines how much trading capital should be allocated to each market. It's designed so that our chances of losing 20 percent in a month are one in one hundred. That's all done with statistics.

IS YOUR APPROACH TOTALLY MECHANICAL?

Yes. The only thing that's not mechanical is when we do the re-optimization each year; there's human evaluation of the results, which is not done mechanically.

I do this in conjunction with Dunn Capital Management, one of the top three CTA's in the world. They manage about 1.5 billion dollars. At this point in time, I'm managing their money and some of their customers' money. There's an article in *Futures Magazine* describing how they've cultivated strategic alliances with other CTA's and I'm one of them.

ARE YOU DOING THE PROGRAMMING YOURSELF NOW OR DO YOU HAVE PARTNERS?

It depends on what stage I'm at. When I get an idea, I used to work it up in my own program called Advanced Trader, or I'd use other commercially available programs. First, I want to see that it's actually doing technically what I expect it to do.

I almost always prototype things in the S&P market, because I like it better than any other market. This is good and bad. It's good because if I get a model that trades the S&P well, that's fine with me. Because the S&P is so volatile and dynamic in its own right and swings so much, though, what works there may not work in other markets. That's the downside, but that's the way I tend to do it.

Initially, I'll look at how the idea performs in a small sample. If I am observing something that's supposed to be trading every couple of days, I would expect the S&P model to trade every couple of days and make a certain amount of money. If it trades every couple of days and does not make anywhere near what I expected it to make, I'll look to see where the biggest wins and biggest losses occurred to see what those were about.

I have a "C" programmer that I've just re-hired. For the more complex stuff, I go to him or another guy who's done stuff for me over the years. When we get to the stage where we're selecting our portfolio and the portfolio weightings, Dunn will code it up. They actually do the trade management. They'll do the testing in a somewhat different way than the way I test. Then, they code it up for real-time monitoring in their own proprietary system.

HOW DO PEOPLE MISUSE OPTIMIZATION?

A lot of people will say, "Let's try some moving average idea and optimize to see what we come up with." They may optimize and find a few models that look really good and completely ignore the fact that most of the rest look pretty bad. I don't consider optimization to be the way to find if a model is good. I won't optimize a model looking to improve its performance unless its performance is pretty decent within what I intuitively consider to be a worthwhile set of parameters to begin with.

DO YOUR ULTIMATE SYSTEMS TEND TO APPROACH ALL MARKETS THE SAME WAY?

It's the same system for every market, but there are different parameters for different markets and there are different weights for each market based on risk. The basic goal of everybody trading futures should be to make the most amount of money with the least amount of risk. It may sound easy, but that's why we go through this procedure of weighting markets. It's so we can achieve optimal returns. In other words, bet the most we possibly can with what we consider to be a safe level of risk.

PLEASE EXPAND ON THE FUNCTION OF WEIGHTING MARKETS IN A PORTFOLIO.

We determine how much to allocate to different markets based on their volatility. We also look at how much to commit to each model based on its risk characteristics.

You can have a good system and still lose money if you don't know how to trade it with the appropriate amount of capital. The minimum thing you have to do with money management is make sure that you don't overtrade. Be sure that you have enough money to weather the storm. The best thing you can do is figure out the ways to leverage your money to the maximum degree and still have enough to survive the worst market downturns.

One of the really important things about evaluating weightings and risk is that it is your prime determinate of how much money you need to trade a system. Most amateurs, and even some professionals, don't do that correctly. One of the most common failings of the amateur is that they way overtrade. They take on positions that are way beyond what they can comfortably afford. It's fine as long as you're winning, but if you get one of those second or third standard deviation losers, then you're weighted way up and just looking to get wiped out. It happens a lot.

It's probably the most common reason why people lose money when trading commodities. Think about it. If you buy or sell off the flip of a coin and you know how to manage your risk and your profit, you should be able to make something. I have a former client who had determined, prior to starting with a system, that he would make some money even with a random trade selection. He called it a money management system—I'm not sure that's what I would call it.

At any rate, you have to ask yourself why people lose so much money trading futures and stocks when by random selection, you should be able to get a fairly even mix of wins and losses. Most people don't ask that question, but it's a good question to ask.

WHAT MARKETS DOES YOUR FUND INCLUDE?

We trade pretty much everything. We trade bonds all around the world...in Asia, Australia, Europe, Britain and the U.S. We trade short and long-term interest rates, stock indexes in Japan, Germany, Hong Kong, Britain and the U.S. Also currencies, some metals. Most of the energy markets in both London and the U.S. We trade some of the "exotics" such as coffee and sugar. This year, we've added meats, beans and corn to our portfolio.

We review our portfolio once a year. We look for certain characteristics of liquidity and volatility over a large universe of markets. If a market is not performing according to our minimal requirements, we don't trade it. We'll add it to or remove it from the portfolio accordingly.

The core of our portfolio is always the financials. They've traditionally been the big markets and I'm sure will continue to be so because there's so many of them and they have such excellent liquidity.

We diversify in terms of systems, markets and timeframes. When all my models are lined up in the same direction, the likelihood that I'll make a lot of money is very high. When they're not, I'm slowly liquidating one side and entering another. I'm not really getting hurt. Right now, for example, there's a lack of clarity as to what direction the markets are going to take. I'm long and short bonds, long and short stock indexes, and I have mixed positions in energy. With those kinds of mixed positions, I'm really almost spread trading. When they resume lining up in the same direction, I'll figure to have winners. That's the advantage of trading a portfolio with different time frames in different types of correlated and inversely correlated markets.

SOMETIMES, WHEN YOU HAVE EXTRAORDINARY WORLD EVENTS, THE MARKETS MOVE IN LOCKSTEP. A WAR CRISIS SCENARIO, FOR EXAMPLE, USUALLY WON'T AFFECT THE INDEXES WITHOUT ALSO AFFECTING THE BONDS, ENERGIES, CURRENCIES, ETC. IN OTHER WORDS, RATHER THAN BEING DIVERSIFIED AREN'T YOU SOMETIMES JUST PUTTING ON SEVERAL TRADES IN THE SAME DIRECTION?

We reserve the right to liquidate positions if we feel something cataclysmic is occurring. We've traded through some pretty cataclysmic events and we've never chosen to liquidate anything, so I'm not sure what that scenario would actually be.

You can decide that you're going to trade $50,000 in bonds. Or, you can decide to trade with one short-term model, one intermediate model and one long-term model. If you're trading your whole position size on one model you're either going to be right or wrong.

However, if you're trading a short, intermediate and long-term model, it's kind of like you get into a third of your position when the first move starts to happen. If it persists, you get into your second position when the intermediate term kicks in, and if it persists more, your long-term model kicks in.

It's not that we're doing that to build our confidence, because we're very confident that the models work. A lot of expertise went into building them, and they've been very successful. But what it does do is provide another very effective level of diversification. If we just traded one U.S. bond model, our risk would be much higher than trading different bond markets in different time frames all around the world, which is what we do. The models on different time frames on different weightings are what really adapt with a finer granularity to the economic climate. If things really don't move, the models won't kick in as fully in the portfolio.

If volatility were to get progressively smaller and then kind of stayed in the smaller range, the models would adjust their entries based on the existing parameters. It's not an arbitrary attempt to adjust to it. The models adjust because of the way they're designed.

WHAT YOU HAVE IS MORE OR LESS DYNAMICALLY KEYED SOMEHOW—TO EXPANDING-CONTRACTING RANGES, FOR EXAMPLE.

A better way to put it would be the nature of the model is dynamic. It's easy to measure volatility. What's hard to do is to effectively integrate the volatility measurement. Some years back, there was a great deal of interest in what was called 'equity curve trading.' People would keep track of a moving average of their equity curve. If the curve took too much of a dip, they'd stop trading and then they'd wait for something else to tell them it was time to take a signal.

I did a lot of work with that when it first became an area of interest and found that it's hard to integrate an equity curve with a model so that the tempos are in alignment. Generally, what tends to happen if you're trading short-term is a big move, say in the S&P's, could be over in two days. If your equity curve trading has slowed things down to where you don't get a signal, or you don't kick in until it's halfway over, it tends not to be productive.

Similarly, I've found that trying to make decisions on what to trade based on volatility changes tends to get in the way of the models.

With what we have now, I've been willing to sell Swiss francs for the last four or five days, but because it's been so volatile, I need a very big move for that to happen. [Because the volatility widens the entry levels]. It's not trending that much right now, so I'm not in it one way or the other. However, if it stays quiet for four or five more days, the entries will get closer and closer to the market and I'll be more likely to get kicked in. The models trade dynamically because of their design.

HOW DO YOU DIFFERENTIATE A LARGE BUT ACCEPTABLE LOSING STREAK FROM ONE THAT NEGATES YOUR PERCEIVED BOUNDARIES? HAVE YOU EVER HAD ONE GO BEYOND ACCEPTED PARAMETERS?

Yes. The day that the U.S. said, "Diplomacy is dead in the Iraqi situation," we were long bonds everywhere, short stock indexes everywhere, long energy and short the dollar. We had the worst day in our trading history. We just decided that's what happens once in a while. We didn't feel there was anything out of the ordinary.

Here's what I think the primary consideration is. Let's assume that you did everything correctly. You tested on as large a data sample as you had available and came up with your maximum drawdown. Even going way back, a lot of people maintain that you should assume that your maximum drawdown is understated. Assume that it is actually going to be at least twice as bad. Certainly in our S&P models, drawdowns have gotten bigger over time, but then, volatility has also increased. The way to distinguish whether the increase is acceptable is that the current drawdown verses the current volatility should be somewhat proportionate to the original drawdown and the original volatility. If the volatility and drawdown both doubled in size, your profit should also approximately double. If that's what you have, that's OK in my book.

If your profits remain the same, volatility has not really changed, and you suddenly have a drawdown that's twice the size of the original one, it doesn't mean the model has failed, but it does mean you'd better find out why. It's a potential red flag.

DO YOU GIVE EQUAL WEIGHT TO ALL OF YOUR HISTORIC DATA OR DO YOU THINK MORE RECENT MARKET ACTIVITY IS MORE VALID THAN WHAT HAPPENED IN MORE DISTANT HISTORY?

What we've discovered over our years as model builders is that to get optimal performance, you need to know that your model is good overall on the biggest possible sample that exists. But also, you want to pay a little more attention to what's going on in more recent times. Really—who cares what the S&P did in 1983? The volatility is so much higher now than it was then. Still, I personally wouldn't want to see a model that made tons of money in the last two years, but did not make money in the last 14 or 15 years. That wouldn't give me a lot of comfort.

SO YOU'RE KIND OF BRIDGING THE TWO. RECENT PRICE ACTION IS PROBABLY THE MOST RELEVANT, BUT YOU'D STILL LIKE TO SEE THE BIAS HOLD UP TO SOME DEGREE THROUGHOUT THE OBSERVABLE PAST.

Right, it's a fine line.

WOULD YOU ALSO LIKE TO SEE CONFIRMATION IN OTHER MARKETS?

I'm a little bit different than a lot of people on that count. Let's say somebody came to me and said, "I've got a bunch of different models that trade a bunch of different markets, and they're all different, but they're all really great." If I looked at the models and saw they were sound, it wouldn't bother me a great deal that they wouldn't work in other markets. Not as long as I felt they were sound in the market they were designed to trade.

Individual market characteristics do exist. When I consulted for Goldman Sachs, they were—and still are— very big in the energy markets. From this work, I learned there is probably more information available about the fundamentals of oil than any other market— probably more than you could begin to imagine. So if somebody had a model that traded crude oil unbelievably well using information that was unique to crude, it wouldn't bother me as long as I understood the rationale behind the model and knew that it was sound.

I don't actually do that, but I know people at Goldman Sachs who were beginning to work with those kinds of models. They used what I would characterize as technical models built with fundamental data. I think that's a fertile place for exploration.

SO YOU ACKNOWLEDGE THE POSSIBILITY OF EFFECTIVE SYSTEMS KEYING OFF A GIVEN MARKET'S UNIQUE CHARACTERISTICS. BUT AS YOU SAY, YOU ALMOST NEVER WORK WITH SUCH TARGETED IDEAS. GIVEN YOUR MORE UNIVERSAL APPROACH, WHAT SIGNALS RED FLAGS IN YOUR RESEARCH?

Since I know that our models are not based on the characteristics of any particular market, it would not be a good thing in my mind if we tried them on 50 markets and they worked in only five. I expect to see them be effective in all markets and perhaps better in some more than others. I think they do better in some markets rather than others not because of the models, but because the better markets are the ones that are moving. If markets don't move, nobody makes money, except maybe the locals.

GETTING BACK TO THE TOPIC OF YOUR PERIODIC RE-OPTIMIZA-TIONS: DO MARKETS CHANGE THEIR HISTORIC CHARACTERISTICS OVER TIME IN MEANINGFUL WAYS?

Yes, they do change in meaningful and impacting ways. Up until 1990-1992, trading currencies was like picking fish out of a barrel. It was really easy for anyone with a system that was worth anything. Shortly after, there was a big change in the markets and trading currencies became really difficult. If you had tested your model on the last three or four years of data in a couple of currencies, you might think, "Well, this isn't my road to retirement." It's easy to fool yourself. That's why it's important to look at the bigger picture—bigger time frames, more markets.

Around 1980, T-Bills were an incredibly volatile market; a primary source of speculative activity. You had a situation where the prime rate had hit something like 20 or 22 percent and short-term interest rates were even ahead of that.

At one point in time, the business community was saying, "We don't care what prime rate is, just make sure it stays there for six months or a year, so we can do some meaningful planning." The market rallied about a thousand basis points in two or three months with big volatility, yet the biggest pullback the whole time might have been 75 points. It made some people very wealthy very quickly. Years before the classic bull markets in the Nikkei, S&P and NASDAQ, I would consider the rally in T-Bills in this period was probably the mother of all bull markets.

After that rather staggering run-up, the T-Bill market kind of flat-lined. I think it still exists as a futures market, but at some point it stopped trading in a meaningful way. I had a business associate who was a floor trader and order filler during this period. He made a record amount of money during the volatile years, but suddenly he was complaining that he didn't know what to do. I said, "If I were you, I'd go to the S&P pit. I don't know what happened, but the T-Bill market is dead."

SOME SYSTEM TRADERS TRY TO ANTICIPATE THAT IN THEIR MODELS AS WELL, THROUGH VOLATILITY FILTERS AND OTHER DYNAMIC TOOLS. OBVIOUSLY, THEY'RE TRYING TO AVOID THE HUMAN ELEMENT EVEN IN THE STEP OF ASSESSING VIABLE TRADING ENVIRONMENTS. DO YOU REWORK SYSTEMS AS A DIRECT RESPONSE TO CHANGING MARKETS?

With my approach, I re-optimize at periodic intervals anyway, but also, with the way we trade now, that market would be beneath our radar screen for volatility and probably liquidity.

THAT'S WHAT I'M GETTING AT. DOESN'T THE SYSTEM SELF-CORRECT WITHOUT YOU HAVING TO MAKE A DECISION AS TO WHETHER A MARKET HAS GONE DEAD OR BECOME INEFFECTIVE IN SOME WAY?

Actually, we deal with that issue in a number of ways. The systems use volatility as a primary characteristic. If volatility changes and stays changed in meaningful ways, it's going to either increase or decrease the size of the entry point. But also, our second approach is to re-optimize the model every year. If there's been a significant change in volatility in one way or the other, we may change our parameters.

The third way we correct is, we look to see if the market is tradable. We don't care if a market goes like this or like this or like this [traces various bull and bear trends in the air]. We just don't want to see one go like this. [Makes a flat-line gesture]. If it goes flat, there's no economic interest in the market, and you really can't trade it profitably.

Liquidity tends to follow volatility. If you have an illiquid market, you will have very few players. So, our last line of defense is, we'll examine whether there is enough movement in the market to warrant being involved, which is something we'll look at in a number of ways. There's always a limited amount of available money. Is somebody somewhere else offering a better return?

We have enough to trade everything, more or less. We've never been faced with a situation where we didn't have the money to trade the markets that we wanted to trade, though I suppose that's a possibility. But the bottom line is, if Commodity B is marginal, and Commodity A is looking really great, why trade Commodity B when you can trade Commodity A? We use a number of check lines to arrive at that.

One reason the S&P has held so much interest over the years is because it has great volatility and great liquidity. Almost all the stock indexes around the world have similar volatility, but they don't all have the same degree of liquidity.

WHY DO SYSTEMS WORK? WHAT MARKET CHARACTERISTICS DO YOU THINK THEY EXPLOIT?

There's no generic answer to the question, "What characteristics in a market does a system exploit?" because different systems exploit different characteristics. The ultimate reason they work is because they give you a mathematical advantage. A good system by definition has a positive expectancy. A good system will work because it's consistent. It will do the same things day in and day out.

DOES IT HAVE SOMETHING TO DO WITH MARKET INEFFICIENCY?

I've never believed that the markets are efficient, but it kind of comes down to what you mean by efficient. If efficient means that a market is always at the perfect price that it should be at in any particular moment, I don't think that's true. The systems that I use take advantage of volatility and the fact that there are persistent trends in the market.

A system can only work if it catches 'runs,' which is a more meaningful term in the intra-day market. In the larger timeframe, you're looking more at trends.

There are things that occur in intra-day data that you won't see in inter-day data. It's fairly unusual to find five up bars in a row in a daily or weekly chart. It rarely happens, yet it's so very common in intra-day bars.

The trend in a daily bar may be up, down, up, up, down, down. You have a lot of swings. Ultimately, the only way to make money trading is to exploit some kind of trend, regardless of bar size, and to hold onto it long enough to make money overall.

To do this effectively, you have to keep your risk measurably constant in some kind of way. Many people will, if a trade looks good to them, put on too much. They'll risk more than normal in the trade. If they're nervous about it, they'll put on too little even though they can afford a lot more based on risk or volatility.

In a system, risk is uniform and constant. I re-optimize models periodically because conditions and volatility change. You have to adapt to that to get optimal returns. Generally, though, we're risking the same tomorrow that we are risking today. Most people will not only vary their risk a great deal, but they'll get very skittish when they actually get a profit.

WHICH OF COURSE VIOLATES A PRIME TRADING DIRECTIVE: CUT YOUR LOSSES SHORT AND LET YOUR PROFITS RUN.

Exactly. I can give you a story that exemplifies the way the typical amateur trades. Years ago when I was a broker, I had a customer who was a very bright guy. He finished second in mathematics in his country and earned a Ph.D. in chemical engineering. But he was a horrible trader. We had a situation where he'd taken some losses in lumber based on these haphazard risk and reward things that people engage in. Finally, he got a winning trade on. Instead of letting the thing run, he kept on moving the stops virtually every 10 or 15 minutes. He gave the market no room to swing. He had managed to sit it out long enough to let a loser turn into a winner, but he was so anxious about it that he, he squeezed it so hard that he wound up making $200 on it. His previous losses were like $700, $800 and $900.

That's typical of the amateur. They're willing to take more risks than they actually should and when they finally get a winner going, it seems so unusual to them that they don't give it a chance to run.

In futures trading, one of the things that I have found is, in general, you're better off letting your profits run as far as they can even though that can be a little uncomfortable sometimes. In contrast, some people maintain that the best thing you can do is to put up a target order and take uniform profits. I have found that only works if the system is highly accurate. Most systems aren't that accurate.

SO YOU'RE NOT REALLY IN FAVOR OF PROFIT TARGETS?

With the systems I've used over the years, targets have made the models perform less profitably. What you might find is, a model that trades a great deal and is highly accurate could be made more accurate by targets. If you've got a model trading 60 percent profitability and it's a good model, the targets might add 5 to 10 percent to it. So then you're right seven times out of ten, and for a lot of people, that's a big difference. They really like being right that often. But that's another reason people don't trade well. They're more interested in being right than they are in just making money.

I've never really cared about accuracy in a model. A lot of people do, and obviously, the more accurate the better, but I've never made that a primary focus in building a model. The models that my current platform started out with were in the area of 45 to 48 percent accurate. They still made a lot of money because they let profits run and the losses were very manageable.

It's a great irony to me that with no effort to get accuracy, my current models are in the 60 to 65 percent accuracy range.

HAVE YOU ALWAYS TAKEN SUCH A LOGICAL INVESTING APPROACH OR, LIKE MOST OF US, HAVE YOU HAD EXPERIENCES WHERE YOU'VE LEARNED HARD LESSONS THROUGH TRADING IN COUNTER-PRODUCTIVE WAYS?

I once had a customer who traded bonds and options on the floor. We became good friends and I showed him models that I was very comfortable trading in S&P's, bonds, crude, soybeans, and silver. We agreed to pool some money and trade them.

We lasted about a month. In that time period, he insisted on picking the signals he wanted to trade. He knew better than the system.

The long and the short of it was we lost money in the account. I said, "Tony, this is stupid. You're making my systems look bad with your stupid cherry picking. I'm not going to do this anymore."

The models, of course, made a ton of money in that time. They probably would have doubled the account. At that point in time, I didn't know enough to say to him, "You can't do that." I figured he was a successful trader and should know better, but that was not the case.

I saw him a couple years ago and he still makes a comfortable living. He's still kind of playing games with systems though. I'm not saying that no one can enhance a system, because I know some people who, in fact, can and do. But they do it in a systematic way.

THEY DON'T DO IT ACCORDING TO WHAT MAKES THEM FEEL GOOD.

Right. They'll look at a buy signal relative to another indicator and figure the odds will be a little better. It's something they observe. I haven't seen too many people with a 'golden gut.' That's why I was determined that I would have a method that would be sound and do all the things that I wanted it to do. The rest would take care of itself.

CHARLIE WRIGHT

"ONE OF THE INTERESTING THINGS THAT WE FOUND IN OUR
RESEARCH WAS ULTIMATELY, INDICATORS DON'T MATTER."

Charlie Wright is the author of "Trading as a Business," *perhaps the last word on mechanical system trading. The content was derived from seminars that he taught under the same heading on behalf of Omega Research, the creators of TradeStation®. Charlie assisted in the early conceptualization of the program, and personally invented two key components, the Show Me study and the Tick chart. He has actively traded futures since 1982 and stocks since 1974. In the 1980s, he day traded S&P futures as a member of the Chicago Mercantile Exchange.*

In 1999, he co-founded Fall River Capital, a Commodity Trading Advisor, (www.fallrivercapital.com) with Rob Friedl. Starting in August 2000, the fund began trading futures markets with a one hundred percent systematic long-term trend following approach.

"I set out to prove that the principles I taught and wrote about worked in real time," said Charlie. "Today, we're using two programs based on those principles."

Charlie has obviously made his point. In its three-year history, the company's original Global Trends Program has produced 32 percent average annual return with a maximum drawdown of 14.3 percent.

It currently trades 69 markets on a perpetual basis. ("We're always in 69 markets.") The portfolio includes stock index futures, grains, exotic futures such as cocoa and coffee, interest rates, currencies, metals and energy.

I conducted this telephone interview with Charlie one day after the August 14, 2003 Eastern United States blackout. I was still smarting from the aftermath of watching a short e-mini S&P position windfall materialize and then fade to nothing from the news. This opened the door to a conversation in which Charlie— a hard-and-fast system trader—won't often indulge—the potential validity of a spontaneous untested market idea.

As the blackout news was hitting the after-hours e-mini S&P market, causing it to open 10 points lower, I found myself standing in front of the screen with a friend saying "this is a knee-jerk reaction that is going to snap back. I should cover my shorts right now." But I didn't, because I'm a system trader and once you give into that kind of impulse, you're sure to be opening a Pandora's box.

Yeah, what you saw was "the waterfall," which goes back to a problem that I always had when I was teaching day trading. Almost every day trading system I tested over long periods, like three or four years, would break even. It was very difficult for me to find something that I could trade mechanically on a one or a five-minute bar chart that made consistent money over given periods because the market tends to change its personality a little bit. So, what I used to say was, the trick to making money day trading is to have a good system that you follow religiously, and then know when to stop when everything is getting out of line.

And how do you determine that?

I had little tricks. One trick that I would always use was "the waterfall," which is what happened yesterday afternoon. I'd be trading the five-minute bar charts and I'd be short, and suddenly, we'd get this huge run in five or ten minutes where the market dropped a thousand points. I'd look at it and say, "That's a waterfall. I've got to get out."

So, I'd get out and stay out for a day or two, because what happens is, it tends to run too many stops too fast and it freaks everybody out. You can expect choppy action for a day or two, which is why I should take my windfall profits, not trade the system for a day or two, and then re-activate it.

THAT SOUNDS PRETTY GOOD IN THEORY. DOES YOUR RESEARCH SUPPORT IT?

No, it doesn't, and that's the issue with day trading. There were times when I knew I should just take the profit and get out. For instance, when I did the statistical run, I noted that out of 21 trading days, I generally had one big loser, two or three big winners, and the rest were break-evens of plus or minus garbage. There were four probable big days for the month either down or up and the rest were sideways. If I had the run where I made huge money two or three days in a row, I knew that was good for the month. When you run statistics on a system, you know when it gets to be an outlier.

This only applies to day trading, though. I wouldn't recommend any of this to anyone doing longer-term trading.

ARE YOU DAY TRADING NOW?

I wish I were. That's my first love, actually. Rob and I are running the CTA now. Fall River has about a hundred and twenty million under management and we've had consistent growth.

WHY DO YOU PREFER THE FUTURES MARKETS?

Non-correlation. They [futures markets] don't all move together over the long-term. Every once in a while, we'll have a string of days or months where everything correlates, but for the most part over the long-term, different sectors tend to be non-correlated. Ultimately, this lowers your risk. As you mix non-correlated markets that aren't moving together, you tend to increase your efficiency.

SO, A LOT OF YOUR MECHANIZATION PROCESS APPARENTLY CENTERS ON PORTFOLIO ALLOCATION RATHER THAN ON INDIVIDUAL SYSTEMS.

Yes. You work on the correlation of the markets that you're trading in order to control the risk.

AND IS THAT PROCESS TOTALLY MECHANICAL?

Yes, you test. Everything we do involves testing. Everything is fully analyzed from a long-term perspective.

PLEASE EXPAND ON THIS CONCEPT. IS IT POSSIBLE TO COME UP WITH INTEGRATED PERFORMANCE RESULTS THAT ARE GREATER THAN THE SUM OF THE INDIVIDUAL PARTS?

Undoubtedly. Our studies have shown that the more trades you can make, whether it's shortening up your time frame or taking multiple trades over multiple markets, the lower your risk becomes. The goal is to pack in as many trades over a time frame as you can.

The issue is not the return; the issue is the risk-reward. If you're simply going for return, the answer to your question is 'No.' [The results] will probably all morph together and give you some return that's fairly similar. The real question you want to ask yourself is, "Can I, by using multiple systems, lower my drawdown and achieve the same return?" If you were not concerned with drawdown and risk, you could be perfectly happy with a return generated by one system.

If you're just looking at return and you're not worried about drawdown and you're not worried about the risk that you're taking to earn that return, one system is fine. If your testing shows that over time the system is going to make money, why bother with multiple systems?

The real issue with multiple systems is, are the return streams non-correlated and because of the non-correlation, are they lowering your risk? In other words, I may be able to get a 50 percent return with a highest drawdown of 70 percent and I'm comfortable with that. But I may be able to add two or three more systems that can give me that 50 percent return and bring the drawdown down to 40 or 30 percent. That would make me more comfortable still. If you go through a 70 percent drawdown after all, the chances of you quitting are very high.

WHICH TOUCHES ON THE REALITY THAT AN EFFECTIVE SYSTEM ISN'T GOING TO MEAN MUCH IF THE TRADER CAN'T OR WON'T IMPLEMENT IT EXACTLY AS IT HAS BEEN DESIGNED.

Right. Trading is a very negative feedback endeavor because for the most part, we're always in drawdown. We know that is going to be true 70 to 90 percent of the time. If we're almost always in drawdown and those profits come in short spurts, then the issue is how do we psychologically deal with the drawdown? One way we can do that is by adding multiple systems and getting the drawdown to the point where we're not worrying about our survival.

If I'm comfortable with a projected 50 percent return and a 40 percent drawdown and the drawdown does materialize at or near 40 percent, then I am trading my expectations. Where I get into trouble trading is when the actual trading does not meet my expectations. When I anticipate a 40 percent drawdown and suddenly I'm in a 70 percent one, I'm wondering if my system is valid and whether or not I'm going to go broke. If I can trade within the expectations that are determined from historical testing, and nothing has occurred that is out of line with those expectations, then I'm comfortable. I can keep putting on those trades. I can maintain the discipline.

ALLOW ME TO PLAY DEVIL'S ADVOCATE FOR A MOMENT. MY OWN REASON FOR GETTING INTO STRICT MECHANICAL TRADING WAS SELF-PRESERVATION. I COULDN'T DO ANYTHING IN THE WAY OF SPONTANEOUS OR REACTIVE MARKET TRADING AND I THINK THIS IS THE PATHWAY THAT MOST EVENTUAL SYSTEM TRADERS FIND THEMSELVES. AT THE SAME TIME, I RECOGNIZE THAT THERE ARE NON-SYSTEM, REACTIVE TRADERS OUT THERE WHO CAN MAKE FAR MORE MONEY THAN I WITH FAR LESS CAPITALIZATION AND FAR LESS ONGOING RISK. THEY SIMPLY KNOW WHEN A TRADE IS WRONG AND THEY CAN REACT ACCORDINGLY. I'M GRATEFUL THAT I CAN DEVELOP SYSTEMS AND HAVE THE FAITH TO TRADE THEM, BUT AT THE SAME TIME, I SEE IT AS A SORT OF CONSOLATION PRIZE—A SECOND-BEST. CAN YOU COMMENT ON THE LIMITATIONS OF SYS-

TEM TRADING VERSES THE MORE WIDE-OPEN POSSIBILITIES AF-FORDED THE MORE INNATELY GIFTED TRADERS?

In my mind, it depends on what your goals are. The problem I have with discretionary trading is that it totally depends on your judgment and ability to maintain your mental state of mind. If you are just trading for yourself, I think you have a choice as to whether you want to add some judgment and you're not necessarily hurting anyone or putting other people's money at risk. I think you have to look at that issue in the context of, are you solely trading for your own account or are you trading other people's money? There's a difference.

BUT, IF YOU WERE GOING TO ADVISE PEOPLE, WOULD YOU BE IN-CLINED TO TELL THEM THAT IT'S PERFECTLY OK TO LEAVE THAT DISCRETIONARY DOOR OPEN TO ONE DEGREE OR ANOTHER?

My personal view is very solid on that subject. I'm a one hundred percent mechanical trader. I don't want to have my mental state affect my trading. If I have a late night or a bad day, or if I have a cold and take an antihistamine that messes up my mind, I don't want any of that to affect my trading. I come to this with a strictly mechanical bent.

I really want to have a machine that spews out trades. I learned that back when I was in manufacturing. [The Fall River Group, the day-to-day operations of which have since been turned over to Charlie's partner's son]. In manufacturing, we designed a product and we set up an assembly line to manufacture that product. This enabled us to sell it to a wide variety of people who would know exactly what they were getting when they bought the product.

What we wouldn't do is tell the people on the assembly line producing the product that they could be creative and paint it a different color or change the design a little bit depending on how they felt during the day. I've taken that same approach to trading. If I'm talking to a potential investor or even thinking about my personal trading, what I don't want to have to convince myself or somebody else is that

I have particularly astute judgment. I don't want to convince anybody that not only are they paying for a system, but they're also investing in my ability, judgment and trading acumen. I feel much more comfortable showing somebody a track record and, if they request it, a hypothetical track record. I prefer to be able to say, "This is what our research shows and we guarantee you we will put on these trades to the best of our ability. If we do that, there is a likelihood achieving some sort of return. It may or may not equal the historical return, but we think that considering all the data we've analyzed, there is a likelihood that [the projections] should continue over time."

HOW WOULD YOU RATE THE AVERAGE TRADER'S CHANCES OF SUCCESSFULLY APPLYING DISCRETION?

Very slim.

WHY?

In my view, the markets represent human behavior. They represent the sum total of human nature—fear and greed. As the fear and greed exhibits itself in the market, we as human beings tend to watch it and as we do so, it starts to stimulate and impact our human nature. The studies clearly show that our human nature is wrong when it comes to trading because we become more prone to fear and greed than objectivity.

The corollary to that is that the most successful traders are able to trade counter to human nature. If we accept the notion that human nature causes us to lose money and that 95 percent of all discretionary traders lose money over time trading off their human nature, then we can make the leap to make money trading, you have to trade counter to your human nature. It's very difficult to do that on a discretionary basis. It's difficult enough to do it on a mechanical basis, but if you have a mechanical system and have the discipline to trade it when your human nature is screaming, "don't take this trade!" and the discipline to stick with it, it's probably going to be a profitable trade. Anybody who has traded mechanically for a long time has told me that the hardest trades to put on are generally the biggest winners. They go counter to your human nature.

We had an example of that a couple of years ago when interest rates were really low. We had been stopped out of our long bond position. We got a re-entry signal to go long again, and I looked at Rob and he looked at me. He said, "Okay, here it comes, we have a mechanical signal to go long when they are at historically high levels and interest rates are at historically low levels." Had we had our druthers, we would have not put on that trade, but because we are mechanical traders, we put it on. It turned out to be a phenomenally profitable trade because interest rates continued to go down for six more months. We never would have put that trade on had we allowed judgment. That was just another vindication of how mechanical trading, in my view, is the only way to do it long term.

DESCRIBE YOUR PERSONAL EVOLUTION IN ARRIVING AT THAT CONCLUSION.

Actually, it started very early. I read a very simple book with a very simple system using three moving averages. The gist of it was that you never take a short position when all the moving averages are lined up bullish, and vice versa, and by following that, you probably never would get hurt in the long run.

That started me to thinking mechanically. I had tried cycles and choosing the bottoms of cycles and I'd tried understanding Elliott Wave and all of that stuff and I hadn't done very well. When I applied that rule of never going against the three moving averages, I started to get the idea that [consistently profiting through trading] was doable.

That was morphed into my manufacturing background, which said that what I really needed was a machine that spews out trades. If I could test an idea over time and prove that it was profitable, I'd be OK.

What I came to realize was that most trading tended to be trend following in nature. I would maintain that all trading is trend following and that it just depends on your time frame. I developed a core philosophy that one of the ways I could make money in the long-term was to always be in the market—always reversing. It goes back to the contention of Peter Steidlmayer [renowned trader-advisor perhaps best known for his development of the Market Profile] that markets exist to facilitate trade. Because of that facilitation, they ultimately need to trend. If they don't trend, the markets will ultimately die because there won't be any money in them and people will stop trading them.

Then, the leap I made was to have the absolute conviction that eventually a market must trend to draw traders in to make money to survive. If it doesn't, the market will die because traders will go to other markets.

If you make the leap that the market is ultimately going to facilitate trade and trend, then you can take the next leap that you should always be in it. If you're always in and reversing, eventually you will hit that big move that will make back all the money you lost in the choppy markets and enough extra to give you a profit. Once I made that leap of understanding, trading simply became a business problem rather than a trading problem.

HOW MANY TIMES DID YOU HAVE TO BURN YOURSELF BEFORE FULLY INCORPORATING THAT CONVICTION?

Hundreds of times. I tried to put judgment in there and then I'd go through choppy markets and lose faith. I'd lose the conviction that it was ultimately going to trend because the market will do everything it can to get you to trade, lose money, and quit. That's the market's goal—to get your money and get you out.

DOES EVERYTHING YOU'RE CURRENTLY USING INCORPORATE THAT THREE MOVING AVERAGE IDEA?

No. One of the interesting things that we found in our research was that ultimately, indicators don't matter. Whether you use a moving average, an n-day breakout, a momentum entry or the MACD or the RSI or whatever—if you're trend trading, it doesn't amount to a hill of beans which technique you use assuming you're comparing the same time frames.

Let's say that you and I agreed to look at a time increment that we'd extend over a longer period. For example, a 40 day time frame on 70 markets and that we would extend it over 10 years. Our research showed that whether you took a 40 day n-day breakout or a similar time frame moving average crossover, momentum or whatever, the profits were all about the same.

AND I ASSUME THE ENTRY POINTS WERE ROUGHLY SIMILAR AS WELL.

That's precisely right— entry points tend to be around the same level. It you look at the CTA universe and look at trend followers who trade between 30 and 90 days, which is probably the majority of CTA's, everyone gets in at just about the same place and time, plus or minus a week.

So, if there is no edge in the entry—if entries tend to be fairly generic—then where *is* the edge in trading? The ultimate success in getting a trading edge is how you manage the risk—how you do the money management on the back end. It's down to what you do with risk control and position sizing. It has nothing to do with the indicators. The irony is that most people who trade and do research spend most of their time trying to tinker with indicators—better entries. We spend literally 90 percent of our research time on money management and risk control. We cede that we aren't going to be brilliant on entries because we've tested entries and have found that they don't make any difference.

HOW ABOUT TRADING HORIZONS? ARE SOME TIME FRAMES IN-
HERENTLY BETTER THAN OTHERS?

I don't think so. I think it's just a matter of individual choice. In one of our programs, we take three time frames and mix them all together. That gives you a mode of diversification as well; you can do short, intermediate and long-term. Some people trade six time frames, others do three, but many successful traders trade multiple contracts.

In our other program, we basically take a long-term momentum filter and aggressively trade short-term in the direction of the long-term momentum. We're basically saying that we want to have enough conviction that there's the potential of a long-term move and once we arrive at that, we want to trade it short-term in that direction.

INTERESTING APPROACH. IS THERE SOMETHING ABOUT THE
SHORT-TERM THAT YOU PREFER?

It lowers risk. The ultimate issue is that we know that we all make money—traders make money when markets trend for a significant proportion of time relative to their overall time frame. Therefore, if you're day trading off one minute charts, that trend might be 10 or 15 minutes. If you're trading daily charts with longer-term indicators the trend could be three years. But a chart is a chart—it doesn't make any difference. It just depends on your time frame orientation.

The issue becomes how you manage the costs during the choppy periods when the market isn't moving in the way that was designed to capture your profits. So what do you do during the two days that the markets are chopping on five minute bar charts waiting for that one-day trend? How do you lower your costs? Again, the business issue is, while we're waiting for the big move that we have faith is going to come, how do we minimize our costs through the chop? It's a business issue, not a trading issue because we've ceded the entries. We know they don't make any difference. We end up trying to manage our risk during the chop so that we don't have costs high enough during that period that we can't make them plus profit back during the trend.

It's no different than running a manufacturing line. You have fixed costs. You have costs of employees, costs of equipment, costs of electricity. Those costs all have to be in line so that when you ultimately make your product and sell it, you've made enough to cover them all and have profit.

I draw that analogy to markets. The choppy periods are your costs. You have to be able to prove that you can make enough when markets trend to cover all of your business costs plus your drawdown during the chop.

LET'S ASSUME THAT SOMEONE HAS MADE ALL THESE LEAPS AND NOW WANTS TO COME UP WITH A REALISTIC BUSINESS PLAN INVOLVING TRADING FOR A LIVING. WALK US THROUGH WHAT THIS PERSON WILL HAVE TO INCORPORATE, INCLUDING STARTUP COSTS ASSUMING HE NEEDS TO EARN $50,000-A-YEAR TO SURVIVE.

A lot of people tend to be non-realistic about their costs. They tend to look at trading costs and drawdown only and don't look at the costs of their time and the computers and office rent, electricity, and all that. So the first thing you have to do is be realistic.

The second thing you have to be aware of is this: the bane of all businesses—the reason 90 percent of all businesses and all traders fail is that they aren't adequately capitalized. The new trader thinks that they can make a whole pile of money by putting up very little. That has to do with the trading level and how much money you have to invest. I think the mistake most people make is they undercapitalize their trading, and they try to make big money on a small amount. They think that in the trading business, you make a million dollars by putting up ten thousand.

PART OF THAT PROBLEM IS ALL THE TRADING LORE OUT THERE
ABOUT THE EXTRAORDINARY INDIVIDUALS WHO ACTUALLY DID AC-
COMPLISH THAT.

Larry [Williams] did do that, but Larry is a professional trader and
had a very well defined money management scheme to control his
risks. He took ten thousand and ran it up to over a million. He was
very methodical and he wasn't shooting from the hip, saying "I'm
going to take ten and turn it into a million." It was more like "I'm going
to take ten, and I'm going to trade it on systems and I'm going to
manage the money in these pre-determined ways and if the markets
do what I think they're going to do, I can make a lot of money." It's
a different way of thinking that most people don't get.

The other thing is that you have to look at the risk of the back
testing as a proportion of the money that you're trading in your account. When we looked at our trading over time, we thought that
having a goal of making 30 percent per year and trying to keep the
drawdown under 30 percent was a reasonable goal.

AND PRESUMABLY YOU ARRIVED AT THAT BECAUSE THAT'S WHAT
YOUR HISTORIC RESEARCH WAS PROJECTING. BUT ARE THERE AD-
DITIONAL AXIOMS TO PROCESSING WHAT YOUR RESEARCH IS TELL-
ING YOU? FOR EXAMPLE, DO YOU PROJECT AN EVEN LARGER DRAW-
DOWN FIGURE THAN ANYTHING YOU'VE SEEN IN THE PAST?

You always have to underestimate performance in order to stay
sane because we all know that our worst drawdown is ahead of us.
No matter what type of results the testing produced, we always know
that there's going to be a worse drawdown coming up.

We basically say that our benchmark is to keep our drawdown
equal to our average return. If we can produce a 1 to 1 ratio—if we
can say that our target is a 30 percent return per year and we expect
a 30 percent drawdown and our testing shows that we can beat that,
then we're pretty comfortable.

If our testing shows that over 20 or 30 years, we can provide that 30 percent return with a 15 percent drawdown, then we have a lot of room for increased drawdown. So we would say, "OK, let's plan on our worst drawdown probably being double what we've seen." I generally use between one and a half to two as a rule of thumb.

A lot of times, investors will ask us, "At what point would you consider your system has busted?" In other words, at what point would we stop trading? Basically my answer to that is if we get a drawdown that is double what our hypothetical testing shows, I'm getting concerned because I've made some sort of error.

ASIDE FROM AN EVERYDAY DRAWDOWN GOING BEYOND THE PAIL, WHAT DO YOU DO ABOUT THE SUDDEN EXTRAORDINARY MARKET SHOCKS—THE EVENTS THAT WE'VE BEEN SEEING THAT TURN MARKET MOVES INTO HUGE HISTORIC OUTLIERS?

That's an interesting issue and it actually happened at the beginning of this year. [2003]. Between January and February, we had phenomenal run-ups in the energy and interest rate markets in anticipation of the war. In March, every one of those markets retraced what it did in January and February. As mechanical traders, when all the dust settled at the end of March, we were up a little bit, which was great, except that we'd had such a huge run-up and then gave it all back.

So the issue is, what was the right thing to do? Several people—experienced CTA's, old-line traders—de-levered at the end of February. They'd had such a big run-up that they took off half their positions—maybe a little more or less. They said, "Well, I've made so much money, this can't continue."

We didn't. We talked about it and decided not to because we are mechanical traders. We stick to our mechanics.

There was a very interesting debate going on in the industry at that time over just this issue. My answer to why we didn't [lighten up] was, if I de-levered at the end of February, and our drawdown was half of what it was, then I have to go back to my investors and convince them that I'm brilliant, that I could do that every time and that I probably wouldn't make a mistake. Then, I'd have to convince them that they were not only buying my products, but they were buying my ability to discern market anomalies and to de-lever and re-lever accordingly.

IT'S FUNNY HOW CLEAR THAT IS TO ME AND SYSTEMS TRADERS IN GENERAL, BUT HOW OUTSIDERS REGARD SUCH STAYING-THE-COURSE AS UNNECESSARY AND FOOLHARDY. I CAN'T COUNT THE TIMES I'VE HAD TO EXPLAIN TO PEOPLE WHY I'M STILL TRADING MY SYSTEM EVEN THOUGH A WAR OR A GOVERNMENT REPORT IS IMMINENT.

Right. We were getting questioned left and right about what we were going to do, pretty much meaning in what way were we not going to stick with our system. Well, the answer is No—We stick to our system.

Being the eternal system tester, what I did then was say, "OK, let's devise an indicator that shows us events similar to January and February." So I went back into research and I came up with one. It said, "OK, when this indicator gets above this level, then we're going to de-lever."

Then we say, "Boy, this is brilliant! We have this market situation that we can avoid now, and we would have missed the pain of March." We looked back [informally] and noticed other situations where it would have helped. "This is great," we say.

And then we ran the numbers. You put it in the tester and say, "When this indicator hits this level, we're going to de-lever." And it ruined the performance. So, you look at the trades and you look at the de-levering and you realize that while the de-levering worked the last three times the indicator was hit, when you go back further, you see something else entirely. The indicator hit the mark, you de-levered, and the markets continued to go their way for nine months and you gave up a thirty percent profit by de-levering.

We found that this was just another sort of discretionary dead end that, over time, makes no sense. You can always find something that works in the short-term, but when tested over a long enough time, generally we found that with a great number of trades, most things don't work.

WHAT OTHER KINDS OF PROBLEMS ARE INHERENT IN MECHANICAL SYSTEM TRADING?

One of the problems I have always faced in doing mechanical trading is the frequent occurrence of data disparities over the long-term when you're putting together continuous contracts. What I mean by that is, you use one continuous contract in research and then when you start trading real time, you're not using the same data. [You trade specific active contract months as opposed to a theoretical continuous field]. That raises questions as to whether the performance on the real-time data is going to match whatever you tested on your continuous contract.

So, what we did at the outset is, we created our own continuous contract data manager. We used the same data stream for both testing and live trading. We can add today's bar [to the existing all-purpose data block] and take a signal.

We've been able to run our testing platform side-by-side with our real-time trading. We can run correlations to make sure that we are producing the same trades in real time that we did hypothetically. We've been running about a 95 percent correlation and we feel very comfortable with that.

That was a huge issue. The choice of how and when to roll contracts and how to put your continuous contracts together has a bearing on your real-time trading. You have to be careful that you can match the data.

Having said that, the longer our track record has become, the closer it has matched the hypothetical track record. We went back 30 years to 1970 to create all of these contracts. We determined the largest return, the largest drawdown and the Sharpe ratio and all of that stuff. We just finished the first three years on our Global Trends program, which was the first program Fall River developed. The statistics on it are remarkably close to our hypothetical trading.

DISCUSS HOW YOU AVOID THE PITFALLS OF OVER-OPTIMIZATION.

One way is to test the idea over multiple markets. The second is to make sure you haven't condensed your testing to a particular time frame or a particular market era. You need to make sure that you're looking at a long enough time period so that you can see multiple market conditions. Third, the parameters surrounding the chosen parameters should all be reasonably profitable so that if there were any drift, it will not make any difference. Those are the basic ways we think about it.

DO YOU EVER ACKNOWLEDGE PECULIAR CHARACTERISTICS OF ONE MARKET OR MARKET GROUP THAT WOULDN'T FIGURE TO TRANS-LATE WHEN YOU TEST OTHER ENVIRONMENTS?

We do not, because remember, we go back to our basic premise that indicators don't matter. Your question basically says, "Should I alter the parameter or time length of my indicator?" We think that that is curve fitting.

In doing our long-term testing, one of the things that we learned about our programs is that when you don't optimize indicators you find that your system works over time. What you also find is that people who have optimized or tested over shorter time frames can outperform you in the short run. Because we didn't optimize our parameters, we have found that the longer we extend our track record, the better our performance looks compared to other CTA's who have used shorter time frames for their optimization.

DO YOU PERIODICALLY OPTIMIZE AFTER A SYSTEM OR PORTFOLIO IS IN PLACE?

We never re-optimize indicators because we realize that's an illusion. We're continually working on the money management and risk control, trying to figure out how to chip away a percentage of drawdown here or there. That is our obsession—research on risk control and money management. We constantly do it, although we haven't made any changes yet in three years. We haven't found anything yet that has made a significant difference, but we're getting close.

IS IT IMPORTANT FOR YOU TO UNDERSTAND WHAT'S BEHIND GOOD RESULTS OR DO GOOD RETURN NUMBERS MERELY SPEAK FOR THEMSELVES?

We understand what's behind our numbers. I think you need to understand it because it's the only thing that gives you comfort. I could never trade a black box. If you look at what we've talked about and go through the logic, you see that at every point, we understood where we were. At every point we started with this assumption, and that led to that assumption, which led to that understanding which leads to this parameter. It goes through a logical step.

You start with the basic assumption that the markets have to trend to survive. That leads you to the question of how am I going to capture the big move, leading to the decision on indicators. Which leads to the realization that indicators don't matter. Then you're there—you say, "OK, I'll pick an indicator that I'm comfortable with."

Then you say, "OK, but if I'm always in the market, and I'm reversing on an indicator, I have huge drawdowns while I'm waiting for the move." That's an observation. So, my business decision becomes how do I limit the risk while I'm waiting for the return? That observation results in either adding multiple systems, multiple markets, working significantly on money management, or probably all of the above.

Again, this all comes down to it being a business decision, not a trading decision. The best chance we have is to stick to our business plan.

LARRY WILLIAMS

"THE CREATION OF WEALTH COMES FROM MONEY MANAGEMENT, NOT FROM SYSTEMS."

Larry Williams is one of the most recognized names on the trading/investment seminar circuit. His many books include the popular "How I Made A Million Dollars Trading Commodities" *and last year's* "The Right Stock at the Right Time: Prospering in the Coming Good Years."

One of his most notable claims to fame occurred when he invested $10,000 in the Robbins Trading Championship at the start of 1987. By October, the account had $2.1 million in it. The ensuing stock market crash trimmed him back to $700,000 before Larry was able to run it back up to a year-closing $1.1 million—an 11,000 percent return.

Needless to say, he won the competition. The feat, however, was not performed without controversy.

"There were rumors that I rigged the contest in some way," Larry volunteered, *"or that I could only handle trading S&P's. But, if you look at the records, you'll see that there was a time where I traded everything, just to show, 'Hey, if it moves, I'll trade it'."*

He took something besides the profit and recognition from the event.

"My money management was way, way too aggressive," he concluded. "On the upside, it got me from the $10,000 to $2,000,000, but the downside (from two million to $700,000) was devastating."

Thereafter, Larry devoted much of his energies to money management; a trading component that he thinks is most overlooked by investors. "The creation of wealth comes from money management, not from systems," he observed. It would be a theme that would resurface in much of the interview.

For over four decades, Larry has been inspiring attendees across the country with his unemotional analytical approaches to commodity markets. His techniques run the gamut from the familiar, ranging from moving average breakouts and range extensions to the more esoteric including some idiosyncratic pattern recognition strategies, with everything in between.

Like a blackjack expert, Larry will consider anything that will demonstrably stack the odds in his favor. Often this involves "layering" several techniques together, or following one percentage play only when it falls within a wider advantageous scenario, which in turn conforms to an even bigger concept, and so on. His Genesis software can simultaneously access several markets as well as additional technical and fundamental factors. The resulting stew has routinely produced results of at least 80 percent accuracy.

Quite frankly, Larry has had a direct, personal impact on me. It was his mechanical trading lectures, some co-hosted by fellow luminary Jake Bernstein, that precipitated my metamorphosis from a chaotic perennial loser to a profitable system trader. One of my early omnipresent strategies was a direct application of his teachings. My wide range of systems, entry techniques and markets became linked by one constant; I'd hold trades over one night, and try to exit the longs on Day One's highs, and ditto for shorts on the previous lows.

That was strictly a Larry-ism, lifted from a concept he introduced as "How to sell the high and buy the low of the day." It was gimmicky, but undeniably effective—as Larry observed, "So what if you're doing it one day after the fact?"

He helped me "tidy-up" my trading. Cut and dry—no fudging, no squinting at charts in confusion. Somewhat naively, I assumed his interview would conform just as seamlessly, but Larry draws different conclusions from his cold statistics. Yes, perhaps mechanics do tell 98 percent of the tale, but occasionally, markets have that maddening way of throwing you the unexpected curve ball. System purists try to deal with that by anticipating everything beforehand. If a market gets too volatile, they might have a circuit breaker of some sort. If the ranges start exceeding anything seen historically, the entries and exits might widen accordingly. Traders might, in short, make their methodologies as dynamic as possible—changing according to all possible market contingencies.

For many, anything non-systematic, i.e. spontaneous or gut-related, is inevitably disastrous. Many people (myself included) are perpetually out of synch with markets. It's a common problem—as one Market Wizard noted, "Markets are like an opponent trying to teach you how to play badly."

That is why some of my questions seemingly may have been egging Larry toward improvisational denouncement. Larry, however, has never proclaimed himself a pure mechanical trader, although it might be forgivable for one to jump to that conclusion. Larry has such a wide arsenal of mechanical approaches, after all. Still, he can apparently process the occasional market shock swiftly and directly.

"You're supposed to drive to the right of the yellow line," he observed. "That's the law. But there's a big semi truck coming at me in my lane and there's a clear space if I cross the yellow line. Do I say to myself, 'Well, I'm going to follow the legal system here' or do I say, 'Uh oh. Some condition has changed?' In my case, I say, 'I'd better acknowledge reality'."

The interview took place face to face, in his Solana Beach, California office, (nestled in a small complex off a hilly, winding road). Despite the upscale nature of the town, Larry keeps his environment modest and uncomplicated—two or three rooms, a reception area, and one receptionist. The simplicity is one of the things Larry likes best about trading.

He greeted me in a casual pullover shirt and jeans, (plus a trendy mustache-goatee combo I hadn't seen before). He offered me a coffee choice—normal or stronger than Starbucks? We talked a little about the two percent of the time Larry thinks it's prudent to override a system, and a lot about the 98 percent of the time when everything else in his vast arsenal is applicable.

REGARDING THE ANALOGY OF SYSTEM TRADING AND DRIVING DOWN THE HIGHWAY: IT'S KIND OF A SLIPPERY SLOPE ISN'T IT? DON'T MOST PEOPLE RUN INTO TROUBLE IMPROVISING THEIR TRADING, EVEN WHEN IT SEEMS INDISPUTABLE THAT THERE'S A TRUCK HEADING TOWARD THEM IN THEIR LANE?

Well, it's an easier analogy when I'm driving down the freeway, isn't it? But in the market, you don't know the future, which is unpredictable, and you don't know if the system has blown up or not. I think there is a time that calls for refining and improving your system along the highway.

WHILE YOU'RE ON THE HIGHWAY?

While you're on the highway.

BUT ISN'T THAT ONE OF THE WORST TIMES TO BE EMOTIONALLY VULNERABLE?

Well, that's right. You'd actually better start preparing when you get on the freeway, preferably in the slow lane. You'd better make sure you have air bags in the car. Check the traffic report. Plan for as many contingencies as possible.

I wouldn't consider it emotional to go back and look at why something didn't work out. "What was wrong with this set of scenarios?" "Oh yeah, this condition existed...I didn't think of that at the time..."

I've learned a bit more about markets now then I knew, say, ten years ago. I try to apply my new knowledge to whatever I'm involved in.

GIVE AN EXAMPLE OF WHAT WOULD MAKE YOU SIDESTEP OR IM-PROVISE.

I get a signal to buy today and Federal Reserve Chairman Alan Greenspan is speaking. Why do I have to trade every day? That would be a good example. I know something is going to happen.

WAS THERE A POINT WHERE YOU WERE STRICTLY MECHANICAL AND A REASON THAT YOU STOPPED BEING SO?

I don't know that I've ever been strictly mechanical. I don't know that I'm that expressly a believer in mechanical systems. I doubt if anybody, if they're telling you the truth, has been 100 percent mechanical.

I'm very systematic in what I do. I came here this morning. I placed my orders, I put up my stops, my targets are in place. You might call that mechanical, but I think of it as more systematic.

I tend to follow my approach 98 percent of the time. But I need to divulge publicly that there is two percent of the time where I think I should, and I think they should, have some space to make a judgment call.

And of course, some people are very intuitive. I've got a friend who has traded since the 1960's. He has done very well just from his thinking and notational interest in the marketplace.

BUT AS A LECTURER, YOU CAN'T IMPART THAT SORT OF EXPER-TISE.

As a lecturer, I think I've got to tell the truth. I've got to tell people, "You've got to find out who you are, what you do. And here's what I do, but you can't be me, and I can't be you."

What I show them is programmable, it's teachable. But people are inevitably going to take ideas and put their own personal spin on them.

Tom DeMark is a dear friend of mine. Some of what he's done I don't even understand, but other stuff I'll try to incorporate in my work. I'll look at things...shop around..." Oh, I never thought of that before, I'm glad I talked to that guy. I'm glad I listened, I can use that."

HOW DID YOU GET STARTED TRADING?

I started in stock trading and read the books at the time that were oscillator based and technical. I believed in all the Gann paraphernalia and Elliott and all that mumbo jumbo stuff. For a long time, I went down that ally, thinking markets were predictable to the 'Nth degree.'

Now, I don't believe that at all. I think the markets are highly irrational, that there's no perfection to them, no hand of God, no manipulators. It's just a game of randomness that overrides longer-term fundamental conditions.

Then, I got into some ideas of my own that I thought made more sense. After three or four years, I got into trading commodities. An old guy in the brokerage business said, "You can make more money trading commodities. Nobody does it, but look at the leverage."

HOW AND WHEN DID YOUR ADVISORY CAREER COME ABOUT?

That was well after the fact, after I had been trading a while and making some money and having some runs. I had some limited partnerships that did pretty well. People were asking me for advice. There was one thing I learned in journalism school. (He earned his undergrad degree at the University of Oregon). My professor was a really brilliant guy. He said, "Make them pay for it." I said, "OK, I should charge for this information."

DID YOU EVER WORRY THAT WIDESPREAD KNOWLEDGE OF YOUR TECHNIQUES WOULD DILUTE THEIR EFFECTIVENESS?

No. I figured first of all, not many people would actually follow them. Second, I didn't think I had that great an ability to promote. Even today, the number of my followers is relatively small.

WHAT PERCENTAGE OF YOUR INCOME COMES FROM ACTUAL TRADING?

Depends on the year. I've had years like 1987 and 1997 where trading made up the bulk of it. Recently it's maybe 50-50.

You don't know when you're going to make money in the markets. Maybe you do, but I don't. A friend of mine, Robert Allen, has done a lot with real estate. He said, "Give me multiple streams of income." I think that's something we can all use.

Why doesn't Bill Gates retire? I'm impoverished compared to Bill Gates. People like to continue working. They like to continue doing what they do. Why do law professors teach and practice law? They enjoy both and both are streams of income.

Why I lecture, why I write books is because I enjoy it. I really love it. I have a background in journalism, it's natural, it is what I learned to do. It's an expression of my heart...where I come from.

GIVE US A ROUGH IDEA OF WHAT YOU'RE DRAWING ON WHEN INVESTIGATING MARKETS AND/OR CREATING SYSTEMS.

I have two views of the market, long-term and short-term. Fundamentals drive the long- term, and short-term fluctuations are caused by emotion.

I first look at the long-term. I look at the conditions that would suggest an up or down move. Let's say the activity of commercials and the public, and the open interest and seasonals are setting up a long scenario. And valuation is important...I'm obviously looking for a market that's undervalued.

Most of the time, according to history, "this" is what will result in the future. Not always, but historically, these moves from these conditions have existed so often off these highs and lows that I'll want to go with them.

On top of that model, I bring in a timing tool. I don't think a market will bottom the same way every time, so I have an arsenal of four or five ways to identify bottoming action. If it does bottom, I'm probably going to catch it. It might be a trend line, a moving average, a channel breakout...one of these things should trigger.

In the short-term, you can see emotions reflected in the chart patterns. Say, for example, you have a day that closes on its low and everybody tends to puke it up on the opening the next morning when it looks so bad. That's generally where I want to buy it. I want to take advantage of the crowd's emotions. An outside day with a down close to me is a really big day. I'd probably want to be a buyer the next day or the day after that.

I wouldn't want to do that if bonds were in a severe downtrend. I'd rather they were in a strong uptrend. I'd prefer to do it near the end of the month when stocks usually rally. And I'd probably prefer to do that if the market itself has been in an uptrend for some time period.

So I'm layering conditions to try and set up good trades.

HOW DO YOU ASSESS THE FUNDAMENTALS?

Every week, the Commodity Futures Trading Commission releases the Commitment of Traders Report. I can use it to evaluate every commodity as to whether it's undervalued or overvalued. I don't mean overbought or oversold, that's technical. I mean truly under or overvalued.

I can measure what the large guys are doing. I can measure what the small guys are doing. I want to see that commercials are heavy accumulators to be a buyer and heavy sellers to go short. I can look at open interest, which is a reflection of commercial activity. Finally, I can look at seasonals. So, I'm looking at five or six fundamental factors.

Then, I measure the number of major advisory services that are bullish or bearish on a weekly basis. I can see when the majority of advisor opinions are really out there. When they get 80 percent bullish, for example, the market could go down.

He then proceeded to give an impressive demonstration. The interview took place in mid- February 2003, during a protracted Iraqi anxiety-related S&P downtrend. Larry noted an 11 percent bullish consensus reading. Since this is a contrary opinion indicator, he concluded that "an incredible buy" could be imminent. After trading lower for most of the next day, the S&P's settled slightly higher. They added another 18 points on the following close—amazing to many who could imagine no reason for the market to go up during a time of such dire uncertainties.

LET'S SET UP A HYPOTHETICAL SITUATION. JOE TRADER WANTS TO BECOME A PROFESSIONAL SPECULATOR. HE'S MOTIVATED AND REASONABLY ADEPT IN HANDLING TRADING SOFTWARE. LET'S SAY THAT HE KNOWS ONLY ONE THING—HIS GUT TRADING HAS ALWAYS BEEN DISASTROUS, AND SO HE'S SOLD ON THE IDEA OF A MECHANICAL MONEY MAKING POSSIBILITY OF SOME SORT. HE'S TOTALLY OPEN TO WHEREVER RESEARCH MIGHT LEAD HIM. WHAT DO HIS CHANCES OF SUCCESS DEPEND UPON?

People say that they want to make a living trading, and that's great, but how much do you need to live on? If you have to make $50,000 a year, then you have to put that in some sort of reality. If a fund does 20 to 30 percent per year on any consistent basis, that is considered really good. They might be up 60 percent one year and down 20 percent the next, but they'll average 20 to 30 percent *if they're good.*

So the guy probably has to have $150,000 for a startup if he wants to make $50,000 and that's still risky. Thirty-three percent return on his money? That's a phenomenal rate of return.

Realistically, you have to run the numbers backwards.

BUT THE INDUSTRY IS NOTED FOR STORIES OF SMALL STAKES RUN UP INTO LARGE ONES. RICHARD DENNIS. YOU.

Yeah, but your scenario is talking about planned consistency. I don't know what the market is going to do today, tomorrow, or next year. People do have spectacular successes, but you don't see them doing it every day or every week. Nobody does that on a consistent basis.

If you have a system that works and you can follow it and you have your emotions in check and you have the time and the money.... you can come out on top. But to predict you're going to score 36 runs or you're going to score one run and both win the game? We don't know what the system is going to give us in a given year.

All of the great stories that we hear about are people who started with small stakes. But I've heard more stores about people who started with big stakes and ended up with small ones.

DURING YOUR HYPER-RETURN TIMES, WERE YOU DOING THINGS THAT YOU WOULD NOW, ON REFLECTION, ADVISE OTHERS AS BE-ING RECKLESS?

Of course, I was young...

SO YOU WERE KIND OF LUCKY IN A WAY?

Yes, although there is a right time to be in phase with the markets. I'm not always in phase.

I'm not a particularly smart guy, but I worked really hard at this stuff. I spent my whole life on these markets, so I do understand them a bit.

I tell people they've got to start small and slow. Learn as you're paper trading. Gradually build your account up.

SOME ADVISORS REGARD PAPER TRADING AS NOT BEING AN ACCU-RATE INDICATOR OF ACTUAL TRADING. THE EMOTIONAL PRESSURES ARE ABSENT.

Well, what causes the emotions is the fact that you're probably over-margined. We tend to be over money-managed. We trade too much. We become emotional freaks.

Money management is emotional management. This is the point that everybody has missed, I think. It isn't the act of trading, it's the over commitment of our money that causes the over commitment of our emotions.

SO YOU CAN LEARN THROUGH PAPER TRADING?

I think so, yeah. If you look at medical students, they don't get to operate until their third year. They're paper trading on cadavers. There was a country singer who won the bareback title one year and he rode the bucking machine all year leading up to it. That's like paper trading. He didn't go to rodeos to get his arms and legs broken. He was *healthy* when he went to Oklahoma City. We go to college to get MBA's and that's paper trading.

SO THE PITFALLS DON'T LIE IN TRADING PER SE, BUT IN MONEY AND EMOTIONAL MANAGEMENT. HOW DO YOU PERSONALLY AP-PROACH THE PROBLEM?

There's no magic formula. Basically I have to know what risk factor I'm comfortable with. I'm 61 years old, and I'm more careful with what I trade than I used to be. I'm basically a one-market trader now because I'm not good enough to focus on three or four markets. I trade the S&P's and occasionally bonds, so my comments all relate to a one-market approach. Although I think they would have application to a multi-market trader. I don't want to risk any more than eight percent of my money on any given trade ever. Somebody else might want to do 20 percent or two percent. If I traded a portfolio, I might risk one or two percent in five or six positions which would be a 12 percent risk if the whole thing blew up on them.

In any event, you have to keep your risk exposure very, very low.

COULD YOU FURTHER AMPLIFY YOUR TRADING STYLE?

I'm a short-term trader. My average trade lasts a day and a half to a day and three- quarters. But that's the S&P. When I used to trade setup markets, it might be 12 to 30 days.

In the S&P's, my system averages about 70 trades a year, so that's about 1.5 trades a week. This year it's signaled 12 times.

My stops are large. The closer you make them, the more times they're hit.

DO YOU USE PRICE TARGETS?

Not as a short-term trader, but as a longer-term trader I like price targets. I like to apply price targets to intermediate-term swings.

Targets probably don't give you better historical returns. The trouble with a system that holds on forever is you have a big run-up where you don't take profits. Then the market goes sideways or maybe down for a month or two. Then, you're in jail. You're in prison.

Then it starts to take off again, but gosh, you probably could have been in a more constructive situation. And this choppy time period is emotionally very draining on you. Although someone could point to a place in the book and say, "Oh, we bought here and got out there" the reality is, with a month or so of pullback along the way, you could not have ridden the trade. It doesn't matter that the system caught it. You won't be able to ride through that.

The average person doesn't have the luxury of the trend following system that bails you out. He can't play the same game that a fund can play.

WHAT DO YOU PRIMARILY LOOK FOR IN YOUR STRATEGY PERFORMANCE STUDIES?

What resonates with me is the largest losing trade. I could have a system that's 90 percent accurate, has a nice average profit per trade, but one losing trade destroys all of the victories of those nine winners. The worst drawdown would be acceptable, but not if it all happened at one time. So, I'm not even a big fan of drawdowns (as a system indicator). What my trading experience has taught me is to be careful of the large losing trade. That's what's going to destroy me.

AND YET YOU USE WIDE STOPS.

Right. I know in the case of the S&P's what my loss has been in historical testing. I figure it's got to be bigger than that in reality.

DO YOU HAVE A RULE OF THUMB FOR LARGEST ACCEPTABLE LOSS?

It varies form market to market, but generally, you can use 100 percent of the average range for the last three days from the entry point. That's a pretty good range in most markets. In the S&P's, it is currently coming in at about $5000 (20 points).

LET'S TALK ABOUT SYSTEM OPTIMIZATION AND OVER-OPTIMIZA-TION. HOW DO YOU AVOID MERELY GIVING A PERFECT RENDITION OF THE PAST WITH LITTLE RELEVANCE TO PROBABLE FUTURE OUTCOME?

Commodity numbers are like prisoners of war. You beat them often enough, they'll confess to anything.

You don't want to beat them up too much. You don't want to over-grind. I'll make a first pass-through and say, "Oh yeah, something is really there." Or, "There's nothing there, forget it, Larry." I'll forget things really quickly.

There's got to be some kind of resiliency in the data that pops up. If there is, I'll say, "OK, let's look closer at these examples." And I'll visually hand-check the patterns. What was going on in the market? Inside days? Outside days? Were there gaps? Is it the first or the last part of the month? What was the bond market doing? I try to build some structure within all that.

A system should be judged on the integrity of what it's about. Is there some logic to it? I judge that, plus the performance. Other than that, it could be very simple, or very complex.

So many of these systems, especially in the old days, would just be numbers run through a computer and the results showed they made money. But there was no logic to it. There was no rationale other than, "Numbers make money." Then, of course, they don't hold up in the future.

SO IT DOES BOTHER YOU, THEN, IF YOU DON'T UNDERSTAND THE RATIONALE BEHIND THE RESULTS.

Absolutely. Things happen for a reason in my life and in the markets. So there needs to be a theory.

ALTHOUGH I'D IMAGINE IF IT HAD BIG ENOUGH NUMBERS, YOU'D WANT TO INVESTIGATE IT FURTHER.

Yeah, walk it forward, do unknown data. Wait a year and see if it holds up. There's always a chance that somebody "cracked the code" right? But primarily, no....there needs to be a reason. There needs to be order. There's got to be a premise. Check the premise.

SO THE MORE COMPATIBLE IT IS WITH YOUR PERSONAL EXPERIENCES, THE MORE YOU'LL LIKE IT?

The more I *might* like it, but again, I'm limited in my knowledge of the markets. Somebody out there might have a system that doesn't resonate with what I know, but it may open up doors further down the road for me to see and understand.

WEIGH IN ON THE FOLLOWING DEBATE: "A SINGLE SYSTEM SHOULD PERFORM ROUGHLY THE SAME ACROSS ALL MARKETS." OR, "EACH MARKET HAS ITS OWN CHARACTERISTICS THAT CAN BE EXPLOITED BY INDIVIDUAL CUSTOM TAILORED SYSTEMS." IS IT MORE THE FORMER, THE LATTER, OR A COMBINATION OF THE TWO?

I'd say it's a combination. There are certain characteristics—clearly if you look at the S&P's right now with a $30,000 margin and compare to cattle with a $400 margin, it's not the same player in the S&P as in cattle. It's a whole different ballpark.

If you have trading rules that you're going to buy the S&P in January, that's different than buying cattle in January because of the Cattle-on-Feed Report and all sorts of other fundamental factors in that marketplace.

I want to have commonality in all markets, but there are unique market characteristics, too. As an example, we don't go to premium in gold, but we can go to premium in the agricultural markets. We don't go to premium in abstract markets. You've got to look at the fundamentals.

GIVEN THAT YOU HAVE A DATA FIELD AT YOUR DISPOSAL FOR THE ENTIRE HISTORY OF A COMMODITY, WOULD YOU INCORPORATE ALL OF IT IN YOUR STUDY, OR CUT IT BACK TO BETTER REFLECT RECENT MARKET ACTION?

I do the entire field, but you still have to take things into consideration. In my S&P research, I use bonds to trigger S&P trades. As you may recall, in the 1980's, there was a huge government report every Thursday, so bonds acted differently on Thursday than they do now. They also had a different opening time. (8:00 central vs. today's 7:20 open). And T-Bills used to be the big market, not Treasury Bonds.

Then you have to remember the S&P contract has been cut in half (from $500 to $250 per point) and that they're a lot more volatile now so maybe my exit point has to be different than it was in 1982. You have to take all of that into consideration.

In short, you have to know what's in the data you're looking at. Math is a perfect thing, but you run into problems when you try to apply that perfect thing to an imperfect world. Still, I like to see patterns that also hold up going back into the past.

DO YOU USE VIRGIN DATA? (DATA LEFT OUT OF THE OPTIMIZATION PROCESS SO THAT AN IDEA CAN BE SUBSEQUENTLY "FORWARD TESTED" IN THAT FIELD).

I like to have at least three years "out-of-sample" data. It depends on whether it's something that occurs a lot. If there are 800 occurrences, maybe my out-of-sample test need only be a year.

WHICH BAR CHART DO YOU PREFER?

The daily. I want to make less trades, rather than more. Every time you pull the trigger, you can get killed in this business. I don't want to be trading one-minute bar charts. With 1400 minutes in a day, that's 1400 times you can screw up.

I'm focusing my attention on you and I have a position in the S&P market. I could go out for a run this morning if I wanted to. I put my stops up and I'm out of here. It's a healthier way to live.

Day trading works. I've taught people how to do it, but it's just not my love. I just don't have those flames anymore. It's a lot harder than most people think or say that it is.

WHY?

Because day traders think that every day they can come in and kill the market. But some days are a lot better than other days. You need to isolate the days that are best to be able to work the markets, really beat up on them.

Day traders tend to be really technical and want to catch every little move. I'd rather catch a large trend within a day as opposed to trying to get in here, here, and there for quick profits. When you do that, when a trend does come, you're probably on the wrong side when it backs off, and then you've lost all those little nicks that you've fought for.

I look to see where the profits come from. The really big money comes from the trades that you hold overnight.

IS TRADING AN ART OR A SCIENCE?

Yeah. (Laughs). You get to use both sides of your brain. The art is in the development of the systems, the creative aspects. "Oh, I'll bet no one ever saw that before!" And then you take that creative idea and apply it to a scientific approach. You get to work with that condition for years and years.

ARE TRADERS BORN OR MADE?

Born mainly. Some people have more of an 'inkling' for it than others. You could wake up one morning and say, "Hey, this isn't my calling, but I'm probably really good at something else."

I say go find what you're good at as opposed to continuing to ram your head against the wall. Look around you. Does the universe agree with you to some extent? If so, great, continue. If not, you've got to face the fact that you're continually bucking the market.

The only caveat would be ultimately, trend is the basis of all profit. People are not aligning themselves with whatever trend they're trying to trade. Traders are intelligent people. They like to argue and they like to argue with the market.

F. Scott Fitzgerald had a beautiful line in one of his novels. He said, "Intelligence is the ability to hold two diametrically opposed ideas in the mind at the same time and still function."

That's what trading is. Fear and greed. Up and down. Two concepts pulling your mind apart. A lot of people get screwed up on that. They go all one way or the other, or they can't function at all.

HOW IS THIS GAME LIKE ANY OTHER?

The number one cause of failure in business is under-capitalization. Number two is lack of experience.

HOW IS IT DIFFERENT?

It's more fun. (Laughs). You don't need as many employees. You can get into the business with no cost. You can find out for free if you're any good at it.

IT IS A PARTICULARLY SAD SITUATION WHEN PEOPLE FAIL IN TRADING, ISN'T IT? I'VE JUST HAD A COUPLE OF FRIENDS BUST OUT WHO HAVE BEEN DOING IT FOR YEARS....MIDDLE-AGED NOW WITH NOT A WHOLE LOT ON THEIR RESUMES.

Hey, if that were me, I'd put that on my resume, "I was in the *pits, man!* I was with the best of them. I was in there *swinging!"*

Any field you're in, turn it to your advantage. That's what I'd tell these people. Look what you learned down there. You learned about emotion and money and people.

What a grand experience to bring some corporate world!

Louis Lukac

"Everything that we have ever developed from Day One has been mechanical."

Louis Lukac is the president and CEO of Wizard Trading Inc., a Commodity Trading Advisor (CTA). He formed the company with Jack Schwager, author of "The Market Wizards" book series as a natural outgrowth of the intensive research the two had been doing for years on mechanical trading systems. Jack left the company in 1998 to embark on hedge fund management while Louis continues to trade portfolios and refine and augment what may well be one of the world's ultimate trading mechanisms.

Louis' involvement with numbers began at Purdue University, starting with a program that he developed for his Master's Thesis in 1985. The subject was agricultural economics and the topic was market efficiency in the futures markets.

"We used mechanical trading strategies to test the theory of whether the futures markets were efficient or not," he recounted.

Louis and his team compared how similarly 12 systems would trade in one, three and five day windows. They also tested them against models of pure randomness—what one would expect to find if there was no bias in the market. Louis handled the programming, as he has done throughout his professional trading life. Others such as Schwager would help in the brainstorming, but Louis was the one who turned the theories into reality.

Like everyone, he started testing ideas on existing software, but encountered problems that are inherent in the commercial products. For one thing, the most popular programs were lacking in comprehensive portfolio management capabilities.

"Also" said Louis, "you get into the role of trying to write Excel spreadsheets, and then mixing this with that, and at that point I just decided I was going to write my own." He's been controlling his research from the ground up ever since.

Several papers were published as a result of Louis' study, which proved the existence at least some degree of market inefficiency— a necessary condition for speculative success.

"The research that was published found some similarities in the trading patterns, so they are somewhat herd-like," said Louis. "For the majority of the periods and systems that we tested, we did find significant profits above what you would normally expect to find, which I had suspected all along.

"We suggested the theory of dis-equilibrium pricing. It says that markets move from one equilibrium to another. As they move toward the new equilibrium, they are in dis-equilibrium, and trends develop as they are digesting information. Therefore trends are nothing more than a natural phenomenon in these markets. And what do trend-following systems do? They capture these trends.

"That's why when you're in a period of higher volatility where you have a lot of uncertainty and markets are moving to new equilibriums, these systems generally do well.

"If you have a period like 1998, 1999 and 2000 where there's relative stability, they don't do so well. It doesn't mean that they've lost their edge or that things have necessarily changed. It just

means that the markets were less volatile so there were less chances of markets moving to a new equilibrium and there was less opportunity for the systems to capture trends."

Louis directly profits from his labor. He's personally invested in the Wizard Capital LL Fund, which trades the model encapsulating all of Wizard's activity. As always, he's also heavily into research; at present, examining trading modifications that he hopes will be a breakthrough of sorts. Rather than scrutinizing individual systems, he's keying on the kind of broad market environments that generally cause some of the worst trading havoc. The goal is to mitigate the normally negative outcome.

He's also in the process of expanding his company's prominence.

"I'm gearing up to do more marketing," he said. "I will become more involved in the selling of the product rather than just doing the research."

The interview took place in March 2003, just before the start of the Iraqi war. The resulting market environment was one in which Louis tends to thrive. As he put it, "volatility is probably the key to the profitability."

WALK US THROUGH YOUR EARLY DAYS OF BRAINSTORMING AND IMPLEMENTING SYSTEMS.

Basically, Jack [Schwager] would come up with some ideas through his **Market Wizards** books and through running several different major brokerage research departments on Wall Street. He'd write down ideas on a piece of paper, type it up, send it over to me and then it would be my job to take those rules and put them into computer code that could be tested and evaluated. This included the individual trading model itself, how it integrated into what we already had, and all of the portfolio statistics of analyzing the strategy across broad time frames and broad market groups.

WHAT WERE YOU USING?

Originally I was using...I think it was a CDC 6000 or 600, something like that at Purdue University. This was back in 1985. Back then, the personal computers just weren't fast enough to do what we were trying to accomplish.

Then I did some programming on an HP mainframe back in the late 1980's. I did programming on a Digital MicroVAX as well, which is like a mainframe. Then in the early 1990's, the technology was good enough to where I could start doing all of my testing and evaluation on PC's, so I've been there ever since.

I write my own programs. It's all in C. It's kind of a hybrid C/C++. I wrote it myself since I never was able to find an off-the-shelf platform that would do everything Jack and I needed it to do. I ended up writing 100 percent of the programs, which included the programs for testing and evaluation, as well as programs for implementation including the programs in the back office to do our checking and positions.

The majority of the system testing that I've done is in open-high-low-close, volume, open interest and sentiment.

How do you measure sentiment?

There are several sources. There's a Market Vane service and a Bullish Consensus service. Some indicators are daily and some are weekly. Jack and I created an index of sentiment based on a weighted average of three different sentiment sources in the industry.

And you kept that completely mechanical?

Right. Once we got the information, we developed trading systems that are completely mechanical off of the sentiment information. Everything that we have ever developed from day one has been mechanical.

So you must have intuited something early on that many traders have had to learn the hard way...often several times. How did you come to the realization that your success was going to depend on 100 percent mechanics— zero percent human interference?

Good question. I still remember it to this day. There was another firm that I was working for, and I won't mention its name. I was with them right out of graduate school, very early in my career. They were trading a very concentrated portfolio of foreign currencies, using a system kind of like Bollinger Bands to determine when markets were oversold or overbought. They were trying to trade inside these bands.

The person pulling the trigger thought that what he was doing was mechanical, but it wasn't. For about eighteen months, he did very well. At that point, he thought he knew the market pretty well and that he had a handle on it.

Finally one month, I remember walking into his office to ask if we could get out of positions that were down nearly 55 percent. He almost couldn't talk...he just could not make the decision. We finally made the decision and got out and lost all the equity. It taught me a very big lesson. If we had followed any system at all, the stops would have been hit, the reversals would have been made, and we actually would have made money during the month.

As it turned out, the gut or discretionary-type trading just completely obliterated the track record and the assets to boot. The program never recovered from that period.

I call it the 'deer-in-the-headlights' syndrome. It's when you just flat-out can't make a decision because you're so far in the hole. You also know that it's on your shoulders that you are in that hole—because of your decision.

At that point, I'd already been through graduate school and done all the mechanical trading. I had seen that it worked. I saw that it had an advantage and saw that the markets were inefficient enough to allow systems to make money. The whole time I was there, we were doing development, and we were preparing to move into mechanical trading, but his feeling was that in a currency portfolio like this, he wanted to apply discretion to this certain system that they had been doing research on for quite some time. One of the worst things that can happen to a trader is to have initial success right out of the box, so that he thinks he knows what he is doing. At that point, of course, the market normally turns. If you're not able to adapt and turn with it, it usually hands it to you.

Whereas a system—being cold and calculated and looking at nothing but statistics and patterns—doesn't care. It's just trying to control your losses so you can trade another day and make it back in the good periods.

It all seems pretty logical to me. Besides, given that Wizard trades over 56 markets globally, there is no way that an individual, or even a group of individuals, is going to be able to keep track of all those markets and stay on top of them, unless you're Paul Tudor Jones. There are Einsteins out there—not very many, but they do exist. I'll be the first to admit, I don't have any crystal ball on trading discretionarily.

OF COURSE, THERE ARE PROBLEMS IN SYSTEMS. HOW DO YOU
GET AROUND A MARKET THAT INSTANTANEOUSLY JUMPS BEYOND
ANY PROJECTED VOLATILITY YOU'VE SEEN IN HISTORICAL DATA?
WHAT DEFENSE DO YOU HAVE AGAINST THAT OCCASIONAL
BLINDSIDE—THE UNFORESEEN SHOCKING EVENT?

There isn't any. If something happens instantaneously like a gap
opening, there's no way you can do anything about it.

One of the worst trades we ever had was a seven-to-nine percent
hit in the Euro Lira. The volatility was running three or four ticks and
it opened 50 ticks against us.

The hit probably represented 10 times what it would normally exhibit, but on the other hand, that was one time in 13 years. Plus, it was
only one market. To get around shocks like that, we diversify across
50-some markets. That's a way of taking care of that kind of event
before it even occurs—by not allocating too many assets to one market.

Beyond that, you have to trust what you can demonstrate. If you
initially test the system over a long enough period of time, across a
broad number of markets, across large timeframes, and then use
'Monte Carlo' simulations to reshuffle your return streams so that if
you do thousands of iterations, you can get a very good distribution
telling you what the system should attain in the future.

PLEASE DEFINE 'MONTE CARLO' SIMULATION.

Let's say that you took Wizard's actual trading returns from 1990
to 2003, and you threw them into a 'Monte Carlo' simulator. That
simulator treats the actual results as a single occurrence of how a
return stream could come out. It just so happens that it is the actual
one. Assume that you were down 10 percent one month and down
six another month and eight another; there's nothing to say that the
losses couldn't all have occurred back to back. That's as much a part
of the model as the potential good scenarios. The simulator continu-

ously re-shuffles your returns to a different outcome to the point where you start to develop a true distribution of your return stream, not merely the one actual occurrence. It's a way of simulating more data.

The result is that your maximum drawdown goes out because there will be one simulation where all of those bad months hit together. What it really does is show you what the true risks and true rewards of a system are, which is always worse than what you initially have in front of you. It drives home the fact that maybe this model is much riskier than you think. The simulation helps you set your leverage more accurately.

Most of the systems in the very long term have a very slight edge over the marketplace. There are pitfalls in systems in the sense that they go through good periods and bad periods. However, one of the keys with Wizard is that we try to combine as many types of trading strategies as we can. This includes counter-trend systems, which we use to mitigate the big high-risk periods like we're in right now.

There is really no control through 'whipsawing' markets. By definition, these long-term systems are going to try to buy most of the breakouts because all of the money is made when the trends occur.

There are only so many ways that you can develop a mechanical trend-following system. Therefore, most of the systems are similar. If you get low volatility and whipsaws in the market, you are going to lose money.

HOW ABOUT SUPPORT AND RESISTANCE SYSTEMS? (THEY'D PROFIT IN THE FALLOW TIMES HE'S DESCRIBING).

They work very well in the long run with longer parameter sets. I call them Channel Breakout systems or the Donchian method. Trying to trade this type of system with shorter parameters is very dangerous though, because in the long run they are best used as long-term trend following systems. Trying to trade them as counter-trend systems in fallow times is a disastrous long-term strategy. Breakout systems and dual moving average systems continue to be the best performing type systems to this day.

Let's say that you are looking at 50 days of highs and lows. Your 'buy stops' are at the highs of the channel and your 'sell stops' are at the lows of the channel. As you move forward, of course, the channel will move with you. So, what that's really doing over a 50, 100, 150 day period—whatever your parameter—is defining your support and resistance levels. That's what it does over the long-term. If you are breaking out above say a 100-day channel, there's a good chance that you are breaking out through resistance that has probably been there for quite some time. This event is potentially a reliable indicator that some change is occurring and that the market is in dis-equilibrium and trying to find a new equilibrium.

It's the same for a dual moving average crossover systems. These types of systems also seem to work quite well over the long run. I'll emphasize again though, there's no doubt that the industry went through a tough period in '98-2000. Systems couldn't seem to make any money. In the case of Wizard, [the equity] just went up…down, up… down. We weren't losing, but it was going sideways, like up 10, down 10. The reason isn't that the systems were flawed. The reason is that we witnessed unprecedented stability. Systems just don't do well when the markets have a low volatility period.

The key to profitability is finding when you're going to be in one of those periods, or identifying when you are in one. Then, you can tailor your system to pull back on the allocation, or widen your parameter sets so that the market doesn't whipsaw you.

ARE YOU TALKING ABOUT SOME SORT OF SWITCH MECHANISM?

Exactly. I'm working on that. I'm trying to accomplish it through options. I've got an idea that Jack and I discussed over many times in the past. I'm just getting time to test it now, and I've got a pretty good idea how to do it.

If someone can come up with that key, that could get you less committed during periods where you have a high probability of losing money, and get you fully committed and allow the system to run in volatile periods, like what was witnessed last year [2002]. Last year, Wizard was up over 80 percent because you had nice dis-equibrium and trends everywhere.

Another way you can try to smooth out your equity curve is to build counter-trend research into your model to lighten up your position as you move further and further along in the trend. The key there, which I can tell you from personal experience, is to build it very slowly over time. Very good examples of this are the currency and bond markets, which just recently turned. The Wizard model was under 20 percent exposed when these markets turned, even though the trend followers were still full long right at the top. Our position had already been drastically scaled back to reduce the risk.

BECAUSE YOU WERE GETTING COUNTER-TREND SIGNALS?

Our signals were *screaming* to us that a reversal was going to occur.

SO QUITE CLEARLY, YOU'RE MORE THAN A MERE TREND FOLLOWER. SOME OF YOUR SYSTEMS PERFORM THE VERY UNUSUAL SYSTEMATIC FEAT OF PREDICTING OR ANTICIPATING MARKET TURNS.

Absolutely. Not only do we have systems that anticipate movement, but also systems that look at how long a move has gone and what that means based on statistics. If a market continues to break out into 200-300 day new highs each day, that is telling you something. When the market is really breaking out and really moving ahead, blowing away highs that are three or four years old and moving straight up with hardly a hiccup, no support or resistance lines, that's another thing the system looks at. That type of scenario sets you up for the 'V' top that we just witnessed in many of the markets. There is absolutely nothing more deadly to a pure trend-following system than a

'V' top or a 'V' bottom. When they occur in currencies, energies....
bonds, all in the same month as they're doing now, it doesn't bode
well for the industry.

We'll make good money in trending periods. Last year, we were
up 80-some percent for the year. This year, I think we're up 11 or 12
percent year-to-date even with being down three to four percent this
month. We are trend followers. We still exhibit the same patterns as
trend followers, but we try to reduce our volatility in certain down
periods. Not in down periods where there's low volatility and you're
just getting whipsawed all over. We'll lose money during those periods just like everyone else. The systems still have to bet on the
breakout. But that's what I'm trying to mitigate with the new strategies I'm working on—those periods of low volatility and false
breakouts.

The type of potentially adverse periods we've accounted for pretty
well is the type of volatility that we're witnessing this month after a big
spike. With the systems we use inside Wizard right now, we have a
very competent system to reduce this kind of volatility. I think being
down three to five percent for the month is going to be very good.
Even the most conservative [trend following] systems are going to be
down big.

In short, there are really two types of risks; the low volatility whipsaw risk and the high volatility end-of-a-run type risk. I'm trying to
reduce the risk of that low volatility period.

**HOW DO YOU INCORPORATE MONEY MANAGEMENT INTO THIS
RATHER COMPLEX MODEL?**

The trading model itself stands on its own. It is a combination of
probably 50 to 60 different types of systems with far more derivations
of each system based on the sets of parameters that I trade on each
one. What happens is, as I trade the systems, each parameter set
gets a weight toward the position that I want. My position or composite forecasts are referred to as position weights. The composite

forecast can vary from +1 to -1 and fall anywhere in between. That tells me the systems can be full long at +1, full short at -1 or anywhere in between including zero, which means that all system parameters are crossed up and I don't even want to be in the market.

That's the part that tells me where I want to be. Also, inside that position weight are some counter-trend systems that also tell me, after big runs, when it's trying to pull positions from my position weight as much as possible. You have to be very careful with that. If you pull too early, you're dead.

Money management is built into the system in much the same way. The system won't allow more than 'x' percent commitment of capital based on volatility. Proprietary money management models try to identify the best risk/reward trades and then try to maintain a sector balance across the entire portfolio.

Of course, watching the systems trade, you would not be able to tell which algorithm is triggering the trade on any given day.

HOW DO YOU ARRIVE AT WHAT INCREMENTS YOU TRADE FOR A GIVEN INVESTOR?

It would depend on one, the size of the account, two, the volatility in the account relative to the portfolio and three, where my trend/counter-trend position weight is in the market at that time. I can tell you from a money management point of view that my model will trade less of a market at high volatility than it will at low volatility. It's all mechanically built-in.

A perfect example of this is the high volatility in the energy markets right now. We're out of that market right now because this type of volatility would allow hardly any positions to go on even if my position weight was heavy one way or the other. The reason is that the relative volatility is just off the scale. My model really tries to stay away from that.

How do you measure volatility?

It's always relative volatility—volatility today relative to where it was at a certain interval in the past. I use ratios of average daily true ranges. Then I smooth the daily average daily true range over a short period of time and then calculate the volatility over a longer period. What I'm really looking for is that ratio.

Is the market telling you everything or is anything arbitrary?

The market is telling us everything and we never over-ride. Ever. Never ever. (Though our disclosure document says that we reserve the right to. I cannot envision all cases, so this statement is in the disclosure document).

Ever been tempted to over-ride when the systems are asking a lot of you?

Gosh, who's not tempted? But you know what the temptation is actually good for? It is good for generating new ideas. When you see a situation that you really don't like, then use that temptation to build a research module that will alleviate it. Jack taught me to do this long ago.

But you've got to do that in the quiet time when you're not under fire, right?

Usually right after the bad event. You don't know what that bad situation is going to be until it evolves. Then you are under fire and not motivated to fix it. I know where I want to take Wizard on the next leap and I have a road map on how I'm going to get there. It will lower volatility and drawdowns in the periods when you're getting whipsawed and it's going to use options to achieve this.

WITH ALL YOUR BUILT-IN COMPLEXITIES, WOULD YOU BE ONE TO DISAGREE WITH THE AXIOM THAT SIMPLE SYSTEMS WORK BEST?

I agree that at the core level of systems, simple is best. The parts are simple. They have to make sense. They also have to be very robust. Putting them all together is where it gets far more complicated.

WEIGH IN ON WHETHER A SINGLE SYSTEM SHOULD WORK THE SAME ACROSS A WIDE RANGE OF MARKETS, OR WHETHER EACH MARKET HAS QUALITIES THAT CAN BE EXPLOITED BY TAILOR-MADE SYSTEMS.

I'll tell you my evolutionary thought on this subject. Originally, we thought that systems should perform similarly across all markets. But remember, our systems don't just use one parameter set, they may use more of a parameter set range. We're taking the average performance more or less of that range. We're not just trying to pinpoint one parameter set.

So when you apply this to several different markets, it really depends on what phase the market is in. The S&P 500 used to trade horribly on a system basis. Then, the thing explodes and trends beautifully for years, which looks great as a system-tradable market. Finally it trends down and you make a lot of money again. If you'd only done your analysis before the bull market in stocks, you might think that you should trade according to that period, which was not good for a simple trend-following system. Consequently, we developed separate systems for some of the markets, mainly Stock Index Futures. Jack thought that they really were different, which seemed logical at the time.

In hindsight, it was a mistake. I've now come full-circle and trade every single market the same and I completely avoid trying to tailor one system to one market. I just won't do it, unless, in the future, I find some input that is exclusive to that market giving me some competitive edge and I only have this information in this one market. Then, it might make sense. But from a long-term perspective; a 15 or 20-year horizon across several different markets, what happens in one market from year to year really doesn't mean anything. It's how the system performs over the long term through the entire portfolio across different market cycles.

I began as a purist. Then, I deviated from that. Then, the stock market changed and the models that we used got clobbered [for the market-specific systems]. Then, I started doing research again, and all we would have had to do was use the exact same model we used everywhere else and it would have performed just like any other market.

Results become very dependant on the market that you choose, and very dependant on the time period that you choose. Given that the futures markets only have 20 to 25 years of good data anyway, that's not much to base it on. Therefore, your only choice is to try to trade it across many, many markets over many, many years to evaluate a system. It just makes statistical sense.

IS THAT TRUE PARTLY BECAUSE YOU HAVE RELATIVELY FEW SIGNALS?

No. Part of that is because I don't consider 10 or 20 years of data to be much data at all.

HOW MANY SIGNALS A YEAR DO YOU AVERAGE, ROUGHLY?

I'm constantly changing my positions. For instance, if I'm at 1.00 position weight and I go to 0.75, I'll peel 25 percent from the position. Then, I may go to 0.5 position weight and peel another 25 percent off. Then, I might go back to 100 percent if the market breaks out and the counter-trend signals clear out. Relatively speaking, the system is fairly active, but it's not because it's buying and selling in and out a lot. It's because it's 'massaging' the overall position as it goes up and down.

Because of this 'massaging' of the position, it is a fairly active program. Commission to equity ratios of eight or nine percent are common with my systems. It's not like an old John Henry type system where if you're full long and then you get a big reversal you reverse short and then you just hold that position until you get another big reversal. Sometimes the brokers complain about my system because it's always doing two, three or five-lot trades. That is what we call 'massaging the position.'

GIVE US AN EXAMPLE OF HOW A RAW IDEA GETS HONED INTO A USABLE INDICATOR.

A perfect example is one of the pattern recognition signals built into Wizard. Jack all along kept seeing this same pattern, and decided that it had to have some validity in the future. He kept writing down the pattern as he saw it and tried to get it into what I would call mechanical format. That is one where mechanically, it can be written into code. There's no more gray area, no assessing it. "This happens, and you're going to do this. This, this, and this happens, and you're going to do that."

That is what he did, and we wrote them down and discussed it to make sure there weren't any "ifs" that were unaccounted for. Of course, when I'm coding the system, I'll find them if there are any.

After I do the first run and put it together, I dump a file that can run in TradeStation® that plots the 'buys' and 'sells' on a graph. From my algorithm, Jack could visually determine whether the system was firing exactly where it should be firing on a trading basis.

Once we determine that it's right, which usually took about two or three revisions, we'd run about two years of printout, with lots of different system-specific indicators and he would go through the graph to make sure it was trading exactly as we wanted it to trade. Once we were convinced that, "yes, that's it," then I'd load it up on all the databases over all of the markets and we'd evaluate it. Mostly, we would evaluate it on its own. Then, we would evaluate it in the mix of systems that we already had to see what effect it had on our portfolio. In other words, we'd include it in the current position weight to measure its effect.

Normally, we could tell from the individual results whether we would be able to use the system or not. Then, we would put it in with the mix. Many times, we would find that what looked decent, as a standalone system would not add any value to the portfolio. It didn't increase the Sharpe ratio. The reason for this is that there were already several systems inside the mix that were doing exactly what the new system was doing.

CAN A MIX MAKE INDIVIDUAL SUB-PERFORMING SYSTEMS BETTER? CAN YOU GET A WHOLE GREATER THAN THE PARTS?

In a "Markowitz Efficient" way. It's the old argument that you can have a system that merely breaks even, but the mix lowers the volatility tremendously when you need volatility lowered. However, this system doesn't hurt the overall performance. That's referred to as a Markowitz Efficient portfolio—after [economist] Harry Markowitz. That's when you have either a higher return for the same level of risk, or the same level of return with a lower level of risk. Either of these cases makes a superior portfolio to the baseline. We have found many times that you can add systems that you would never trade on their own, but in the mix, you would.

SO YOU'RE CONSTANTLY LOOKING AT REVISIONS, RIGHT?

Yes. In fact, we just completed a pretty major revision to the portfolio analysis.

EXPAND ON THAT, PLEASE. GIVEN THAT YOUR SYSTEMS ARE KIND OF TIMELESS, APPLICABLE ON A BROAD SPECTRUM, AND NOT FITTED TO A SPECIFIC MARKET OR TRADING ENVIRONMENT, WHY WOULD ONE, IN A SENSE KEEP RE-EXAMINING THE WHEEL? IS IT BECAUSE THAT'S WHERE YOUR PASSIONS LIE, OR IS SUCH A DYNAMIC APPROACH ULTIMATELY NECESSARY FOR SURVIVAL?

It's not necessary in the sense that you're always looking for a better trend-following model. I basically have quit looking at trend-following models themselves. What I'm working on now is a systematic basis for developing portfolios to trade certain markets when they exhibit higher volatility patterns that would be conducive to making money and removing markets that don't exhibit this pattern. That's been my latest revision to the trading models. All of my accounts are traded the same, so they all get adjusted accordingly.

The new idea that I'm working on with the options is not a pure system trading approach but rather, an approach that modifies the current trend/counter-trend models with money management overlays.

I think you have to re-examine [your approach] in order to evolve and survive. Most firms are looking for you to increase Sharpe ratios and so on. But, it is also my passion.

BUT WHAT HAPPENS IF YOU DON'T REVISE? DO THE MARKETS DRIFT?

They don't drift, but I just think that I can always do better. If this statistic is robust and makes the overall results better, let's use it. I'm always looking to mitigate maximum drawdown and increase Sharpe ratio.

To tell you the truth, though, since we've set the trend/counter-trend and pattern recognition systems and so forth—once we've put all that stuff together, we haven't taken anything out. What I'm always trying to do is enhance what I have with new ideas. That's different than if you were trading with System A and then you replace it with System B and then a few years later replace it with System C. Yeah, I'd say you might have a problem then.

However, when you start with System A and you keep System A and you have a different idea that you might call System 1A, which you integrate with System A and now you have a blend of the two, it's a different story. All that's saying is that you're evolving. You're not replacing or changing it, but rather, trying to make it better.

HYPOTHETICAL—A WOULD-BE TRADER DOESN'T KNOW MUCH EXCEPT THAT HE GETS HURT EVERY TIME HE TRADES DISCRETIONARILY. HE'S SOLD ON THE IDEA OF MECHANICAL SYSTEMS, AND HE'S DETERMINED TO FOLLOW ANY PATHWAY WHERE RESEARCH LEADS HIM. UPON WHAT IS HIS THEORETICAL SUCCESS GOING TO DEPEND?

The first thing will be his ability to evaluate and eventually write his own software, or at least have access to somebody who can do it. If you could get to where you could get the systems programmed and you did long enough simulated runs with out-of-sample results and you did the 'Monte Carlo' simulations to develop the distributions on "re-shuffling the deck" to determine what they would really look like, you could then turn your limited 10 year data stream into 100 years. Granted, it's still coming from the same basic return stream, but that's a heck of a lot better than just one return stream.

WHERE WILL HE HAVE TO GET HIMSELF PSYCHOLOGICALLY?

If he's a system trader, he only has to become comfortable with his ability to develop. From there, he should just let it go. The only reason he should be concerned is if during his actual trading, some performance aspect—say volatility, maximum retracement, Sharpe ratio—starts to go outside his 'Monte Carlo' simulation. That's when I would say he's got a problem.

HOW OFTEN HAS THAT HAPPENED TO YOU?

It hasn't. I would say our worst drawdown was in the high 20's percent. We knew from our simulations that Wizard could draw down in the high 20's, which is something we psychologically held onto as we were reaching our worst point. The market stopped within our projections and held true to form, the snapback was off the scale. Our equity probably ran 130-140 percent off that bottom, and it just stopped running this month, by the way. This is the first down month of any significance we're going to have since that run began. My recent revisions to the model should hold future maximum drawdown in the low 20's.

THAT MEGA-SNAPBACK SCENARIO FOLLOWING A DEEP DRAWDOWN IS PRETTY COMMON, ISN'T IT? YOU HEAR STORIES ALL THE TIME ABOUT TRADERS LOSING FAITH AND PULLING THE PLUG JUST BEFORE THEY WOULD HAVE ENJOYED SPECTACULAR RECOVERIES.

Yes, but look at any asset class. The bonds have been down 20 percent. Stocks have been down 30 to 40 percent. You have to put it all into perspective. There's nothing magical about commodities that says they are not supposed to draw down 20 to 25 percent on a system basis. If you did your research right, you should almost expect it. It's going to happen at some point, especially if you trade for over 13 years like we have.

Again, the 'Monte Carlo' simulation really shows you what that nasty case is going to look like. My old adage is, "Your worst drawdown is always in front of you." At some point, the market will probably deal your system a low volatility period or a big reversal that your system hasn't seen before and probably...*probably* you'll have your worst drawdown ever. If I trade long enough, I will see the low 20s percent drawdown that the 'Monte Carlo' simulations project.

THERE MUST BE TIMES WHEN EVEN YOU HAVE TO GEAR YOURSELF UP PSYCHOLOGICALLY.

Oh, all the time. Jack was probably better at that in the long run by saying, "Look, it's not deviating from any of the patterns, it hasn't exceeded this, it's going to go through that" but when you are losing somebody else's money and accounts are closing, it's human nature to try to stay positive and try to concentrate back on the research.

I probably feel a lot better now than when we were at the depth of that drawdown. Now, I can look back on it and say, "Yeah, it was a bad one, we did approach the high 20s percent but the comeback was also just about what we would have expected. And now, it's performing closer to the norm." But when you're in it, the psychological effect is brutal.

HOW ABOUT THOSE SCENARIOS LIKE THE IRAQI SITUATION WE'RE IN NOW, OR IMPENDING FED ANNOUNCEMENTS—TIMES WHEN YOU KNOW THE MARKET IS GOING TO DO SOMETHING BIG AT PRESCRIBED TIMES. DO THOSE OCCASIONS ALTER YOUR APPROACH IN ANY WAY?

No. We don't override.

The biggest temptation I ever had was in the Canadian Banker's Acceptance market a few years back. The Canadian Banker's Acceptance, which is the short rate, is traded on the Montreal Exchange. At the time, an eight or ten point move was huge.

There was an impending referendum vote and the market gapped down something like, I think, 70 points. Seven-zero. We had a *huge* short position. The temptation was to get out [and take the windfall]. I remember calling and Jack agreeing with me, but he said we have to stay true to form, so we didn't do anything. Lo and behold, the next day it was right back up where it started and the opportunity was gone.

It was obvious that the move was overdone. Eurodollars weren't doing anything. It was a knee-jerk reaction to the impending vote. You can't do anything about it. If you're a system trader, you're a system trader.

Of course, there were countless times when the outcome was just the opposite. There were lots of times during these recent moves in energy, currencies and foreign bonds where if I had discretion, I would have said, "Man, we've got to get out of this, it can't run any more." Then, the market runs another 15 percent. It's a dual edged sword. You've got to be careful. We've chosen to just never cross that bridge.

KEITH FITSCHEN

"I CAN SHOW YOU THAT YOU NEED THOUSANDS OF TRADES IN YOUR
DEVELOPMENT SAMPLE BEFORE YOU CAN HAVE ANY STATISTICAL
CONFIDENCE THAT IT'S GOING TO TRADE THAT WAY IN THE FUTURE."

*Keith Fitschen is the president of TradeSystem Inc., a com-
pany that markets the renowned Aberration system. The long-
term trend following approach tracks most commodity markets
except for the equities. Keith developed it in 1986 and privately
traded it successfully through 1993, the year he offered it to the
public.*

*Since that time, it has become one of the worlds most her-
alded commodity methodologies. On each of three occasions when*
Futures Truth Magazine *published its list of the top ten trading
systems of all time, Aberration was included. Anyone is free to
buy the system, complete with a full disclosure of all rules, or
trade it as part of one of Keith's multi-sized portfolio funds.*

*Aberration is the cornerstone of Keith's work, and judging
from the interview, an obviously comfortable fit for its developer.
Keith's main criterion for determining a system's validity is
whether or not it contains an abundance of trades in the data
sample, preferably in a variety of market environments. Aberration trades across almost all market sectors. (Sufficient volume
and diversification). It exploits the characteristic Keith views as
the most timeless and robust—long-term market momentum. It
thrives in the supply/demand driven markets as opposed to those*

that are tied into psychology. Consequently, Keith can't imagine how it will ever stop profiting, save for an unlikely scenario in which all the markets change their fundamental characteristics.

TradeSystem Inc. also markets two other systems—Aztec, (Keith's creation) which trades shorter- term trends, and I-Master, (developed by system colleague Murray A. Ruggiero Jr.), which trades the equities indexes. As Keith explained, the indexes don't trend like the other markets. I-Master actually trades counter to the prevailing move—it buys weakness and sells strength.

Keith frequently lectures across the country on the subject of system development. His three-hour seminars cover all the pitfalls of market research, including how to mathematically measure the validity of a system, and how to avoid the pitfalls of curve fitting.

HOW DID YOU GET INTO SYSTEM DEVELOPMENT?

I graduated from college in 1968 with an engineering degree. Rather than face the draft, I went into the Air Force and went to Viet Nam. When I came back, the Air Force decided they wanted to get me a masters degree, so I got one in stochastic estimation. That's the reason I'm doing what I am doing today.

Stochastic estimation is the process of extracting signal from noisy time series data. All data has some noise in it. The signals we were working with for guidance systems were noisy and we had to filter out the noise to get the true signal content. I got an education in doing that. There's nothing noisier than equity and commodity data. In the early eighties, I decided to put my education to practical use and started playing with the data.

Around 1986, I developed Aberration, which is a system that I started marketing in 1993. It's been sold commercially for ten years, although I've traded it since 1986. In real time, it's performed very well.

Aberration is a basket system. In my seminars I can prove that the best way to trade the true commodities—grains, meats, metals, energies, currencies, financials, softs—everything but the stock indexes, is with a trend-following technique. The best, most profitable trend-following techniques are longer term, which is what Aberration is. It trades all of the markets except the stock indexes. We do, however, trade the Nikkei Index, which is the Japanese stock index. It trends very well.

WHAT IS IT ABOUT THE INDEXES THAT MAKES THEM RESISTANT TO PURE TREND FOLLOWING?

Here's my explanation. The pure commodities are absolutely supply and demand markets. There is a physical deliverable bar of gold, bushel of corn, whatever. There are true hedgers on both sides of the markets. There are supply hedgers like the farmers and the end users like General Mills. Big time money is hedging positions on both sides of the market and price is really kept in line with the fundamentals. In that condition, if the market has something behind it that causes supply and demand to get imbalanced, it'll trend. That's what we're trading in the futures.

In the equities, it's entirely different. There is no deliverable. There's a certificate of stock which has no pure value associated with it. There are no hedgers on either side of the market and nobody knows what the true value is.

The concept of the efficient market has been shot in the butt in the last three years. The CEO's lie. The companies that do the audits lie. The analysts that pass judgment on the value of the companies lie. Nobody has a clue what the value of a company is. Therefore, the equities and the indexes that are based on the equities are a psychological market, not a supply/demand market. When psychology comes into play, people are moving prices up and down.

If you look at the S&P during a great economy, a yearly move might be 500 points. We routinely have 50-point range days in this market. What fundamentally could change in the United States that would cause a 10 percent of an annual range to happen in one day? It happens all of the time.

BUT SHORTER-TERM, YOU DO GET THOSE KINDS OF HYSTERICAL MOVES IN OTHER MARKETS TOO, RIGHT? FOR EXAMPLE, WEATHER MARKETS IN THE GRAINS.

Right, but they're based on supply-demand, not psychology. There are blow-off moves, but they only happen after a huge supply-demand imbalance that causes prices to go way up or way down. But in the equities, it happens every week. There's nothing causing it other than traders running the market up and running it down. If there's a true value and you get two hundred points above that true value, it's got to come down. That's why, yeah, it's overbought and then it corrects and comes down—maybe gets oversold and corrects back up from there.

That's why the index markets are best traded with a counter-trend strategy. All the good index systems are basically counter-trend where you're looking to sell strength and buy weakness.

YET, YOU SAY THE NIKKEI DOES TREND?

There's a different psychology over there. I've looked at all the world [equities] markets. The Nikkei is the best trending market and the U.S. indexes are the worst trending. The other indexes, the DAX, the CAC, the FTSE, even the Hang Seng Index fall somewhere between trending and non-trending. In my opinion, those indexes are actually the hardest to trade because you can't effectively use a trending or counter-trending technique on them.

WHAT MARKETS TREND THE BEST?

The currencies and financials.

DO YOU TRADE YOUR TREND SYSTEMS OFF DAILY CHARTS?

Yes. The only commodity markets I believe you can trade intraday are the indexes—the S&P, the NASDAQ and the Russell.

HOW DID YOU ARRIVE AT THE CONCLUSION THAT MOST MARKETS BEST LEND THEMSELVES TO LONG TERM TREND TRADING?

You have to do what the market gives to you. If the market can be traded only in a trend-following manner, you can't be trying to counter-trend trade it. If a market is amenable to counter-trend trading, you can't trend trade it as easily as you can use a counter-trending method. I try to find whether the market is trend or counter-trend. It's easy to do. You just roll data forward each month.

If you're looking for trend following capability, you'll buy into everything at the first of a month that's above a given average or [relative strength indicator] and then sell at the end of the month and re-invest. I've done that in equities and I can prove that over millions of trades, you're better off buying weak stocks than strong stocks. It's like a two to one return over buy and hold if you just buy the below average strength stocks. You'll under-perform by a third if you buy above average strength stocks. With that dynamic in the marketplace, you're a fool to try trend following.

I always trend follow in the commodity markets and I always counter-trend trade in the equities markets.

SO OBVIOUSLY, YOUR TREND-FOLLOWING METHODOLOGIES ARE GOOD ENOUGH TO CAPITALIZE OVER AND ABOVE THE CHOP AC-TION THAT ALL MARKETS GO INTO ALL TOO FREQUENTLY.

That gets us to the problem with trend following systems, which is that markets only trend maybe a third of the time. But that's plenty. The four portfolios we offer with Aberration have never had a losing year. We've had drawdowns every year and we always will, but the markets trend enough that if you put enough hooks in the water across a wide enough array of market groups, you'll get one that trends enough to make up for everything else.

Furthermore, Aberration is not always in the market. It just looks for strong trends. That's where the name comes from—we're look-ing for aberrant price trends. We only want to get in when prices are strongly trending one way or the other. The rest of the time, we're out.

IS THAT KEYED INTO SOME MARKET DYNAMIC SUCH AS AVERAGE DAILY RANGES?

Well, that's what [our subscribers] are buying—the logic that fig-ures that out. But I'll tell you that we statistically measure the strength of the trend. When it crosses a certain generic threshold, we go in the direction of the trend.

DO YOU USE PRICE TARGETS OR LIKE MOST TREND-FOLLOWERS, DO YOU ULTIMATELY GIVE BACK A PORTION OF YOUR OPEN EQUITY AS THE TREND CHANGES?

A basic trend-following system always gives back equity at the end of a move. You don't know when a move is over. If you're trend-follower, you acknowledge that the market has it's own head, which you don't try to figure out or predict. We just follow the market.

The mechanism most people use is a trailing stop of some sort. Our basic system does not have anything like profit targets, but we do wrap-around money management for our large traders who are trading a multi-lot strategy of more than one contract per each trade. We scale out at various profit targets. There are generic profit targets that get us out of half our position. The benefit is that when the open equity giveback hits, maybe you're only experiencing it on one of ten contracts. The rest, you would have exited near the price peak. That reduces drawdown.

YOU'RE TRADING ONE HUNDRED PERCENT MECHANICALLY, RIGHT?

Absolutely.

COULD YOU WEIGH IN ON THE PROS AND CONS OF THAT APPROACH VERSES JUDGMENTAL, SPONTANEOUS TRADING?

If you can look at a chart and use it to tell you discretionarily what's going to happen next, the argument there is you can always adapt and make money on the fly. That's truly a great gift.

I don't have that gift. I can't look at a chart and tell you what's going to happen next, so I've got to be mechanical. Generally, those [discretionary] traders will denigrate us and say, "We've never seen a system that has made money continuously." On the other hand, we don't denigrate them. I wish I were one of those people, but I'm not. I have to rely on raw science, a big data field, a lot of numbers and a lot of trades to make my decisions and I go with them.

Let me say this about discretionary traders. Again, if they can chart read and figure out what's going to happen next that is a great gift. The problem with it is that you're always second-guessing yourself. The comfort I have is when I go into a drawdown, I know exactly why I went into it. I stick to my knitting. I keep the same size on and know I'm going to come out of it.

People who discretionarily trade have the problem of struggling not to change what they're doing, which is very hard emotionally when you're in a drawdown. Similarly, when you're in a run-up and you want to plunge—take every signal that you see, you're going to over-commit. I think that a mechanical trader has an advantage during drawdowns and run-ups because he's going to have less trouble maintaining his usual approach.

DID YOU FIND OUT EARLY ON THAT THAT'S THE WAY YOU HAD TO GO, OR DID YOU HAVE TO BURN YOURSELF A FEW TIMES?

I never was a discretionary trader. I didn't know what was going to happen. When you try to figure that out, you're guessing. I knew I had to have something behind me to tell me why I believed what I did. If you're a trend follower and the markets are going up, then you can say, "I'm going with the trend." At least you have something behind what you're doing.

I'm of the opinion that 95 percent of a system's profitability is determined by the entry. I only know eleven [effective entries]. If you go to one of my seminars, that's what you'll hear me say. I've been doing this twenty years which means I find one every two years.

If you're confident with your development platform—TradeStation® or Metastock® or whatever—and somebody gives you a valid entry, you can develop a 95 percent solution in a manner of hours. There's just so much you can do once you have the entry. But it takes forever to come up with the entry. There aren't that many great ones.

BUT ON A LONGER-TERM WHEN A MARKET IS ONLY TRENDING A RELATIVELY SMALL PERCENTAGE OF THE TIME, DON'T ALL TREND-FOLLOWING SYSTEMS PRETTY MUCH HAVE TO BE BUYING AND SELLING IN THE SAME GENERAL AREAS IN ORDER TO BE SUCCESSFUL?

All longer-term trend-following systems get aboard the trend at a certain point. The question is, can you get aboard the trend early enough to capture a half or two thirds of it, and late enough to avoid being chopped up?

That's what *Futures Truth* is about. [The magazine staff] monitors three hundred systems and they tell you that there are few of them that are great and the rest of them are mediocre or losers.

SO A LOT OF THEM ARE NOT GETTING INTO THAT THEORETICAL "MUST GET ABOARD NOW" WINDOW TO CAPTURE PROFIT.

Actually, the problem with most of them is that they're curve-fitted. Among the ones that aren't curve-fitted, some have a better set of entries than others. The best of the best get in early enough to enjoy enough of the trend and late enough to avoid the chop. If you're in too early, you're in every trend that's more than a day old, and you'll get stopped out of the market a lot.

I give one or two seminars a month. They involve a couple things. The first part deals with curve fitting. We give two anecdotal pieces of evidence to show what curve fitting is and what it isn't. Then, I present a quantitative method to measure the degree of curve fitting in a system, which really revolves around the number of trades in your development sample.

Every system is developed on past data. It's not like gravity or relativity where you can say in theory how the markets work. Markets are too noisy for that. What you have to do is go over past data.

Most people develop a system on one chart. That might produce a hundred trades. That's not enough. I can show you that you need thousands of trades in your development sample before you can have any statistical confidence that it's going to trade that way in the future.

I go through that for 45 minutes, then I show people how I develop systems to keep them minimally curve fit. I show them entries, stops, filters, measurement metrics—how you measure whether a system is good or not—and then we tie it all together by developing a system in the session step-by-step. We give the participants that system to take home.

OTHER THAN MAKING SURE YOUR SAMPLE IS LARGE ENOUGH, HOW ELSE DO YOU GUARD AGAINST CURVE FITTING? DO YOU FORWARD TEST IN VIRGIN DATA?

No, you really can't. Walk forward testing is nice in theory. People say "keep half of your data back when you test." The problem is, there's generally not enough data to generate the thousands of trades that you need for statistical validity, and so if you keep half back, you're making the problem worse. There are 57 worldwide commodities that I use to do development on. Most are U.S. markets, but there are some London metals and world bonds.

INCLUDING SOME MARKETS, ACCORDING TO ONE OF YOUR SITES, THAT I HAVEN'T EVEN HEARD OF. DRIED COCOON FUTURES AND THE BALTIC FREIGHT INDEX TO NAME A COUPLE.

Right. You're always looking for a market that isn't highly correlated with anything else. We develop across a basket of 57 commodities. The problem is, half of those commodities don't even go back to 1980. So, there are about 5000 bars in each commodity. Five thousand bars are going to generate about 100 trades. If you leave half out [to create virgin data], you've got 50. Fifty trades is nothing—I say you need thousands. I won't believe anything that shows 50 trades. It's not even worth looking at.

I would rather put all the data in and get a thousand trades than put half in and get 500. I need thousands to believe it's going to trade that way in the future.

DOES THAT MEAN YOU WOULDN'T BE INTERESTED IN DEVELOPING SOMETHING THAT EXPLOITS CHARACTERISTICS PECULIAR TO ONE MARKET?

I would do that if I had enough data to believe it. We developed our I-Master program specifically on the indexes. The entry has 4000 trades behind it so I believed it. I didn't develop it on cocoa or soybeans, but specifically on indexes.

THE BOTTOM LINE IS, AN ABUNDANCE OF TRADES IS WHAT YOU'RE CONCERNED ABOUT, REGARDLESS OF WHETHER IT APPLIES TO FEW OR MANY MARKETS.

Right. Day trading systems have one advantage over longer-term systems that hold overnight; you can get a lot of trades. The S&P

futures have traded since 1982. If you traded every day, you could have 5000 trades in your back test.

HAVE YOU EVER HAD SITUATIONS WHERE A SYSTEM GOES BAD ON YOU BEYOND WHAT YOU'VE SEEN IN HISTORICAL DATA? IF SO, AT WHAT POINT DID YOU START LOSING FAITH?

Well, you're asking, "Do you ever go beyond historical projections?" The answer is, you *always* go beyond. Mathematically, you have to go beyond. If you've developed something on 20 years of data and you've got an infinite amount of time ahead of you, you're always going to have a bigger maximum drawdown in the future. Does that mean the system has busted? No.

I would bet that Aberration never goes bad because Aberration is a very elegant trend following method on a supply and demand market. That supply and demand market is never going to change.

Individual commodities may change. I believe the British Pound has fundamentally changed. It used to be the greatest trend market of all the commodities in the '70s. I haven't had a commodity system that can make money on it since 1992.

SO MARKETS DO CHANGE.

Individual markets do change. The whole character of the commodities markets doesn't change and so trend-following systems will always work to a greater or lesser degree. In order for the whole thing to go bad, the fundamental aspect of commodities would have to change.

Index systems always go bad. The reason is again, that they are psychology driven markets and constantly evolve. When the S&P came out in 1982, I used to trade it with trend-following methodologies and it had no problem making money until 1987 when we had the Crash. Then it became a counter-trend market. In the early 1990's, there was tremendous volatility. In 1997, they halved the value of the contract from $500 a point to $250. Also, that was the year of maybe the biggest change of all—when they introduced the Globex session.

Before Globex, 95 percent of the S&P change occurred from the day session open to the day session close. Now, almost half of it occurs overnight meaning that systems trying to trade the S&P have half the range they used to have. The last change occurred in March 2000 when we entered the bear market. When one of those things happens, the systems that were capable of trading it stopped working and new things started working.

Systems that trade the indexes will constantly go bad. I had a system that traded the S&P called Acendex. The bear market ended its effectiveness. It made great money until March 2000 because it was developed on a market that was constantly up from 1982 with a couple of brief exception periods. When we went into a bear market, it couldn't survive. I threw in the towel and I told the users that it wasn't going to be able to handle a bear market.

In a case like that, you know when it's broken. You know what fundamentally changed in the marketplace that would prevent it from working. There are a lot of systems including our I-Master system that is having trouble trading the indexes. A lot of people are scratching their heads, but I'm pretty sure I know what the problem is. The problem right now is, we're in a period of almost six-year low volatility in the S&P. We haven't had volatility this low since 1997. Even back in 1997 when we had the small ranges, it was $500 a point—twice what it is now.

Systems make money on range. If the market doesn't move, you can't make money.

THE FUNDAMENTAL CHARACTERISTICS OF A MARKET TELL YOU
WHETHER THE DRIVERS BEHIND YOUR SYSTEM ARE CONTINUING
TO BE VALID. BUT YOU DON'T INCORPORATE FUNDAMENTALS IN
YOUR ACTUAL TRADING, DO YOU?

It's not the fundamentals of the market, it's the market. What is
the market doing? If it's in a bear market and you are aware that you
developed a system in a bull market and it's not working, that's your
clue that something's wrong.

Everything I do is mechanical and technical, which are the same
to me. You test and find out what works. But you don't have to be a
trader to know there's a drought in the Midwest or to know that there
must be a shortage of coffee because the price is going up. I know
this stuff, but I don't pay attention to it. The system decides everything.

As a private trader or even as a part of a big company, I'll never
know the true fundamentals like the true insiders. I'll never know
what General Mills knows. Some of these guys that sample all over
the Midwest still won't know what's happening in Argentina or Australia, but General Mills knows. I'll never know the fundamentals like
they know them, but I will know price the same second they do.

DO YOU PERIODICALLY RE-OPTIMIZE YOUR SYSTEMS?

No. At the beginning, I get my thousands of samples, and from
there, that's how I trade. I don't go back and do it again. Aberration
has a single parameter value, which relates to the number of bars that
are used to make our decision. In 1986, we decided to use 80 bars,
and that's what we're using now. I developed it on 35 markets then.
Now, I test on 57 or 58, and the bar count is still 80. That was the
right number to start, and I determined that because I had enough
samples to get an idea of what the right number should be.

HOW DO YOU APPROACH PORTFOLIO ALLOCATION?

We start with our smallest portfolio. We put in the performing best grain, our best meat, financial, energy and so forth. That provides diversification. Our second concern is size—we trade a one lot. Then, look at risk. We take trades with a risk of less than $3000 although we give the client the ability to pick any number he wants us to test to decide what he likes best.

We have portfolios for all account sizes. We have a starter portfolio for ten to thirty thousand, a mid-sized account from thirty to fifty thousand, a full-sized account from fifty to one hundred thousand, and then a global portfolio for greater than $100,000 accounts.

Our sectors are equally balanced. We have the same number of currencies as we do financials. We do that even though some trade better than the others. The dollar index trades better than live cattle. People sometimes ask, "Why not leave the weak sisters out, like the meats, which are the worst trending markets?" I tell them they can do that, but I discourage it because the fundamentals of the meats are independent of everything else. If the fundamentals are in place for that one sector to move, nothing else will necessarily move except the meats. Right now, we're in a $7000 live cattle trade. It doesn't happen often, but when it does, it can carry the whole portfolio.

HOW ABOUT YOUR APPROACH TO MONEY MANAGEMENT?

It's straightforward. You never want to pyramid. The only time you'd want to do so is if you had a system that had a higher expectation of profit further down the trade than at the start. I know of none of those, so it doesn't make sense to me to put more on later.

In our seminars, we prove that it's best to scale out of multi-lot positions. That gets you out of part of the position at the peak, and minimizes drawdown.

We know how much we're willing to risk on each given trade. That projected risk determines whether we're going to include that trade in the smaller portfolios, and how many contracts we're going to assign to it in the bigger portfolios.

I'll grant you that you can have the occasional overnight price gap. If it gaps beyond your stop level, you don't adjust, you just get out. It's not like you're sitting there day after day wringing your hands.

SOMETIMES THOSE GAPS CAN BE HELLACIOUS THOUGH. HAVE YOU EVER BEEN ON THE WRONG SIDE OF A SHOCKING EVENT LIKE 9-11?

The thing about the catastrophic events is they'll find a way to hurt you no matter what positions you have on even if you're diversified. When the Hong Kong melt happened, [1998 collapse of Pacific Rim markets], I got messed up in something I never would have thought could be an Achilles Heel. It turned out to be the Mexican Peso. It gapped down, I believe, six cents, or three thousand dollars a contract. Catastrophic events will manage to somehow hurt you. They're out there, but I don't know any way around just trading through them. But on the other hand, we actually were on the right side of 9-11. We made a windfall.

HOW IS TRADING LIKE EVERYTHING ELSE IN LIFE AND HOW IS IT DIFFERENT?

Trading is like everything else in that if you want to be good, you have to work. I spend untold hours on it. You're not going to get good at it reading somebody's book.

This doesn't necessarily mean you can't make money following someone else's system. If you want to gain skill and understanding, though, you have to work at it.

It's different because you're constantly under stress. It's not like a normal job where you might have a normal day 80 percent of the time and 20 percent of the time you have a stressful day because you did something wrong or something happened. In trading, you're pretty much always in run-up or drawdown, so you're pretty much always at the high end of your emotions.

WAYNE GRIFFITH

"ANYONE WHO HAS DEVELOPED A SYSTEM HAS TO ADMIT THAT THERE
ARE SITUATIONS THAT THE SYSTEM DOES NOT COVER."

Wayne Griffith is the inventor of the "Anticipation" system, a mechanical approach that is well known to many in the futures industry. It is the most highlighted product offered by Advanced Systems, Inc., a CFTC registered commodity trading advisory company located in Greenville, South Carolina.

Unlike other system creators, Wayne doesn't manage funds, (although he plans to soon), nor does he provide an advisory service in the traditional fashion. He sells a subscription service, which brokers and other industry insiders can use to access the signals. They have not received full disclosure of the exact system mechanics, however. Although willing to provide an overview, more than once Wayne pulled back before revealing too many specifics about his methodology. To everyone but Wayne, some aspects of the approach are simply going to remain a black box—an arrangement that has evidently satisfied advisor and clientele alike since the program's 1993 inception.

Although "Anticipation" produced theoretical profits across several markets, Wayne decided early on that coffee was the best vehicle for it to trade, largely because it was one of the few markets in the 1990's that was not subject to protracted periods of price inertia. For 20 months, Wayne watched in anonymity as his system racked up real-time profits. Then, he submitted it to Futures Truth and they began to track its performance from May 1995. The system topped the prestigious Futures Truth Performance Table bi-monthly ranking for over six uninterrupted years and has dipped below top ranking only five times since independent monitoring began eight years ago.

In 2000, Wayne saw the coffee market drying up, so he moved "Anticipation" into the thriving stock index futures. Today, Advanced Systems offers three variation of "Anticipation" in addition to the original system, all were created by Wayne. "Anticipation II" is "Anticipation" modified to give more consideration to trend. "Anticipation First-Born" is a variation with counter-trend more emphasized and "Anticipation Mid-Point" is a hybrid of the two. The diversification provides more phasing into and out of the markets than a single version would allow.

Two aspects of Wayne Griffith make him a counterpoint to most of this book's other interviewees. For one thing, in an extroverted business, Wayne is reticent if not shy. I found myself asking considerably more follow-up questions than usual to compensate for frequent short, unelaborated answers.

Two, he is not a system trading purist—he believes that he can and will successfully augment his systems with judgment. He hasn't started yet, and acknowledges that his endeavor may fall short of expectations. Still, while many have decried the hybrid approach as being the road to ruin, Wayne is confident that his years of experience will mitigate the pitfalls. Besides, at age 60, he figures people should pursue activities in life that bring them joy. Aside from family, markets are Wayne's near-sole passion. He wants to be engaged in a way that the "cold numbers game" of system trading simply doesn't allow.

YOU'RE WELL-KNOWN THROUGHOUT THE INDUSTRY AS THE IN-VENTOR OF THE 'ANTICIPATION' SYSTEM.

Right, the 'Anticipation' System is what most people know of me. I owe a lot of that recognition to John Hill of *Futures Truth* magazine. When I was in his seminar, he said that the charts tell you everything that you need to know. He emphasized that you have to anticipate the market, which is what inspired me to name my system "Anticipation."

The system looks to get in on a rebound after a retracement. I go with a range breakout in a counter-trend setup. I'm trying to go with the trend, but I'm waiting for movement in the opposite direction first. If I'm looking to buy, I'm looking for it to go down first, if I'm looking to sell, I want it to go up.

SO YOU'RE ENTERING ON LIMIT ORDERS?

No, I've found that however fractional the amount is, you need some sort of movement off the opening to go with.

WHAT'S YOUR TIME HORIZON?

We can change positions intra-day, although when that happens, it's usually not a happy day because it means that we started out wrong. Generally though, that doesn't happen—we stay the same way in a trading day. The trade times vary—about two days is the average.

IS THERE ALWAYS A POTENTIAL SIGNAL OFF THE OPENING?

No. You use chart setup as a filter to determine whether you trade or not. If the setup is OK and the market has gone down and the chart indicates that there might be an upmove according to our programming, then we might get an entry.

ONCE YOU'RE IN IT THOUGH, PRESUMABLY, YOU'RE EXPLOITING A TREND.

Right, that's what we're attempting to do.

HOW ABOUT THE STOPS?

They key off of chart patterns. Every day you're in a trade, there's always a "liquidate" or "reverse" point based on the chart pattern. Since the charts change, we don't know today what tomorrow's exit point will be. It doesn't lend itself to pyramiding in the way some people favor—that is, put on so many contracts because the risk is 'X' amount. 'X' changes as the trade progresses. We do have a fail-safe money management stop in case the chart pattern makes the stop too far away. That's also mechanical and keyed into market activity.

ONE THING THAT MY PARTNER AND I HAVE NOTICED ABOUT COUNTER-TRENDING SYSTEMS—SUPPORT AND RESISTANCE, RANGE TRADING, ETC.—IS THE DIFFICULTY OF APPLYING NON-ARBITRARY STOPS. A LONG SIGNAL WILL PERSIST EVERMORE AS A MARKET CONTINUES TO DROP, WHICH MEANS THAT EVEN AS YOU GET STOPPED OUT, YOU'LL STILL BE IN BUY MODE. A MOMENTUM SYSTEM BY DEFINITION DOESN'T HAVE THAT PROBLEM—YOU'RE ONLY BUYING AS THE MARKET GETS STRONGER. BUT AS A FADE SYSTEM LONG DETERIORATES, YOUR BUY MANDATE, IF ANYTHING, ONLY GETS MORE INSISTENT. IS THAT A REALITY YOU ALSO HAVE TO WORK AROUND?

To a degree, but not completely. A market will go back and forth and generally, the more it's going in one direction, the more ready it is to go in the other direction. If it has too much steam, however, we squelch wanting to go in opposition to it. Normally we would reverse if the setup was right. If the market was too strong against us though, we would liquidate.

PLEASE SHARE SOME OF YOUR PERSONAL BACKGROUND.

I'm an informational CTA. My formal education is in math, physics and psychology. My first job was in the space program in Huntsville, Alabama. I went immediately into modeling and simulation. I programmed the model of the propulsion system of the second stage of the Saturn V moon rocket, a model to determine radiation exposure of the Saturn V lunar orbiter, simulated Apollo Space Telescope orbit and determined time-phased electrical power to be generated by solar cells, designed a polynomial manipulation language for use in control system design and analysis—did various scientific modeling like that.

My next employment was with IBM doing commercial data processing. For an electrical utility holding company client, I programmed a system to generate commercial and residential electrical rate schedules for all the individuals and businesses within three southern states. We had to adhere to government regulated profitability allowances and billing equitability requirements. For that same company, I programmed an econometric model to determine when to issue bonds, preferred stock and common stock, quantities, yields, etc. I did various things of this nature until I began full-time trading in 1987.

WHY IS IT THAT SO MANY PROFESSIONAL MECHANICAL SYSTEM TRADERS COME FROM THE SCIENCE SECTOR RATHER THAN THE BUSINESS WORLD?

I would think it was due to the formula orientation.

SO THE SCIENTIFIC METHODOLOGY IS APPLICABLE?

Yes, I think it's key. You're doing the same thing. You're looking at the markets and saying, "What are the forces here and what are the rules that define them? What are the probable outcomes?"

I had no way of knowing that this would all lead to something I was really interested in. Where I am now, the most important criterion of having reliable products is being able to back test and [construct] valid models and simulations.

I had first started trading commodities in 1969. I went full-time in 1987, making my living by trading OEX options and no-load mutual funds. On the weekend before 'Black Monday', I went around telling people that the market was going to crash on Monday. I was so new at this that I didn't perceive what a once in a lifetime opportunity it was going to be. I had made correct moves—I'd liquidated any long positions and had bought puts and written calls, but I could have done it to a much larger degree than I'd done. I came out well, but I had passed up a really good opportunity.

HOW HAD YOU ARRIVED AT YOUR CONCLUSION THAT THE MARKET WAS GOING TO CRASH?

I was dead sure of it. I know it sounds ridiculous, but I was. There are a lot of people who can vouch for the pronouncements I was making that weekend. It was because, instead of looking at trading as a hobby or something part time, I woke up in the morning, and the first thing I'd do was turn on FNN, which was what CNBC was at that time. I was absorbed in everything everybody said, all the market moves and everything [connected with trading] from the time I woke up until about 10 or 11 at night. And I was doing it every day.

AT THE TIME, HOW MUCH OF WHAT YOU WERE APPLYING WAS ME- CHANICAL? OR TECHNICAL?

Nothing. It was all gut.

WHICH APPARENTLY WORKED FOR YOU, UNLIKE THE MULTITUDES OF OTHER PEOPLE WHO MOVE TOWARD MECHANICAL TRADING AS A MEANS OF SURVIVAL.

Right. I think being so immersed in everything going on is what made it all so clear to me. I haven't done that sort of thing since then. It's interesting you should be bringing this up, because that is where

I'm headed now. I miss that. [Discretionary trading]. I long for it. As a result of doing the system development and system trading, I've become somewhat of an emotionless robot. The fun and joy—the pursuit and the challenge—I don't get that in the system trading. System trading is just a numbers game.

You have expectations for how your model will turn out over the long-term. You might be disappointed, discouraged or depressed over a particular day, week or month of system activity. Still, you're somewhat detached from it. You're just running a numbers game, waiting for it to be your time.

HOW DID YOU GET INTO THIS "NUMBERS GAME"? OBVIOUSLY, MAKING A LOT OF MONEY ON 'BLACK MONDAY' WASN'T EXACTLY AN INCENTIVE TO VEER OFF INTO A NEW APPROACH.

I got into mechanical trading because I did very poorly during the time right after the crash. It was a period of extreme volatility and wild moves. I shouldn't have been trading then. But still having a "job" mentality where you are supposed to work every day, I thought that I had to trade every day. The full-sized stock index contract moves were mega-dollars then. You had a choice of either unreasonable dollar value stops or reasonable sized stops triggered almost instantly, sometimes almost by the bid-ask spread.

It was too stressful and I wanted to reduce the stress. I backed off and took about three months to assess how I wanted to continue trading. I knew I didn't want any approach based on fundamentals, which I knew meant that I'd always be trying to keep up with a wide array of information that other people would always be ahead of me. I knew that I would always be at a disadvantage.

So I went in the technical direction. I figured long-term trading would be the easiest but I didn't choose it for two reasons. One, I didn't like the [wide] stops that are associated with long-term. You'd have to give back so much money. Two, I wanted to make a model that I'd have faith in, and I knew I'd have more faith if more trades were generated. I needed a large amount of trades to give me a larger foundation of confidence for the future.

I started doing research; doing exploratory data analysis using Data Desk Professional and other statistical [software] packages. I was seeking an understanding of how the markets behaved. I'd look at stops, range expansion, open-high-low-close, a variety of charts—all for the purpose of understanding the characteristics of the market. After several years of doing research, I started turning what I had observed into trading rules.

HOW ARE YOUR CUSTOMERS PARTICIPATING? IT'S NOT THAT THEY'RE IN AN ACTUAL FUND, RIGHT?

They subscribe to trading signals. Rather than actually give an individual the black box signal generator program, we give it to a system-assist broker. The subscriber then has the system-assist broker trade the signals for him.

Previously, we had provided the signals to any individuals and brokers who wanted them, but then we had overtrading and slippage. We had people cheating. More system-assist brokers than not were trading for people they shouldn't have been trading for. They were trading more contracts than they were authorized to trade. I didn't want the slippage that would result from that, so I just shut everybody off.

Today, we provide the system but we don't sell the system. We don't give anybody the capability of generating the signals except people we trust.

DO THE PEOPLE WITH THE ACCESS KNOW EXACTLY HOW THE SYSTEM WORKS?

Generally. Not totally.

DO YOU MANAGE ANY MONEY NOW?

No, but I plan to. I have been telling people that I was going to start this summer. But I haven't yet, (been too busy), and I'm not sure how soon it will be.

My plan is to utilize the systems and system knowledge that I have as the basis of a trading program, but I'd also want the ability to override and interject my own knowledge. I expect that sort of approach to do better than simple system trading and it would provide more opportunities than simple gut trading.

OFTEN WHEN PEOPLE MARRY DISCRETIONARY AND MECHANICAL TRADING, THEY WIND UP WITH THE WORST OF BOTH SIDES. WHAT EVIDENCE DO YOU HAVE THAT YOU WOULDN'T SUCCUMB TO THAT PITFALL? HAVE YOU BEEN TRACKING THE MARKETS TO SEE HOW YOUR DISCRETIONARY IDEAS WOULD HAVE PERFORMED?

No I have not, because it would take the dedication that I once gave it to do it for real. Just a whimsical look now and then wouldn't really tell me anything.

YOU'VE DONE VERY WELL WITH YOUR MECHANICAL APPROACH. WHY RISK THAT WHICH IS SO HARD TO QUANTIFY?

Anyone who has developed a system has to admit that there are situations that the system does not cover. I know when my system has a good feel of what's going on, and I know when it doesn't. So why sit here and refuse to supplement that which isn't programmed?

When you're system trading, you have to endure the consequences of trades that you know are blatantly wrong. If you were [using both approaches], you could sidestep those. Of course, you would sidestep some you thought would be wrong that turned out to be good.

**DON'T YOU FIND THAT THE TRADES YOU FEAR THE MOST ULTI-
MATELY TEND TO BE THE BIGGEST MONEYMAKERS AND THE APPAR-
ENT NO-BRAINERS CAUSE MOST OF THE TROUBLE?**

Yes, but I *know* that, which I think would play to my benefit rather
than my disadvantage. I wouldn't want to squelch the ones I fear the
most. I would want to squelch the ones that are in a dull, ho-hum, do-
nothing dead situation.

I don't mean to over-emphasize my desire to include judgment.
My main focus will continue to be systems. I just want to augment
what my program knows with what I know.

**HOW WOULD YOU BE MARKETING THIS? ISN'T IT TRUE THAT IN-
VESTORS TODAY TEND TO BE SOLD ON THE IDEA OF MECHANICAL
SYSTEMS AND THAT DISCRETIONARY FUNDS ARE MORE OUT OF
FAVOR?**

You bring up a valid point. I have wondered what my response
would be when I tell prospects and existing customers that it's going
to be part mechanical and part discretionary. I don't know how that
will sell. I just know that I want to do it for me and for my money—
for my retirement money. It will either be accepted by prospects and
customers or it won't.

**ASIDE FROM YOU NARROWING THE ACCESS OF YOUR SYSTEM, HAVE
THERE BEEN OTHER CHANGES IN YOUR APPROACH IN THE TEN YEARS
SINCE THE INCEPTION OF 'ANTICIPATION?'**

When I created 'Anticipation' in 1993, it worked overall on most
of the markets, but some markets would go through periods of low
volatility. They wouldn't lend themselves to the kind of track record
[I was hoping to achieve] in Futures Truth. Coffee appeared to be the
most promising market, so in the early 1990's, that's all we were
trading. We were doing well enough that I wasn't paying much attention to other markets.

NEW YORK MARKETS HAVE A REP FOR BAD SLIPPAGE AND FILLS. WAS THAT A PROBLEM FOR YOU?

At different times, we had good market action and brokers that were very good and we'd come out well. Then, we would have periods of bad slippage. That was somewhat unpredictable. We altered the program so that the signals wouldn't be generated if the prices and average daily ranges fell below a certain level. Even though the signal might be theoretically profitable, in reality, we knew we'd have trouble executing it, so we wouldn't let it generate in those circumstances.

SO YOU STARTED WITH COFFEE AS A WAY OF LEADING WITH YOUR STRONGEST SUIT. OF COURSE, THE '90S WERE THE TIME OF AN ULTIMATE MEGA MARKET. DID YOU CONSIDER PLAYING THE STOCK INDEXES?

At that time the S&P contract was too big to trade. (The minis weren't available until 1997). I didn't want to take the loss size that an individual trade would have to take based on the size of accounts that we traded. And then, we were much too slow in recognizing that the e-mini S&P contract was such a liquid, well-traded market. We didn't start trading it until the coffee market went dead.

At the beginning of 2001, we switched to the S&P and NASDAQ minis. The Midcap and Russell minis are also growing in liquidity and we added them to our trading this year.

DO YOU TRADE ALL MARKETS THE SAME WAY?

The basic program does, but in order to provide a little diversification, I purposely changed some stop and profit objectives as well as the time of the day the systems started trading. Some continued to trade at the open, but others would be restricted until midday or mid-afternoon. As a result, we have 12 trading versions of the same basic system—three versions each trading four stock index markets.

WAS THAT STRICTLY FOR DIVERSITY'S SAKE, OR WAS IT ALSO IN-TENDED TO ACKNOWLEDGE SPECIFIC CHARACTERISTICS OF INDIVIDUAL MARKETS?

Mainly for diversification. Even though our current markets are all stock index futures, there are occasions where we're long one and short another, which the alterations helped make possible. There are occasions when we're flat. Right now, [July, 2003], the Russell is doing a lot better than the others because it's had a volatility expansion while the others are still dead.

What we found is that people who wanted to pyramid positions were adding contracts to exactly the same thing. That would result in too many contracts trading at the same time. We had experienced slippage in coffee associated with that happening. We didn't want that here, although again, we had underestimated the liquidity of the stock indexes. We were overly cautious in terms of how many contracts we would let be traded.

PHILOSOPHICALLY SPEAKING, WHY DO SYSTEMS WORK?

For both psychological and technical reasons—the psychological aspect of systems is that they keep you from making decisions based on fear and greed. From the technical standpoint, the system hopefully gets you in the market at some advantaged price.

HOW WOULD YOU DISTINGUISH BETWEEN A BAD RUN THAT IS WITHIN ACCEPTABLE SYSTEM PARAMETERS AND ONE DRAMATIC ENOUGH TO CAUSE REASONABLE DOUBT REGARDING THE SYSTEM'S VALIDITY?

There are two ways to look at it. One, the system has in reality bit the dust. The other, it has done so according to the perceiver. I think it's usually according to the perceiver. That has to do with timeframe and confidence in the system. I've been watching 'Anticipation' perform in real time for roughly ten years. I've seen more examples of disappointing time periods than most people, but I also have more perspective on how it comes back. So, I know what I think of it and believe to be true about it. Somebody new that gets aboard might be more inclined to say, "I'm out of here!" after taking some heat.

We try to keep subscribers from doing that. It seems to be a function of how long they've been in the markets and how mature they are.

HOW CAN YOU DETERMINE WHETHER OR NOT THEY'RE CONTINU-ING TO STAY ABOARD WITH YOU?

If they re-subscribe, we presume they're continuing to trade, and if they don't, we presume they aren't.

WHEN YOU'RE IN RESEARCH, ARE EYE-POPPING RESULTS ALONE GOOD ENOUGH FOR YOU OR DO YOU HAVE TO UNDERSTAND SOME-THING ABOUT WHAT'S BEHIND THEM?

I don't look at the good numbers first. I look at the worst drawdown and the number of times a significant drawdown has occurred. If I've had one drawdown in 10 or 15 years, that's a lot different than having 15. Only after determining that the number of occurrences of drawdowns is satisfactory do I become interested in the net profits.

I tell people that if they gave me a day—a week at the most, I could make them a system that looks much better than 'Anticipation'. It just wouldn't have anything to do with the future. It would be an optimization of the past. I do care what's behind the numbers—I won't use moving averages, oscillators or such to make the numbers fit the past.

YOU'RE VERY COGNIZANT OF ROBUSTNESS.

I am. I always start with a market premise. I never just start running against the data just to see what it looks like. It needs to be based on something I know, such as contraction follows expansion and expansion follows contraction. Unless you base your program on some rule or action that you know will continue into the future, then yes, you should be very suspect of good numbers alone.

WHAT ELSE WOULD TELL YOU THAT A SYSTEM IS ROBUST?

When I make a data run, I look at how smooth the performance history was. If you've made all your money in a short period of time, that wouldn't be robust. I also do sensitivity analysis on everything. I'll change the variables on whatever I'm testing left and right. I'll want to see the system hold up through a wide range of such changes.

LET'S SAY SOMEONE WANTS TO BECOME A PROFESSIONAL TRADER. THEY BELIEVE THAT THE MECHANICAL APPROACH IS THE ONLY WAY THEY'RE GOING TO BE ABLE TO SUCCEED. WHAT ARE THEY GOING TO NEED IN TERMS OF STARTUP, PHILOSOPHY, TECHNICAL CONSIDERATIONS, ETC. IN ORDER TO BE ABLE TO MAKE IT, ASSUMING THEY NEED TO MAKE $50,0000 A YEAR TO LIVE?

Are they going to have this as their only income, or are they doing it in addition to other income?

LET'S SAY IT'S GOING TO BE THEIR ONLY INCOME.

I hate to be so persnickety about my questions, but do they have to have income flow every year or can they miss it this year and make a hundred thousand next year?

HMM. I GUESS I'D LIKE TO LEAVE THAT AS OPEN AS POSSIBLE AND HAVE YOU TELL ME WHAT IS REQUIRED IN WHICH GIVEN SCENARIO. I'M LOOKING FOR A GENERALIZED OVERVIEW OF WHAT IS NEEDED FOR A TRADER TO REALISTICALLY APPROACH A PROFESSIONAL PATH.

Don't do it at all if you must have a steady stream of money. If it can't be, like I said, where you make some, go through a flat period, maybe lose a little and then make some later, then just forget about it. You have to be ready for periods that are better and worse than what you expected. It's hard to look at as some sort of substitute for a job income.

WHAT OTHER PITFALLS SHOULD A TRADING HOPEFUL BE AWARE OF?

A mistake that I made right after the Crash was, when I'd lose, I felt like I had to make it right back. That is a sure road to disaster. Now if I lose, I let it hurt my feelings and I look the other way. I do not try to rectify it. That one approach will go a long way toward saving someone. It's potentially disastrous to try to make up losses too quickly. If you lose, you should cut back on trading. It doesn't matter if you think the next time you're going to win, because obviously, you could be wrong.

It's just as bad if you make a lot of money quickly. Then, people regard their successes as a given and want to escalate their trading too much. I guess it gets back to greed. It applies more to discretionary trading, but I've seen it in system trading as well. People who have made money quickly trading 'Anticipation' have gotten into trouble by rushing to increase their positions.

From my observation, even system traders often fall victim to fear and greed. If you're going to quit when you lose, don't get involved at all. That's a loser's game. It can be hard to follow a system. It comes down to how long you've been trading it and how much you believe in it. 'Anticipation' can be especially hard to trade, because it's often buying when it looks like it should be selling, and selling when it looks like it should be buying. If you understand, though, that's what you need to be doing, it's easy rather than hard.

IT SEEMS LIKE YOUR LIFE IN GENERAL IS TIED INTO TRADING. DO YOU HAVE ANY OTHER INTERESTS? IN MY LAST BOOK, PEOPLE WHO HAD SURVIVED TRADING DEBACLES STRESSED THE IMPORTANCE OF HAVING BALANCE IN LIFE. ARE YOU BALANCED?

I'm not balanced. I would like to be balanced, but there's only so much time. I guess my wife and family and trading constitute the majority of my interest and time. That works for me. I guess maybe I love it more than most people. I don't want to retire. The idea of not being associated with the markets would just be horrible to me. I would hate not to do this. I would probably pay to do it instead of being paid for it.

I'VE HEARD YOUR RELIGIOUS FAITH HAS ALSO PLAYED AN INTEGRAL PART IN YOUR TRADING EXPERIENCE.

It has. After 1987, when I was trying to become mechanical, every time I'd get discouraged, along would come a gift. It might have been a gift of knowledge or a gift of money—but something that kept everything on track.

IT WAS SOMETHING THAT WAS HELPING YOUR DESTINY.

Yes. [Pause]. I really do believe that.

Tom DeMark

"THE BOTTOM LINE WAS, AFTER SEVENTEEN PROGRAMMERS AND
FOUR OR FIVE YEARS OF TESTING, THE BASIC FOUR OR FIVE
SYSTEMS WORKED THE BEST."

The following quote by Tom DeMark appears on at least one of the numerous websites devoted to his services.

"I have added a caveat to the phrase 'the trend is your friend.' It is 'unless it is about to end'."

The original "trend is your friend" may well be the ultimate trading axiom—the idea hammered over the head of everyone who enters a trading pit or peruses an investment primer. System traders are particular disciples of the philosophy. After all, almost all mechanical approaches exploit some aspect of market momentum.

By contrast, Tom DeMark's techniques have been anticipatory in nature from early on. They forecast rather than attempt to get aboard existing trends. Specifically, they are tools for picking market tops and bottoms.

"The problem with trend following systems is that they're too late," said Tom, "and too competitive if you want to buy size [big positions]. You get price gaps and slippage."

For over thirty years, Tom has been advising and managing funds for some of the industry's biggest financial names. His list of trading relationships includes George Soros, Michael Steinhardt, and the Goldman Sacks Investor Group. He was an official in such renowned companies as Tudor and Van Hosington and a partner of the late Charlie DiFrancesca, who was one of the Chicago Board of Trade's most noted size traders. Currently, he is working with SAC capital, the nation's number one hedge fund that has $4 billion under management.

His techniques pervade investor software including CQG, ILX-Thomson Financial, Aspen Graphics, FutureSource, Bloomberg and Investment Software Systems (www.tomdemark.com). They feature several original proprietary indicators such as TD Sequential ™ which forecasts market directional changes based on price relationships, and TD Combo ™ which helps confirm the sequential signal. Both incorporate a set number of adjacent bar chart prices in a "setup" and a "countdown" sequence.

On top of all that, Tom is an author. His celebrated books include: "DeMark on Day Trading Options," *(co-written with son Tom Jr.),* "The New Science of Technical Analysis" *and* "New Market Timing Techniques."

His ascension in the trading industry was nearly immediate. After attending law and business graduate schools, he joined a Milwaukee, Wisconsin investment company that had $400 million under management. Tom was the market-timing developer, a job that introduced him to a wide array of research ideas and influential people. Four years later, the funds had mushroomed to $4 billion.

He determined that most of the popular advisories of the time were offering largely the same sell-oriented sentiment-based techniques. He set off on his own research course, which led to an involvement in the commodities markets. "That's where most of the thinkers, the creative people were," he observed. He also

118

liked the leverage that those markets provided. He found a kindred spirit in commodities expert Larry Williams. The two formed a lasting friendship and reciprocal trading idea sounding board.

He turned his attention to the burgeoning International Monetary Market (IMM) branch of the Chicago Mercantile Exchange, which housed currencies, interest rate and financial markets. By that time, he was well involved in equities fund management. He looked to futures as a way to trade something else on his own without conflict. However, his personal trek became more than a mere diversion once he discovered how readily his futures methodology translated to the stock portfolios.

YOU'RE CLEARLY NOT A RUN-OF-THE-MILL TECHNICAL ANALYST. HOW DO YOU FUNDAMENTALLY DIFFER FROM THE AVERAGE SYSTEM PLAYER?

First of all, I don't consider myself a technician. I'm a market timer. Technicians are subjective; chartists are "chart artists." I'm a chart scientist.

Most of my work is an exhaustion type of approach where you're buying weakness and selling strength. I've done a lot of statistical work and the conclusion that I came up with is; markets make lows not because of smart buyers but because of the lack of selling. Conversely, markets make highs because of a lack of buying...the dissipation, if that's the right word, of buyers.

As a market moves higher, more people buy at the high and less resources are available. Unless there's a fundamental change that would enable a whole new set of buyers to enter, markets will top just by default. They will either move sideways or decline due to the lack of buying. This is totally opposite what most people think.

GIVE US AN EXAMPLE OF HOW YOU CAPITALIZE ON THIS PHENOMENON.

There are relationships in the markets. First of all, you've got to identify the environment. Are you looking for a buy or a sell? There's a pattern that seems to exist whether it's a one-minute or monthly chart.

On a daily chart, if you have a series of nine consecutive closes lower than the close four days earlier, you've identified a potential buy environment. If it's greater than the close four days earlier, you've identified a potential sell environment. This works on one-minute, daily, or monthly, regardless.

Once the setup process is completed, the countdown begins. Once you've accumulated 13 closes, less than or equal to the low of two days earlier, that gives you a point of downside exhaustion in the market. That's usually where markets turn. TD Combo ™ has additional rules. Sequential is somewhat imperfect because it doesn't catch the exact tops and bottoms. Combo does, but Combo doesn't speak as often as Sequential.

There's one additional Sequential requirement. Either the low price bar eight or price bar nine must be less than the lows of both price bars six and seven, and vice versa for sells.

That sets up the environment. Sometimes markets turn right there, but often it's complicated; it might turn on countdown thirteen. But you've got at least a short-term move in the market once the sequence is completed.

HOW ELSE DO YOU APPLY THE CONCEPT OF PRICE RELATIONSHIPS?

I use opening prices a lot. People use yesterday's close as a reference, but a lot of things change between the yesterday's close and today's open.

If, say, the ten-year bond had a close of 113-00 and there was good news after the close, so it opened 113-16. Then closed that day at 113-08. The spin perpetrated by the media is that there was a quarter point up move for the day, when in fact the open to the close reflected an eight point decline as opposed to the eight point advance, if you base it from the close to the close.

One of the indicators I've got is called TD Camouflage ™. If the market closes up for the day, but down from the opening, and if the high is above the true high of two days earlier, it's pretty revealing even in a chart that the movement the next day projects lower.

Conversely, if you go back to September 21, 2001, the S&P's closed down on that day. Everyone was bearish because of the media talking about it being down, but in fact, it closed above the opening. Also, its low was less than the true low two days earlier. That falls under TD Camouflage™. It tells you that the next day you are more likely to trade above the high of that camouflaged low day than you are to go below the low. I consider that a low-risk buy opportunity. The critical price is really the open, not yesterday's close.

When I left Tudor Trade, working with Paul Jones, I went to work with the biggest trader at the Board of Trade, Charlie DiFrancesca. He traded 40,000 bonds a day, but he never carried a position overnight. I taught him camouflage, and something called TD Diff™, which enabled him to hold trades overnight.

There are other ways to measure buying and selling that people don't even think about. You can use other comparisons to yesterday's close. For example, if you compare yesterday's close to today's high, or today's low to today's close, that's looking for buys. The reverse of that is from yesterday's close to today's low is selling. So is today's high to today's close. That's the kind of stuff I do...look for relationships. It helps to incorporate that into your analysis.

Here is an example of TD Diff™. If I have two consecutive down closes, I'll look at the buying pressure, which is the relationship between the low and the close. If the current day's difference between the close and the low is greater than the difference yesterday, that means there is more buying. At the same time, I'll measure the selling pressure by looking at the true high verses the close for both the down days. If the difference between today's true high and the close is less than yesterday's, that means selling pressure has diminished. I look for days when that's decreasing at the same time buying pressure is increasing.

REMIND US AGAIN—WHAT IS "TRUE HIGH?"

You fill the price gap. If today's high is less than yesterday's low, that is a gap. If today's high is less than yesterday's close but above yesterday's low, that's a "lap." (That's a term I invented).

If your high is less than the previous day's close, you fill that cavity. You're considering today's high or yesterday's close, whichever is greater, to be the point of selling pressure, because you've come off of a high. Same for today's high versus yesterday's low when the low is greater. You remove the price gaps so that the higher price is the one that you're considering.

I'll use two consecutive down or up closes as a short term tool. I've also got hundreds of long-term indicators that I have created.

SINCE YOU LEAN SO HEAVILY TOWARD ANTICIPATING MARKET TURNS, DO YOU CONSIDER ANY OF THE STANDARD OVERBOUGHT-OVERSOLD INDICATORS?

People make mistakes there, too. They misuse divergences. Divergences are a symptom, not a cause.

Take the RSI [relative strength index] for example, which is a misnomer as well. It's not a great indicator because it's exponential from close to close. If for some reason the exchange closes early—an electrical failure say, or presidential assassination—with that short day, you get a closing price that contaminates the data. It's an artificial day, and if it's an exponential calculation it's in there permanently. It diminishes with time because it's exponential, but as long as it is in the data, which would be until the contract or security stops trading, it's always going to have that skewering effect. An arithmetic oscillator would be better.

A lot of people think a market is overbought-oversold based upon where the market is versus the threshold that defines overbought-oversold. [Twenty to twenty-five percent is a standard oversold reading and seventy-five to eighty traditionally means overbought]. There's actually a distinction between mild and severely overbought.

We've done testing on this and have come up with more appropriate thresholds. To use the RSI as an example again, which I'd never actually use, if you're above 70 on a nine or fourteen day time period or whatever for six or more trading days, that is a severe overbought market. If you're below 30 for six or more trading days, that's a severe oversold market. If you're above overbought levels or below oversold levels for five or fewer days that is mildly overbought or mildly oversold.

When you've established a mildly overbought-oversold condition, if the market has backed out of the extreme zone on a closing basis before day six, then the market should turn. Once the market has become severely overbought-oversold, what has to happen is, the oscillator has to go back into neutral, redefine itself and go back into overbought or oversold, but only reside there in the zone for five or fewer days.

The problem with the way people normally look at divergence is they could have severely overbought readings five times in a row. If you were to have just one thrust into overbought....a single time for five or fewer price bars, then you could produce a sell signal.

Or say you're overbought for something like 10 days, you pull into neutral and do your second trip up there. The frequency isn't as great, but the time is less. As a result, you have a declining oscillator with an ascending price.

That's when meaningful divergence appears. It has nothing to do with the way people normally use it, it's linked to the amount of time the indicator spends in overbought-oversold. It's just a different concept...a different approach.

PLEASE ADDRESS THE PITFALLS OF GUT TRADING.

It's all trend following because the emotions are dictated by what other people are doing. It's too competitive. Also, the news of the day seems to influence people. You want to be totally removed from that.

In my work, I don't even look at the chart headings; I don't care if it's copper or bonds or IBM or Microsoft. I just remove the label and analyze it that way.

SOUNDS LIKE YOU'RE ANTICIPATING A LATER QUESTION OF MINE. I'VE BEEN ASKING MY SUBJECTS TO ADDRESS WHETHER A SINGLE SYSTEM SHOULD HOLD UP IN A BROAD VARIETY OF MARKET ENVIRONMENTS, OR WHETHER IT'S MORE REASONABLE TO ALLOW INDIVIDUAL SYSTEMS TAILOR-MADE FOR THE UNIQUE CHARACTERISTICS OF EACH GIVEN MARKET.

My belief is that a system has to be universal. It's got to be simple. It can't be optimized, obviously.

HOW DO YOU AVOID OVER-OPTIMIZATION?

Make certain that a system works in all time periods and all markets. Everything I've got works that way. Whereas some people, because they're subjective, change their approaches and their results. My stuff is static. It's always there—remains the same. I haven't re-tooled any of this work in years.

SO THE MARKETS HAVEN'T REALLY CHANGED EITHER.

They don't change. It's all a function of fear and greed. It's reflected in the price movement.

ALTHOUGH THERE ARE SOME SURFACE DIFFERENCES, AT LEAST THE S&P DAILY RANGES ARE CONSIDERABLY GREATER THAN THEY WERE 15 YEARS AGO.

I'm still using the same technique on them. TD Sequential ™ was created in the seventies before the introduction of the S&P futures. Not only that, it has application to one-minute bars. And the technique hasn't been re-tooled at all.

There have been one or two imperfections that I've modified. Day eight or day nine being less than both six and seven. There's also one other thing that's come up in the meantime when you go through the countdown. The low of 13 has to be less than the close of eight. That's evolved in the last 20 years, but the application is there.

The same one-minute chart that I look at now wasn't even created then. Computers didn't even exist and you couldn't look at a one-minute chart. But the technique is the same—the data was holding up even back then.

Most people get caught up in the idea of creating a cattle system or a financial system. All it is optimized. They've retrofitted it.

DO YOU EVER HAVE AN IDEA THAT TESTS WELL, BUT THEN DOESN'T CONTINUE TO PERFORM IN REAL TIME?

When I come up with an idea, I go back three or four years and I'll test historically from three or four years back. Then, I'll apply the idea to current markets.

SO YOU USE VIRGIN DATA. BUT WHAT HAPPENS IF IT DOESN'T PERFORM BEYOND THAT?

I'll throw it away. But most of my work seems to be up-sloping longer-term. Some of it may just move sideways and you'd throw it away.

I make certain that it works in all markets. I'll take a cattle chart, Microsoft, the bonds or S&P's put it all together in one portfolio and do the testing from back three or four years ago. Right now, [March, 2003], I'd go back to maybe 1999 and then go back in time from there to maybe the mid seventies. From there, I'd project it into the "future." What has it done from 1999 to the current time? From there, I'd test it six more months in real time. If it doesn't work, it's not going to work back then and it won't work now. I think most people just make it too complicated.

Simple does work best, doesn't it?

Yes. When I was at Tudor, I created four or five systems for Paul Jones. Subsequent to creating them, they brought in guys who do optimization models, artificial intelligence, everything possible that was upper level math. The bottom line was, after 17 programmers and four or five years of testing, the basic four or five systems worked the best.

Some people get caught up in moving averages, and some get caught up in trend following techniques. They come up with the best percentages to use and for the breakout ratios. They've got the ideal moving averages. But what people don't realize is, in a trending market, any moving average will work. In a trading range market, overbought-oversold indices work. The key is determining how to distinguish the two.

We did testing and found that 73 percent of the time markets are in trading ranges and 27 percent they're in trending markets. Fifteen to 17 percent of the time markets will trend up and 10 percent of the time approximately, they'll trend down. Why they trend down less often than up is because people who buy like to add to their positions and reinforce the trend. When they sell, it's one decision they're making, not a multiple decision. If you don't like it, you don't like it at all. So it comes down faster. To the upside, there are varying degrees of "like," which is why up markets trend slower.

When you're doing your final strategy analysis, what resonates the most with you? Net profit? Return on account? Percentage of win trades vs. losses?

Yes, all of that. Sharpe ratio. We've got thresholds on all of that. I do not know what they are off the top of my head, but my programmers do. All of them have to be at minimum levels; they've got to meet certain requirements in a broad universe of testing.

There's logic to most of the stuff that we do. Without an apparent theory, we'll think about what it's doing and usually come up with some reason.

Most of what we look at is price patterns and relationships. We don't just look at something that has profitability for three, four or five months. We really test it for 10 or 15 years and in a broad universe of markets.

HOW DO YOU DETERMINE YOUR STOPS?

There's something I use in TD Sequential™ and TD Combo™ based upon the relationship of the high to the low of the extreme low or high day of countdown. Let's say I get into a low risk buy as price is coming down. I isolate the day that had the lowest price with the deepest downside thrust. Then, I take the true high of that day and subtract that low...obviously you won't need to consider true low since that will, by definition, be the lowest price. I take that true range and subtract it from that extreme low. That will give you a reflection of what the maximum downward thrust of the move was. We're looking at that number as a potential setup for a stop.

There are other qualifiers. Often, closing prices can occur under the influence of, say, a big trader or group of traders selling size on the close. I look for confirmation on the next day's open. The market has to open lower than that close. What frequently happens when you break out is, a market gets out of equilibrium on the close, and then it re-establishes equilibrium on the next open. But if the market opens lower, and then—another requirement—it's got to trade one or two ticks under that, then you could make your exit. That last qualifier would keep you in if the market opened on its low.

Your stops are not just arbitrary numbers.

Right, the market tells me what to do. You'll find that throughout all of my work. Furthermore, I don't believe in changing things. My work is pretty static. It takes a long time for me to become convinced that the markets have changed. They really don't.

And why is that?

Because they reflect human nature. Fear and greed. I don't see that changing.

Do you recommend paper trading?

You've got to do that. Most people are lazy. I'd say 99 percent of the people don't have an opinion. The one percent that does doesn't have anything concrete or logical to back it up—no reasons behind it. Invariably, they'll take hard-earned after-tax dollars and invest it based upon someone else's advice. Most people would just as soon rely on someone else.

So they'll look at my work and get excited about 13's, which are usually indicative of tops or bottoms. They'll go out and buy a position based on that. Invariably, it'll be their first trade, and they'll have put on too big a position. And it'll be wrong—nothing's perfect. Then, they become disenchanted and they won't trade it anymore.

You've got to paper trade. If you're going to follow a system, you've got to understand everything behind why it works. If on the other hand, you develop your own system and understand it completely, then, paper trading wouldn't be necessary. It's all down to understanding what you're doing.

ANY FINAL OBSERVATIONS ON HOW TO ARRIVE AT THIS UNDERSTANDING?

Technical analysis does not work, but market timing does. Technical analysis does not work because it's subjective.

There are three levels of analysis. The first is looking at a chart, which is where most technicians operate. They go with whatever their attitude is at the time, which is highly interpretive.

The second level is indicators. You go back and test them, and if it's successful in identifying turning points in the past, you can extrapolate and say they're going to work in the future.

The third level is systems. To go from indicators to systems is a small step. For me personally though, I don't want to go from indicators to systems in my books or in the work I do with other people because I'd be doing their work for them. People can just take that small step on their own. Plus, I don't want to have interference from the CFTC, NFA and the SEC.

SO YOU'RE SOMEWHAT PROTECTIVE OF YOU METHODOLOGY?

People have criticized me because everything is "TD this, TD that." Two of the bigger law firms in Chicago told me before I published to have everything with a TD and to have everything trademarked. They anticipated well—there have been hucksters out there who have cited DeMark methods and TD this, TD that—who were totally wrong, and I had to stop them. There are a lot of people in the business who have stolen other people's work.

COPYRIGHT CONSIDERATIONS ASIDE. DO YOU WORRY THAT IF PEOPLE KNEW TOO MUCH ABOUT IT, IT WOULD DILUTE THE EFFECTIVENESS?

No. Right now, the biggest traders in the world are using it. There are 20,000 users on Bloomberg right now. But buying strength and selling weakness is a tough methodology to follow. It's tough for me.

And it's such a wide universe. There are different markets and different time periods. Some people are using one-minute bars. Some are using five, eight, thirteen, whatever. Some are using daily, some weekly. Some try to anticipate, going with the 12th bar instead of the 13th, for example. There are lots of different personal applications. So, I don't see any risk. The markets are too big.

MIKE DEVER

"I CAN'T STRESS THIS ENOUGH. YOU DON'T WANT TO BE MAKING
SINGLE STRATEGY, SINGLE MARKET BETS IN A PORTFOLIO IF YOU WANT
TO SURVIVE OVER A LONG PERIOD OF TIME."

*Mike Dever is the chairman and director of research of
Brandywine Asset Management, a company that he founded in
1982. Today, it holds investor funds of just over $100 million,
and has recently enjoyed a 15 percent annual average net return
to investors.*

*The firm applies a diversified array of totally mechanical strat-
egies to numerous markets, including global equities and interest
rates, traditional commodities, currencies, and even mutual funds.
It touts a universe of "alternative investments," a reasonable
summation considering the unorthodox makeup of its markets
and approaches. Any methodology that can be quantifiably determined to be a likely candidate for repeatable performance is
fair game for inclusion in the company's portfolio.*

*In contrast to other mechanical system proponents, good his-
torical performance numbers alone are not enough to inaugu-
rate a new system component. Throughout the interview, Mike
stressed the importance of understanding the return drivers—the
trading concepts behind any given strategy performance.*

133

The two cornerstones of Brandywine's investment approach are diversification and non-correlation of strategies and markets. Mike is ever cognizant of the need to minimize "event risk," or the odds of a single market shock affecting too much of the portfolio too adversely all at once. Consequently, the firm regards systems as mere building blocks. The real key to Brandywine's success is how the systems all interrelate in the unified program.

As a related corollary, the company is currently launching 1777 Capital, an investment management firm that will extend the base of Brandywine's products and services to the general investing public. In keeping with Brandywine's overall investment philosophy, 1777 Capital products have been especially designed to exploit absolute return strategies; i.e. performances that are independent of macro bull and bear market conditions. This concept was especially intriguing to me, considering how difficult I've found it to separate systems from the overall market environment. The fact that Mike Dever and company can master such an approach seemed like a natural interview entree.

PLEASE EXPAND ON THE CONCEPT OF "ABSOLUTE RETURN STRATEGY."

We are looking at returns independent of any single market action. Gold might be up and our returns might be down. Bonds might be down and we might be up. The stock market might be down and we might be up. We are looking for returns that are generated solely from the underlying return driver for each individual strategy that we employ.

We are diversified, systematic managers. Systematic meaning that we are looking for repeatable ideas that we can backtest and apply on a uniform basis going forward. We don't want to have any day-to-day discretion in our operations. But in the development of the strategy, there's a massive amount of discretion, trying to determine what really is a valid strategy. I don't feel that simply backtesting and coming up with results is sufficient in determining whether or not something is valid. I think you have to understand the return drivers, or the concept behind the strategy. If you feel that it is valid, then you go forward and back-test it as sort of a final validation.

For an example, people look at the stock market and very quickly off the top of their head determine that there's an intrinsic return in owning stocks. Our philosophy is, we don't want to just accept that as a given. We want to find out what the drivers are. Why is there an intrinsic return? So, we'll back test it against a number of different factors and try to determine what drives stock prices.

WHAT DOES DRIVE STOCK PRICES?

You can really break down stock price action into two primary components over time. In the long term—say 30 years, it's the earnings growth that drives the stock price of a company. It has a very high correlation—over 90 percent. In a less than eight-year term though, the stock price has far more to do with the changes in the P/E ratio than the actual growth or shrinkage in the E portion. Short-term, it's really driven much more by the price-earnings ratio. That's essentially saying that it's the whims of the crowd of investors that drive any individual stock price more than the individual earnings of that company.

So what you're able to at least figure from this is that if you have a strategy that is trying to buy stocks based on earnings, you'd better be prepared to give it at least eight years to work or else hedge out the other influences on stock prices. Otherwise, more of your return is going to be derived from the whims of other investors than from the actual performance of the stock that you pick.

One of the things that we do once we clearly understand that is in our market neutral equity strategy. For example, isolate the factors that we're trying to capture. If the factor is corporate growth, we'll take that element out of the equation to the greatest extent possible, the investor enthusiasm component. Under the market neutral strategy, we buy stocks based on what we think are the long-term return drivers and sell stocks that we think are junk or overvalued based on long-term return drivers. We try to match them in the same industry systematically so we are capturing what it is that we want to capture. In this way, we are avoiding or at least limiting the profitability of that strategy being influenced by factors outside of our control—those whims of the crowd that I spoke of.

SO FUNDAMENTALS ARE ENTERING YOUR MECHANICAL APPROACH?

Absolutely. Our philosophy is that we want to have as many return drivers in our portfolio as possible. We want them to be as diversified as possible so that they're not all subject to the same kind of external events. Our most diversified product is our Brandywine Alliance Fund. Alliance has strategies that are broadly diverse. There are fundamentally driven strategies such as I just described in stocks. There are fundamentally driven strategies in commodities as well, looking at supply/demand equations. There are sentiment-based strategies utilizing government-required reporting such as insider stock purchases and sales, and the Commitment of Traders Reports in commodities.

Exactly, and that's the intent; to take strategies that people would traditionally look at and say "You need discretion to apply these." We're saying, "No, you don't." With our approach, if you can't quantify it and accurately test it, then you don't have a repeatable strategy. Our whole philosophy is to develop things that are repeatable.

**HOW SPECIFICALLY FITTED ARE YOUR APPROACHES TO GIVEN MAR-
KETS? DOES AN APPROACH FOR ONE MARKET ENVIRONMENT AP-
PLY TO OTHER ARENAS TO ANY SIGNIFICANT DEGREE?**

It depends on the strategy type. The simplest example of a transferable strategy type is momentum or trend-following strategies. Here you are capturing the emotional whims of investors. A lot of people try to explain it away by saying something like, "Well, we think trend-following works in the currencies because international capital flows take a long time to happen and that creates long trends." Or they'll say trends work in the grains because of the seasons. Their opinions come from rationalizations, which unfortunately are false according to everything we've seen. The trends are really based on the changing emotions of the crowd.

The type of a trend-following strategy shouldn't change no matter what market you're applying it to. Our philosophy is when we've got a trend-following momentum type strategy, we'll find a broad range of parameters that appear to identify when a trend is in place and apply that to every market that we are trading. We don't differentiate and say that for sugar we're going to trade shorter-term and that we are going to trade longer-term for bonds. They all trade the same broad parameters because, based on our research and philosophy regarding this type of strategy, it's not the underlying commodity or market that's a special factor driving these returns. It is the whims of the investors and that doesn't change regardless of what market they are trading. This is opposite to what we are attempting to capture in other strategies, such as the market neutral stock strategy I was talking about. That strategy takes information that's specific to a company's corporate activity.

WHEN YOU'RE DOING THAT SORT OF NARROW CASTING SPECIFIC TESTING, HOW DO YOU KEEP OVER-OPTIMIZATION FROM BECOMING MORE OF A PROBLEM?

Again, that comes down to understanding the underlying concept. We feel that system testing should start just like the scientific method. You start with the hypothesis and quantify it...

SO IF YOU SEE FANTASTIC NUMBERS THAT YOU DON'T UNDERSTAND, THAT ALONE DOESN'T MEAN ANYTHING TO YOU?

Right, it doesn't mean anything to us.

Once you identify the underlying concept that you think is valid, then you just use standard scientific research and back-testing methods. You identify the primary variables and you vary them over a broad range. You're looking to make sure that the strategy is robust—that small changes in the parameters don't effect big changes in the outcome. We're just applying that premise, which is pretty straightforward.

Identify the most primary parameter sets. In any strategy, no matter how simple it may appear, there are really a dozen variables. I've had many discussions over the years with people about strategies that they're using. They'll say, "It's a trend-following strategy, it's not optimized and there's only one parameter—a moving average crossover."

Well, let's dissect that statement. First of all, if it's a crossover, there has to be a couple of parameters. You've got two averages; one crossing over the other. I'd say, OK, what are the look-back periods for each of the averages? What are the calculations behind them, are they simple, exponential or what? When it crosses over, do you put the trade on immediately when it crosses over? They might say yes—OK, that's also a parameter. It's a 'zero' time parameter, but it could have been a delay where you wait one or two days. Is it set up so that it must cross over by a certain amount? Again, maybe they just happen to select a 'zero' parameter for that.

What commodities are you trading it in? That's definitely a parameter. When are you rolling over those commodities? First notice day? Last trading day? In some markets, that's a *significant* parameter, such as when there are seasonal tendencies.

As you start identifying the actual makeup of a strategy, you may realize that you've got a half dozen, maybe a dozen fairly clearly definable and significant parameters. Our philosophy is to make sure that we have clearly identified and understood all of them. We need to determine whether any of the parameters are significant, because even if we don't back-test them, they will still have an effect on the results of that strategy.

Some researchers feel that if they do not test different variations on a parameter, then they did not curve fit or optimize it. In reality, by not testing a parameter, they settled blindly on a parameter. I would argue that is worse than actually testing in order to determine the robustness of the strategy. When you get down to the testing, you want to make sure you understand, first and foremost, the strategy—where the return drivers are coming from and all of the variables that are inherent in that strategy.

INTERESTING. IT'S NEVER AS SIMPLE AS IT SEEMS.

It really isn't! People make it sound simple, but the reason that it's simple to them is because they simplify it. They didn't look at it in its full measure. What they're saying is, "I don't really understand what this strategy is."

By doing that, you will find that parameters that you have totally ignored or that you arbitrarily assigned a value to might be a significant parameter that you should have been testing the strategy for—like rollover dates. It might sound contradictory at first, but although our overall philosophy is quite simple—to incorporate multiple strategies exploiting diverse return drivers into a balanced portfolio—it isn't always simple to understand the specific details inherent in each strategy.

OBVIOUSLY, DESPITE THE HIGH POSITION YOU HOLD WITHIN YOUR COMPANY, YOU'RE STILL VERY MUCH INVOLVED WITH THE RE-SEARCH.

Absolutely, and that's another difference in philosophy compared to some of the other firms. I remember discussing some research that we were doing years after we had started trading. I had some people come up and say, "Well, what are you researching? What *is* there that you could still possibly be finding?" They were trading pursuant to a specific style and didn't see the need to diversify beyond that. It comes down to the firm's philosophy. We didn't go out, identify a system and start trading that. We went out and created a structure and a philosophy that really requires us to continue to diversify port-folios more and more. We need to accomplish this by identifying new strategies that can add value to the portfolio.

To us, it's a very basic kind of mandate. Once we have the struc-ture in place, it allows us to properly diversify—to keep balance among the different strategies and markets we're trading. It's a pretty straight-forward process.

DO YOU RE-OPTIMIZE PERIODICALLY?

Yeah, I like to refer to it more as "re-balance." Our feeling is that we don't want to be optimizing for risk-adjusted returns strictly using mean variance modeling. We want to create portfolio balance that will lead to the returns being most predictable.

I think there are four criteria you need to take into account when balancing a portfolio: two that are completely objective and two that are extremely subjective. The first two are the same inputs used in basic mean variance type modeling: the return profile of each strategy and the correlation among strategies. This analysis can be totally mechanical. The main reason to look at the mean and variance of returns of each strategy is to normalize for the variance so that you are comparing "apples to apples" when looking at the return of each strat-egy. Certain strategies are just very low volatility strategies as op-posed to, say, a leveraged trend-following system applied to the commodity markets which is a higher volatility strategy. You've got to normalize for that.

The last two other parts of allocation adjustment have a subjective nature to them. One part is to understand the significance of returns of each of the strategies. We put a weighting on that according to what we think it should be worth, all other things being equal. We may decide that this strategy gets twice the weighting of another strategy because the former is more robust, the returns are more significant, and we expect a higher probability of them persisting in the future.

The significance of returns takes into consideration how many variables are primarily driving the strategy's performance. How significant and stable do we think varying those parameters is for those different variables? What look-back period are we considering and to how many markets does the strategy apply? You want to make sure that you don't fool yourself with a strategy that looks great because it's a fundamental strategy that uses sugar supply and demand data and yields great numbers, but is only trading once every year and a half, not counting rollovers.

You don't have many data points and it's a single market. It might look really good, but the significance of the results is far less than the significance of a sentiment-based strategy that is trading in 50 commodities markets. The returns might look great, but you can't weight that strategy at the same level based on its mean variance as you would weight the sentiment strategy with all other things being equal.

BUT WOULD YOU USE THAT STRATEGY?

We'd absolutely use it if it has a valid return driver and has significance of returns because it provides value. We would use it, but it wouldn't get the same weighting that a more significant strategy would get.

GETTING BACK TO THE COMPONENTS OF ALLOCATION ADJUST-MENT...

Right, the fourth is the concept of event risk. That's where we ask if, due to the nature of the underlying drivers, a group of strategies is at risk for the same event. In that case, they might get an across-the-board lower allocation in the portfolio. An event that occurs may bring all the performances of the strategies down in a way that wasn't reflected in the back-testing.

Let's say that you have four strategies that are designed to trade equities utilizing market neutral techniques. Their performances may look historically uncorrelated, but by understanding that they're all subject to, say, a declining interest rate market or a rising revenue market or GDP increases, you can understand that there is event risk. If something comes as a shock to the system, that's going to have an impact on the return driver, one return driver could affect all four of these strategies simultaneously.

A lot of times, the historical track record of the correlation of the strategies doesn't adequately reflect risk in those strategies in relation to each other. Correlations over time are an average. Investors really don't care about the average if you have an immediate event shock that takes their portfolio down ten or twenty percent when on average they were only expecting it to be down five. You've got to take the event risk of the different strategies into consideration.

On the level of allocating to strategies, you have these four elements coming into play, two of which are very much systematic and two of which require a subjective assessment of the strategies themselves. But, once the allocations are set, they would not be something that would change day-to-day on a discretionary whim.

Those give you the strategy allocations in a portfolio. The second half of the portfolio balance equation is the generation of the market allocations. The strategy allocations for us are fairly static. They are re-adjusted when a new strategy goes into the portfolio, but they're not something that I would change on a regular basis. The market allocations—how much we put into the different stocks or commodities that we're trading—varies every month. That's based on the changing correlations of the various markets and the volatility of each market. If we are long in the grain markets entering a drought period, sometime over the next 30 days, because of the increased volatility, there's almost certainly going to be a decrease in our position size in those markets to adjust for the extra risk.

HOW DO YOU DIFFERENTIATE BETWEEN A STRING OF LOSSES FALL-ING WITHIN ACCEPTABLE SYSTEM PARAMETERS AND THOSE THAT ARE OFF THE PAGE—NECESSITATING RETHINKING THE STRATEGY?

I've been in seminars before where I've asked that question to the group. I'll give you a sense of the responses I got plus my own feelings.

One CTA [Commodity Trading Advisor] said that his company looked at the last three years performance of every strategy in every market. If [a given strategy] hasn't made money in a given market, they drop the market from the strategy.

On the same panel, someone else argued that they liked to go *with* strategies after a three-year losing period because they felt there was some [impending] reversal of long term mean performance. In other words, they expected such a market to outperform at that point. There are two completely opposite opinions to the same question.

My answer to the question is that with every strategy, you have to understand the underlying basis for any given return. What is the nature of the return driver? Is the concept that you think is in place to provide an inherent return on that strategy still valid? If it is, stay with it. A losing spell is a good red flag and certainly gives you an opportunity to evaluate whether the return driver is still valid. If you evaluate it and say, "You know what? It *is* valid." Then don't change anything. You have the luxury of being able to do that if you're trading across multiple strategies.

But if you're only trading one strategy, it forces you into making a very hard decision at the worst possible time. "I just lost a pile of money, and I can't afford to lose any more." You may not be making a rational decision about whether the strategy is still valid and whether you should stay with it. It could be an emotional decision. You may be deciding that you just can't take it any longer.

I had an interview in the early eighties with a CTA on the West Coast. They were looking for someone to come in and do research for them. I was a young guy and thought it would be pretty exciting. They were an established name. They showed me a strategy performance without giving me the specifics behind it. They said, "Look, we developed the strategy. Everything is sound—it trades these markets and projects this return. We started trading it and in the first six months, it had a worse drawdown than in any period throughout the history of our testing. What do you think is the problem?"

I responded with a three or four page letter stating that to me, it really pointed to a high-level of probability that there was a flaw in the research methodology. The parameters in their strategy were almost certainly curve fitted to the historical data. The odds that the six-month period where they actually started trading it was going to deviate that substantially from the decades of back testing pointed toward the poor performance being more than just an anomaly in the market.

The lesson is that in doing this kind of performance analysis, you've really got to make sure that what you're trading is in fact a valid strategy; that you didn't fool yourself. That you didn't back-test it and curve fit it and add filters to make the back testing look good. That you remembered, and kept in mind at all times, that all that matters when you finally put money behind it is, is it going to make money? You've got to be super honest with yourself on that. If you know that what you've done is valid and you combine it with a multi-strategy approach, it makes it that much easier to get through those drawdown periods.

WHAT ABOUT THE MARKET BLINDSIDE THAT SUDDENLY SKEWS YOUR HISTORIC PARAMETERS? FOR EXAMPLE DURING BLACK MONDAY, THE DAILY RANGE AND NET CHANGE OF THE S&P FUTURES WAS INSTANTLY SEVERAL TIMES LARGER THAN ANYTHING THAT HAD HISTORICALLY HAPPENED PRIOR.

First of all, if you are truly diversified in a portfolio, an event like that should have a minimal impact even though it might be a big outlier. I can't stress this enough; you don't want to be making single strategy, single market bets in a portfolio if you want to survive over a long period of time.

The second thing is, I talked before about allocating to different markets. You need some sort of systematic dynamic adjustment to say, "Wow, volatility has really ratcheted up!" There was a small amount of warning going into October 1987. For about a week before the Crash, volatility was picking up somewhat. Obviously, it went to a massive extreme on the day it happened.

I know a lot of futures traders during that period who lost a pile of money in the equity index markets. Their systems didn't flip them fast enough. They were looking at end-of- day stuff or even end-of-week stuff. They lost a ton in index futures, but they made a pile of money in short-term interest rate futures as those markets rallied.

GIVE US A SNAPSHOT OF WHAT WOULD TYPICALLY BE IN YOUR PORTFOLIO.

I'll send you a typical snapshot. [An actual past day of holdings for the firm]. It includes, I believe, about 70 stocks with a fairly good balance between longs and shorts. There are probably about 20 or 30 commodity market positions. There are some currency positions. There was a small equity component in there as well. Also some mutual fund positions—all long, because we can't short those.

I'D IMAGINE THAT THE FORMULAS YOU'RE COMING UP WITH FOR YOUR TOTAL APPROACH HAVE GOT TO BE GARGANTUAN.

Actually, each individual one is fairly simplistic.

WHICH SEEMS TO VALIDATE WHAT IS SAID ELSEWHERE ALL THE TIME—THAT SIMPLE IS BEST. SO YOU AGREE WITH THAT STATEMENT?

Absolutely. Each individual strategy is as simple as we can possibly make it. Ironically, keeping a strategy simple is often more complicated than it sounds because it requires extensive research of all significant variables to understand the true return drivers. But in the end, we don't have these huge multi-factor or variable models. A lot of the traders in the equities markets that are practicing more of a systematic methodology and some of the 'stat arbitrage' market neutral traders, for example, have come up with some huge multi-factor models and run them through various optimizations. They've come up with some pretty complicated formulas. Our philosophy is that you sort of lose sight of what the basic underlying return driver is when you do that. So each of our individual strategies is fairly simplistic.

Our philosophy of keeping things simple stretches pretty much across every strategy in the portfolio. The significant difference comes with the varied ways that we plug the independent systems into the portfolio. That's where the higher level of sophistication comes in because that's controlling the returns—how much you allocate to each strategy and how much you allocate to each of the markets. The whole intent of that model is to maintain balance so we don't get disproportionate returns from any single strategy market combination. This is the key to our approach. Over time, we want the fundamental strategy in sugar to make the same contribution to the portfolio as the trend-following system in a currency or the market neutral strategy in a stock.

HAVE YOU EVER TAKEN A FLYER, GAMBLED, OR OTHERWISE VIOLATED YOUR PROGRAMS?

Historically I have but not in the last ten years. It's something we've learned that no matter how good it might feel at the time, ultimately it turns out to be the wrong thing.

YEAH, WHY IS THAT?! WHY ARE WE JUST SO OFF-KILTER PSYCHOLOGICALLY?

It is pretty amazing, but you know, our whole philosophy is to capture the emotional mis-pricings that occur as investors react to news or economics or geopolitical events. You can try for a while to stay out of sync with the rest of the world, which is what you need to do to be successful as a trader. Ultimately though, I think people want to be *in* sync. There's that little disruption or dichotomy thing going on that's just tough to fight forever.

So in the past, I would do that—I would have runs that just felt great, we'd be dead-on and I'd be sitting there able to beat a system. Ultimately over time, though, the system is taking out these little pieces systematically. What it's capturing is opportunities created by the other investors who are acting emotionally. The only way I can see having some persistence of returns and some predictability of returns is to make sure that we follow the system to take those little pieces of emotion out of the market and not become one of them.

The question of "why are people like that" is probably one for someone else. Why do people succumb to the emotional dark side? I really don't know for sure. I just know I've seen it happen to others over and over and it has happened to me in the past.

WHAT WOULD YOU ADVISE SOMEONE WHO IS DETERMINED TO MAKE A LIVING THROUGH MECHANICAL TRADING? LET'S SAY THEY NEED TO MAKE $50,000 A YEAR. WHAT WOULD THEY NEED IN TERMS OF STARTUP CAPITAL, PERFORMANCE OBJECTIVES, MODELS, ETC?

Fifty to survive—you have to step back and figure out realistically what kind of portfolio size you need. You have to take into account that the more you leverage, the lower the probability in any given time period you're going to hit your target returns, so you may have a year where you actually lose money. If you still have to take $50 thousand out, you're now leveraging more. You've taken money out, you had no return, and so you might well have your principle depleted.

First, you have to be realistic concerning what the capital requirement is to give you the return you want over a reasonable period of time. To do that, you have to fully understand the strategies that you're employing. I would definitely say start out with a couple different systems in place. I wouldn't just follow one because any system, no matter how good will fail over certain periods of time. Those failure periods are obviously the time when it would be the most difficult to follow it, especially if you're not capitalized properly. Then, you're in danger of abandoning it at the turning point where it's ready to come back and help you. So, you really need to have a systematic multi-strategy approach.

The second part is, make sure you don't fool yourself when you're developing that system. Over and over, I've seen people who, for whatever reason, lose sight of the fact that they're developing a system to perform well in the future. They get so caught up in making the system test well on back data. They do that through optimization and curve fitting techniques and changing and selecting specific parameters for a specific market when that strategy concept should be applied evenly to all markets. They may have a basic system that's working well, but it's a little too volatile so they'll put a filter in.

Trend following in the futures markets is a great example. You get leverage and a diversity of markets and a very simple strategy. But if you use any trend following strategy on a very small group of markets—say five or ten, which is what you'd likely be limited to with most investor portfolios even of reasonable size—you're going to have drawdowns of 20 percent or more pretty easily if you're using any kind of reasonable leverage.

If you develop the right strategies and you are diversified across strategies, I believe that is possible to make 15 to 20 percent net. Your focus should be to make sure you have a very conservative drawdown. If people were willing to stomach higher volatility, conceivably if they have decent strategies in place, I'd still have to say they're going to need a few hundred thousand to make [$50,000 a year] happen with any reasonable degree of probability.

BUT WORKING AGAINST THAT KIND OF PRUDENT APPROACH IS ALL THE LEGENDARY FOLKLORE ABOUT COMMODITY TRADING—THE STORIES OF THE WIZARDS WHO TURNED CHICKEN FEED INTO VAST FINANCIAL EMPIRES...

Yes, and some did. But it funnels down—you've got one million that start that way, and two that you can name who became legendary. The odds are that purely by chance some investors, who take great risks at the start will survive and produce huge compounded returns. I'm not saying that some of these market legends didn't have some skill sets. I think they did—and do. There was also a hell of a lot of luck, though, especially in the early stages when they were risking their entire capital base on a series of a few trades. People can do that, but you've got to recognize that it's a gamble—not an investment.

Somebody came to me about three years ago. It was right after the market peaked. She had taken a ten thousand dollar stock account up to over two million. Over the course of—I believe 1998, when the market backed off—it dropped down to a few hundred thousand. Then, she ran it back up again to like one and a half million.

When she was sitting down to talk with me, she was back where she started. The margin calls from her broker took her out; otherwise she probably would have been well under water. Her question to me was "How do I get it back"? I said, "Well, you don't have it! The market doesn't owe it to you. You *can't* get it back!" There was an individual who, if by chance, had just pulled the plug on her position when she was up, people could point to and say, "Well, *she* did it!"

I think that you have to say that the people who took a small amount of money to make a large amount of money or who are consistently making 100 percent returns on their capital every year are the extreme minority. Most investors have to face the fact that the odds of that happening are very, very low.

This is the beauty, though, where you get into investor psychology. If you ask them what the odds are of them achieving that, they will always massively overestimate them. Everybody thinks they're better than the average, which is really interesting.

EVERY INVESTOR WHO PUTS ON A TRADE THINKS IT'S GOING TO BE A WINNER, RIGHT?

Yes and that's one of the problems. You really need to take the attitude when you put a trade on that each one is going to lose money and plan for where to get out of it. If, on the other hand, it works out, just be surprised and happy. Take your trades with a better attitude of how the system is going to perform going forward.

BO THUNMAN

"I HAD HUNDREDS OF CALLS FROM PEOPLE WHO OPENED UP BY SAYING, 'LISTEN, JUST GIVE ME THE NAME OF A SYSTEM THAT WORKS CONSISTENTLY'."

In an environment where charlatans are all too omnipresent and hopes and dreams get exploited with depressing regularity, Bo Thunman has served as a sort of consumer watchdog. For years, his publication, **Club 3000 News,** *has offered its members a central clearing house of information on systems and the people who promote them. The specific forum was a published letters column, which Bo edited.*

He has had plenty of experience with opportunists and the skewered services that they offer, but he's quick to observe that they don't create one hundred percent of the industry's problems. There are plenty of unrealistic expectations held by much of the general trading public.

Bo was born in Stockholm, Sweden in 1925. Twenty-eight years later, he found himself stationed in the U.S. as a trade developer for a major ship owner.

"I had been trained as an electronics engineer," said Bo. "They originally hired me to do that, but soon realized that my real talent was as a businessman. So I worked for them as a ship broker and later, in management, with emphasis on developing new business."

He continued his entrepreneurial life for several years, with a few noted detours along the way. In 1967, he began learning computer programming through IBM. He became fluent in BA-SIC, the bellwether code of the time, which is still in wide use.

That set the stage for online technical analysis, something few people of the era were able to master. Bo began trading stock options in 1977, and a few years later, at the urging of a broker, he moved into trading commodities. He enjoyed near-immediate success via his self-developed analysis. The exploding computer universe of the early 1980's served as a natural entree.

It soon became apparent to him that other investors were not so nimble. They were not only not flourishing, they were getting victimized by the new environment. Bo founded **Club 3000 News** *as a result. For 17 years, his technical skills, combined with the success of his newsletter, made him one of the premier voices on investment consumer advocacy. In a lawsuit happy society, Bo would frequently go out on a limb, publishing complaints from club members that he deemed credible. Not surprisingly, he occasionally had to endure the wrath of the accused, although Bo notes with satisfaction that he was never sued during his tenure.*

Partly as a result of increasing industry regulation, Bo retired from the newsletter in 1997. He and his wife enjoy the placid life on his Augusta, Michigan farm. He has gone full-circle and is again trading equity options for his personal account.

How did you decide to start Club 3000?

I started working with computers in the early eighties, back when people didn't understand much about them. The common perception was that the computer could beat the market, but the individual could not. As a result, people would pay $3000 for trading systems and equipment that were in most cases worthless. That led me to start Club 3000, which was in particular, a user's group for commodity traders. That was something I did for 17 years. I retired in 1997.

It was an apparent need that had to be filled and I was there at the right time. It was quite successful. Toward the end, though, the CFTC [Commodity Futures Trading Commission] started to insist that in order to discuss trading, you had to be a registered broker—a certified trading advisor.

I read as much on one of your online sites, which I found a little perplexing. It can't be that I'm going to be in trouble discussing commodities in a book because I'm not a CTA!

According to their reasoning, "Yes." I was told by the CFTC attorney that this is the CFTC's interpretation of the Commodity Exchange Act. They apparently haven't heard of free speech.

They threatened me with five years in prison and a million dollar fine if I didn't quit. That put a damper on the exchange of information in Club 3000, which kind of petered out after a few years as a result.

Didn't they give you the option of playing ball with them—registering as a CTA or whatever?

They told me I'd have to take the exam and become a registered CTA [trading advisor]. Then, I could discuss commodity trading. We never gave specific recommendations—we never mentioned a price or said "buy this" or "sell that" in any particular commodity. We certainly were not commodity advisors, but that's what they said we were.

The Institute For Justice took our case and won. The court ruled that this was a free speech issue and wasn't trading advice at all. The CFTC appealed that decision and lost again. Perhaps, now they've heard of free speech.

THROUGHOUT YOUR INVOLVEMENT WITH CLUB 3000, YOU WERE TRADING YOUR OWN ACCOUNT. ROUGHLY WHAT PERCENTAGE OF YOUR INCOME CAME FROM YOUR TRADING?

Oh, it varied anywhere from 10 to 100 percent. The club was quite a bit of work. Since I had enough members and enough income from that, I didn't vigorously pursue any trading. I was more interested in keeping the club going.

WHAT DID THE CLUB TEACH YOU ABOUT MARKETS, INVESTOR PSYCHOLOGY, ETC.?

That people are completely foolish about trading. They think that there's only going to be profits, no losses, and no risk at all. I had hundreds of calls from people who opened up by saying, "Listen, just give me the name of a system that works consistently." Finally, my wife would walk into my room and say, "Bo, why are you *talking* to people like that?!"

That was the kind of thing we were preaching against. "Don't you understand that it runs both ways?"

Some people were simply obscene when I told them that. One particularly obnoxious guy said, "Listen, never mind the newsletter, just give me a system that works consistently. I want it so my secretary can run it and I figure she can make $5000 a week with it."

I said, "Now, wait a minute, you don't understand." And he just broke into a stream of profanities. I ended up hanging up on him. Totally hopeless.

I used to remind people that silver was once limit down 23 days in a row. If you had been long at that point, where would you be today? They would say, "Oh, you're kidding!" They were just completely unrealistic about it.

What really angered me were the vendors who stepped into this vacuum and sold fairy tales. There's the saying that there are those that know, there are those who don't know, and there are those who don't know that they don't know. Some of these vendors fell in that last category.

They never mentioned the risks. Maybe an individual did turn ten thousand dollars into one and a half million in x number of days but it is not generally discussed that first, he ran it up to two and a half million and then lost a million. People didn't understand that you are putting your *house* on the line...you're putting *everything you own* on the line. Maybe that is possible for some people to do maybe once in ten thousand times, but it is not possible at all for the average investor.

We had the ability to exchange information like that. If you do it in a private telephone conversation, you're not necessarily risking being sued by anyone. In some cases, I did publish letters from others. That was how the club's newsletter was written, with input from the members. If I felt they were telling a straight story, I would publish their letter. It led to some near-fistfights.

I think we cleaned up quite a bit, if I may beat my chest for a minute.

IF SOMEBODY IS SERIOUS ABOUT GETTING PAST THE PIPEDREAM MINDSET, WHAT ARE THE REALISTIC TRUTHS THEY NEED TO FIND?

Success takes two things, again, which people don't realize. There is the system itself, and then there is you. Say I could give you the perfect system. How do I know that you have the courage to take the signals?

I could not recommend a system today. I know one man, whom I won't name, who is absolutely and definitely successful trading the S&P futures. He was kind enough to show me everything including his account statement. I know that he continues to be very profitable.

This friend charged some students a nice fee to learn his successful system. The students would go home and two or three days later, would call him saying " I see a signal here. Should I take it?" He finally gave up taking on students at all.

THE STORY EXEMPLIFIES THE IDEA THAT YOU'RE EITHER TRADING A SYSTEM 100 PERCENT THE WAY IT WAS DESIGNED, OR YOU'RE IN EFFECT, NOT DOING THE SYSTEM AT ALL.

Right, if you're not doing what the system says, then you are not trading the system. That is unfair to the system designer, really. If you take just this and that and the other now and then on some kind of a random judgment basis, you're not trading the system.

Given the current lack of information, system trading is the best chance you have. In *Wall Street Week*, they talk about price-earnings ratios, trends and so on. None of that really exists in a fast-moving market.

That's why you get into technical analysis. It has a rule that says that if you tell me the price, I'll tell you the news. If heating oil goes up, you can probably look out the window and see snow. If you have a very warm March, then heating oil is going to go down. And from there, when heating oil goes up, the stock market goes down, and when heating oil goes down, the stock market goes up. That is fundamental analysis, which is to me impossible in commodity trading.

GIVE US A GENERAL OVERVIEW OF YOUR TRADING WORLD.

I use technical analysis of my own design. I started out using moving averages, which is all I had heard about. Then I gradually learned about volatility, volume and things like that. The amazing thing was that even though I knew almost nothing, I did quite well with exponential moving averages.

I've never stayed with anybody else's systems. I've gone to a couple of seminars and looked at a couple of other systems, but never stayed with one more than a few months.

I don't use anybody else's program. I have tested many others, but none impressed me. I used to test trade some systems that were being offered and were made available for me to review. I couldn't even print the words that I wanted to use.

I haven't traded futures for some time. I day traded the S&P five years ago, but my eyes couldn't take looking at the screen eight hours a day. Now, I'm retired and trading puts and calls.

I don't use any fancy techniques. I'm not a backgammon player or great mathematician. I keep it simple. K-I-S-S—I keep it simple, stupid.

HOW OFTEN DO YOU REVISE YOUR SYSTEMS?

I fine-tune little things basically every day, but I make a major adjustment maybe once every two years. You learn as you go along. "Well, I should have foreseen that, so I'll program this." It helps that I was a trained programmer to begin with. I was able to systematize everything I do. I never trade on guts.

IT'S UNUSUAL TO FIND SOMEONE TAKING A MECHANICAL APPROACH TO OPTIONS. DO YOU HAVE TO TREAT PUTS AND CALLS IN A UNIQUE WAY OR CAN THEY BE COMPARED TO NORMAL OPEN-HIGH-LOW-CLOSE MARKET ACTIVITY?

It's about the same thing. I use the same formulas. It's just a little wilder in commodities.

In the early days, I just took [option closing] prices out of *The Wall Street Journal*. There weren't any data services in those days. When I started trading commodities, I used data from the broker. They simply called me and gave me 40 or 50 high-low-close quotes in the various commodities. Much later on, I started using some of the data services. Today, I use a data service from the stock market.

I wait for overbought-oversold. When IBM goes to 125, someone will take their profit. When it goes to 80, someone will decide, "Hey, I can afford 100 shares of that." Then I'll just wait for a while until it goes up again. So many markets swing from overbought to oversold. That to me is good two ways. At the extremes, you have volatility coming almost for certain. Also, you have the useful "buy low-sell high" syndrome.

WHAT'S A PERFECT MARKET ENVIRONMENT FOR THE TYPE OF SYSTEM THAT YOU USE?

A market that has any kind of consistent movement. In the S&P futures, you can see how people are speculating this way and that and you can play against them. When they're long, you take the profit or go short and vice versa when they're short. In stocks, you have a time frame on the calls and puts, and you're betting on the price going to some level within the time frame.

WHAT SIZE TRADING BARS DO YOU PREFER?

I trade with daily data. Other people trade with instantaneous data, which is not instantaneous with regards to what happened two minutes ago. To be on the floor and seeing what's happening is necessary in wild situations.

If Saddam died or won the war, we'd have a reaction in the futures market within ten minutes. There's no way if you're not on the floor that you can follow that.

AND AT THAT MOMENT, YOU'RE SUDDENLY OVER-LEVERAGED.

Right, and you put stops in, of course, but sometimes the market is so fast that it will run your stops. That is the main problem that makes an amateur be an amateur. He doesn't have the gumption to be in that kind of situation.

OFTEN YOU SEE SOMEBODY SHUTTING DOWN AFTER SOMETHING LIKE THAT AT THE WORST POSSIBLE TIME.

Yes, and they blame somebody else. They blame the broker or the floor clerk or whatever.

WOULD YOU AGREE THAT DESPITE THE PAIN, BEING IN THE MIDDLE OF A CRISIS IS NOT THE TIME TO BE THINKING ABOUT RE-VAMPING METHODOLOGY?

Right, you're not supposed to. Also, mathematically speaking, it's not good to have too many rules either. You can add a rule every day because you saw something that you had not anticipated, but then you get a system that doesn't have any degree of significance. This isn't actually possible, but the best system would be one rule for a hundred trades. A bad system would be a hundred rules for one trade.

OBVIOUSLY, YOU WANT SOME VOLATILITY, BUT IS THERE A POINT WHERE VOLATILITY GETS TOO GREAT, I.E., TOO RISKY, OR TOO IN-ACTIVE FOR YOU TO BE INVOLVED?

In radio technology, there is something known as "squelch." If there's no signal at all, just a hum or hash, the speaker shuts off, and then when you get a signal, the speaker turns on again. So, I simply filter out the noise in the market just like we do in electronics. Noise is when the market isn't going anywhere, which is when there's no point in trading.

WHAT DOES ONE NEED TO TRADE SYSTEMS?

Intelligence, courage, and some mathematical skills. This friend I've been talking about seems to understand [something intangible]. We sit there talking, just as I'm doing with you, and suddenly he says, "Look!" Then he picks up the phone and places an order. That skill has been honed over many years, I suppose. He's basically bright, sensible and honest. Maybe being honest with yourself is also a big factor in trading success.

You have to realize, "OK, this trade didn't work...now why didn't it work?" So you change something and you get better and better at it.

BUT ON THE OTHER HAND, YOU'RE AN ADVOCATE OF THE STRICT MECHANICAL APPROACH, WHICH COULD RENDER INNATE TRADING ABILITIES IRRELEVANT. ARE TRADERS BORN OR MADE?

If you're born intelligent, you can do better. Some people can do things without physical effort at all. But if you have the ability to be disciplined, like if you went to Annapolis or West Point or something like that, you can become a "made trader." You've been taught to follow a certain set of rules even though you realize that you could get killed in the process of doing it—financially in our case, and physically in the case of soldiers. Some people are born soldiers. The Eisenhowers and the Halseys were not only taught, they were born to it. They absorbed everything they'd ever heard about soldiering and then they applied it.

I've seen gifted traders, particularly one, who is simply an intuitive trader. He reacts based on his own charting. He has the courage to not hesitate one second before he executes something.

He was a former Navy Seal who fought in a war. He knows that you have to decide right now what you're going to do. If you don't kill him, he'll kill you. That is trained [behavior]—not inborn.

EXPAND OF THE CONCEPT OF OPTIMIZATION AND OVER-OPTIMIZATION.

You can optimize to a certain degree and test something to death, but then you'll find that what worked in one time period will not work in another. It's better to decide that you're going to nail it to this given number or particular procedure and stick with that. Then you have to try to decide what the market's going to do given certain situations. If we go to war, we know pretty much what the market's going to do. If Saddam dies tomorrow, we know another thing. We have a way of measuring that by our system based on the addition of fundamentals.

SO, DO YOU INCORPORATE FUNDAMENTALS SOMEHOW?

Not mathematically, other than the fact that if you see the moving averages moving upward, you'll probably have a rising market at least for a while. If you're smart, you're taking some of the profit. Maybe the market will go even further, but as they say, you can't go broke taking a profit.

SOME WIZARDS HAVE ARGUED THAT AXIOM FLIES IN THE FACE OF LETTING YOUR PROFITS RUN, CUTTING YOUR LOSSES SHORT.

There's a proverb, "grasp all, lose all."

SO DO YOU INCORPORATE PRICE TARGETS?

Yes. I use day orders. If they're filled, fine, if they aren't, that's fine too. They're based on excursions, in other words, overbought, oversold in my case.

IN RESEARCH, WHAT DO COLD NUMBERS SOMETIMES NOT TELL YOU?

They're not telling you the emotions. They're not telling you who's going to be murdered today. They don't tell you what the market and gold will do. They don't tell you if George Bush has a heart attack. They don't foretell spurious events.

161

YOU'VE TOUCHED ON THE FACT THAT SYSTEMS CAN BE OUT OF SYNC WITH HUMAN PSYCHOLOGY.

Right. I think most people are just dreamers. Years ago I sold mutual funds. I sometimes called on people who thought that at age 64, they could put in a hundred dollars a month, if they could get that much money together, and live happily ever after as they turned 65. There are many people who get into commodities because you can make a hell of a lot of money. But equally fast, you can lose that much. "Ever think of that?" "No, that can't be."

WHAT IS IT ABOUT THE TRADING EXPERIENCE THAT MAKES IT SO EASY FOR US TO DO THE WRONG THING?

Uncertainty and last year's losses. It has been said that the first thing you do when you crash in an airplane is immediately go up in another one. That may work, although I may tend to worry about whether I knew how to fly at all considering I'd just bailed on an airplane. (Laughs). But that's what makes the difference between successful and unsuccessful traders—the ability to get past that fear.

HOW DO YOU HANDLE MONEY MANAGEMENT?

It depends on the results. If it's going badly, you tend to stop for a while and then go back in. I don't have a mathematical money management system. I use common sense. You don't bet the farm on anything. If you made a little more money last week, you can be a little more daring this week. If you lost, you're not quite so courageous any more.

There are books on money management. There are backgammon players who claim they're able to make a great deal of extra money because of money management. I've never been impressed with anything along those lines that I've programmed into my system, however.

Weigh in on the paper trading debate. Is it viable because it is something you can learn from, or is it not viable because the emotional pressures are absent?

There's no emotional pressure in paper trading and very few people in my experience can coordinate the feel of fear and what they see on the paper. That's one thing that's wrong with these trading contests. They are theoretical. Like say I took one million and turned it into 50 million in six days. But nobody thinks of the risks that were taken to accomplish that feat. They were risks that are beyond the capacity of almost anybody to accept.

Expand more on your options trading. Are you always long? Short? Some combination?

Long. That's the best way to do it, in my opinion. In the futures market, you have no idea what your actual risk is because it's unlimited. In options, I know that if I pay $750, that's my risk. Either I can afford that and I'm willing to take it or I'm not.

How is trading like any other endeavor and how is it different?

It's nerve-wracking and demanding. To work for someone else who takes all the risks is a calmer situation, but I've run across many people giving up that security. I have found masses of doctors saying, "I want to get out of the medical business, I want to trade. Tell me how to do it."

And, being highly intelligent and able to go through medical school and be successful, they had a potential to be good traders. But some weren't. Some people think the world owes them a living. "I'm a doctor. I trained to be a doctor, I ought to be very highly paid."

HOW PROTECTIVE ARE YOU OF YOUR METHODOLOGY? DO YOU OPENLY SHARE YOUR TECHNIQUES OR DO YOU FEEL THAT SUCH OPENNESS IS COUNTER-PRODUCTIVE SOMEHOW?

I could, of course, write a book on it. I'm not sure I'd want to expend the effort to do it. The first thing somebody says after you've laboriously explained how you tradet is, "Oh really? That wouldn't work." And here I am, living comfortably, driving a nice car, and they're saying, "No, no, no." What, are you kidding me? I don't walk around showing my checkbook or anything, but I've got to chuckle at people like that.

If you do sell a system, the customer will be very, very angry when the first loss occurs. "The system doesn't work!" So whatever you describe might give somebody out there an idea, but more than anything else, it will get you some ridicule.

That's why I'm not comfortable revealing exactly what I'm doing.

BILL DUNN

"I just looked at charts and without applying anything sophisticated at all, I said 'this couldn't be random'!"

In a game so defined by controlled methodology, Bill Dunn may well be the ultimate market scientist. His background includes a bachelor's degree in engineering from the University of Kansas followed by a Ph.D. in high energy theoretical particle physics at Northwestern. From there, a research grant directed him to the University of California to work with a team of physicists. Unfortunately, the grant ran out of money, and Bill began questioning the pragmatics of his career trajectory.

"I decided that this was a poor way to earn a living," said Bill, "and even if I were good enough to win the Nobel Prize, it would just be so long in coming that it just wasn't worth the wait."

After briefly teaching at Pomona College, Claremont, California, Bill began looking for jobs that would incorporate his ability to construct business models. He discovered that any applicable companies were inevitably linked to the Department of Defense. "I ended up taking a job at the Center for Naval Analyses, Arlington, Virginia," he said.

It was the Naval equivalent of the more familiar Air Force-affiliated Rand Corporation. For seven years, Bill worked on projects shrouded in mystery. Security dictated that each participant was given a mere puzzle piece—the effect being akin to the old adage of the blind man trying to describe the elephant by grabbing a small part of it.

"You never saw the connected end-result," said Bill, "and you never found out whether anything you thought or wrote about actually happened or didn't or why, etc. I didn't see accomplishment. I frankly found it very unsatisfying."

By 1971, Bill had discovered a way to utilize his talents in a more all-encompassing, controlled way. "I became interested in technical analysis of the equities markets. There had been books and journals written essentially saying that the random walk or efficient market theory was not necessarily to be trusted. There was something that could be learned from the historic patterns and studies of the behaviors of stocks, bonds, etc. over a long-term period. You could determine this objectively with computers."

Soon, he realized that he could apply the same approach to futures—an arena that would have the added benefits of greater liquidity, lower commissions, and no short sale-adverse uptick rule. In futures, it was also easier to cover the broad overall trading universe via a few well-chosen contracts.

Bill developed a portfolio model for 15 commodities. Unfortunately, a $200,000 account was mandated in order for his risk management qualifiers to be met— an amount that was far beyond his reach. The only alternative that he could see was to solicit and manage funds for others.

Such was the genesis of Dunn Capital Management. Twenty-nine years after its 1974 inception, the company is managing one billion dollars in strictly mechanical, computer-based futures port-

166

folios. By Bill's estimate, there are 250 individual investors in various Dunn Management partnership accounts as well as approximately 15 large, primarily institutional clients with funds extending into the hundreds of millions.

There is also, Bill proudly notes, considerable customer loyalty. "Compared to most of my competitors, I don't think we have many clients, but we have a lot of quality clients," observed Bill. "They've been with us a long, long time."

Consistency may have a lot to do with that. Since it's 1974 inception, Dunn Capital Management has achieved a net compound annual rate of return of over 23% for its partners and clients. Purportedly, no other futures manager has averaged such a high composite rate of return over such an extended period of time.

The firm's trading approach has been similarly unvarying. The flagship system that was invented at the fund's beginning and one major addition incorporated several years later, have never been tinkered with in any significant way. Through 28 years and all types of market environments, the same methodology has been utilized.

WHY IS THE COMMODITY FIELD YOUR TARGETED INVESTMENT ARENA?

The leverage in the futures market is both easily adjustable and free. You're never borrowing money. You just put up good faith earnest money or initial margin, but even that initial margin doesn't have to be cash. It can be in either T-Bills or a T-Bill equivalent. If you put up cash, the broker will credit the account with the overnight T-bill rate. So, there's no cost of money in the whole thing; in fact, the money is so cheap that amateurs are tempted to use too much leverage and soon rue the day.

Back in 1974, if you compared the dollar value of the contracts traded just on the Chicago Board of Trade to the dollar value of what was traded on the New York Stock Exchange, the futures exchange was about ten times higher. This was essentially because there was no cost in changing your position. If you didn't feel good about your position, you could stand aside or swap positions and the commissions were so low and you could use as much leverage as you wanted.

WHAT IS THE GENERAL NATURE OF YOUR APPROACH?

The original program of 1974 is described as a long-term trend-following reversal program—"reversal" meaning always in the market, it is trading. We're always long or short, never on the sidelines. We're looking to benefit from long-term trends, which don't very frequently occur, but when they do, there is a whole lot of fun to be had with them.

The original challenge was that while it's easy to find a way to get on the long-term trend, the hard part is balancing the fact that 80 percent of the time, it's not doing that, and how do you keep that from eating you alive? Can you break even in those periods? If so, when the good news comes, you get to put it all in your pocket.

That concept—that approach—has not changed since October, 1974, but the portfolio has, in that over 90 percent of it is now in financial futures that didn't even exist back in 1974. Only about 10 percent is left in the agricultural futures that we can trade.

Then, back in the late 1980's, we developed a second program. It's called TOPS, for Targets and Opportunity. It was also looking to benefit from long-term trends, but it also used previously observed patterns that had a weak predictive ability to say that there was going to be a trend. It would go into the market in the indicative way, but if it didn't work out for us quickly, it just knocks us out of the way. Then, we're on the sidelines. If it does move with us, then we use a profit target. If it does something in-between, like it aims in the right direction, but doesn't quite get there, we use trailing stops similar to the trend following stuff. It takes us out when it falls short of the target and reverses.

The TOPS program is on the sidelines an average of 40 percent of the time. It takes many more opportunities than the long-term trend-following system. We developed it because it's different than, and somewhat complementary to the original program. It's going to make its money when the other system does; when there are long-term trends. But the fact that it's also out of the market a lot saves a lot of grief.

Those are the only two programs. Both are diversified in the same way; 10 percent in the physical commodities and 90 percent in the financials.

WALK US THROUGH THE EARLY DAYS OF DEVELOPING YOUR MODEL.

I built these models and put them all together into a portfolio. At that time, I had to go to a mainframe computer to do the daily balancing and risk control. I hooked it up and ran it, and I liked the results. But when I looked at the question of the gambler's ruin, you have to capitalize it enough so that when the inevitable and predictable dips in equity came along, they didn't knock you out of the game. You're still there playing and the odds favor you to win providing you don't get knocked out of the game. So you have to have enough capital and make your bets small enough so that it's not conceivable that you're not going to be able to continue to play every day.

IS THERE A HARD AND FAST FORMULA YOU USE TO DETERMINE THAT?

It's a statistical measure that incorporates standard deviation. You say, well, this is what I'm doing so now how much money do I have to start with so even if I go out past five standard deviations I'm not out of the game? I want to still be left in and come back—this is the nature of the game. That would be an incredibly rare event, but I don't want even rare events to knock me out of the markets.

SO, YOU WERE BALANCING GOOD OVERALL PROJECTIONS AGAINST THE ELEMENT OF SHORT-TERM RUIN.

Right. I put this all together and decided that it's beautiful except for one thing. The way I have it laid out, I would need $200,000 before I could start trading this. And there was no way on earth I was ever going to have $200,000 to try it out. That was the object—to get some savings together and invest it. Well....not this way...I needed $200,000 to start. I would have been hard pressed to get two or three thousand together.

So, it was either back to the drawing board or...I said well....I think maybe this is good enough that maybe I know five people who do have $200,000 in risk capital and do know me well enough and have known my character and my research. I knew I could show them how I came up with this. They're intelligent people. Surely one or more of those five would say, "Yes."

This may come as a shock, but they all said, "No." (Laughs).

DID YOU DISCLOSE YOUR WHOLE METHODOLOGY TO THEM?

Not the nitty-gritty details, but I told them the results. But they all said, "No." I guess because I'd never done this before in my life. But I've never done a lot of things in my life until I do them.

Here's a funny story. One of the five was very technical and computer oriented. He was running some service for tracking mutual funds, and he was also trading for his own private clients as well as helping me. One of the things that he told me was, "Bill, you can not tell people that you can make those kind of [high] returns." I said, "Well, I'm just giving them the results of the research." He says, "Yes, but you've got to do something about it." I said, "I'm not going to lie. How am I going to tell them it's a number other than what comes out?" He says, "Well, you're going to have a hard time."

So he said, "You just give me the signals for six months and we'll track how it's doing. We've got plenty of money, if it works, great, we'd like to have something like this."

My boss at the time suggested that I put together a partnership. "Go to all the guys you've been working with, family and friends. Maybe we can scrape up the $200,000."

So, we put together a small partnership [prospectus] and we had about $100,000 committed after a couple weeks. Then, I got a call from one of the original five. He said, "Bill...we want to know a little bit more about this. Why don't you get all your stuff together, get on a plane and come talk to us?" So I did.

They sat me down in the president's office. After the introductions, we talked for a couple of hours. The president was asking "on this day in this market, what would your system do?" I went flipping through pages and would come up with an answer for him. Then he'd ask, "What about this other day? How long did you hold this and that and the other?" And of course I'd be able to tell him what the system would be doing.

Obviously, he was asking me about time periods and events that were important to him, but they didn't mean anything to me. In the end, he said, "I think we might be interested. What would it take to get this going?" I said, "You're one of the ones I came to in the beginning trying to put this thing together and you said, 'No,' so I'm trying to put a partnership together. We've only got half the money, so if you want to come in on the partnership with $100,000 we could be off and running by the end of the week." And he said, "But, we could do the whole thing ourselves in a private account, couldn't we?" I said "Sure...(laughs)..you could do that...that would be OK." He says, "Let us think about it. You go back home and we'll be in touch."

They called a few days later and said, "That's what we want to do, have you trade a private account for us." They were able to set it all up because they were the second largest futures broker in the world at the time. Their name was Heinhold Commodities.

What they knew that I didn't know was that there were about a half dozen people already doing what I was trying to do and doing it very well. Some of them were clearing those trades on Heinhold's books. And for the first time, this was a deal where everybody won. The clients, the broker and the advisor all won. That had never happened before. They had always burned and killed all their clients.

So, they didn't know whether I could work this out for them, but they did know that it could work. They put their $200,000 in a house account and told me to run with it. The object for them was to establish an audited track record so that they could go out and organize public funds. They would be the broker and I would be the trader.

They were the first ones ever to do an S1 registration with some other traders. After four or five years they came out with one that was kind of innovative. It was a $30 million futures fund, the largest that had ever been organized at that point.

In the meantime, my private partnership was told that Heinhold Commodities was my client, and they brought the total up to $137,000. I said, "That's close enough, we'll go." Suddenly, I had two accounts and we were off and running. That was October 1974. And we have never turned back.

CAN YOU EXPOUND ON WHY, WHEN SO MANY OTHERS COME TO MECHANICAL TRADING THROUGH A WINDING, IF NOT TORTUROUS PATHWAY, YOU WERE ABLE TO INTUIT SO EARLY ON THAT THIS WOULD BE YOUR BEST CHANCE FOR SUCCESS. DID YOUR SCIENTIFIC BACKGROUND HAVE SOMETHING TO DO WITH THAT?

Yes. Almost all of the people that were doing similar research—back then and still to this day—have backgrounds in science and engineering. They knew their ideas could be tested.

Almost anybody and everybody using my approach to market analysis did not come from business or economic backgrounds where they taught the random walk or efficient market theories. They were trying to prove that nothing of value could be learned from studying the past. I just looked at charts and without applying anything sophisticated at all said, "This couldn't be random! This is not the way ideal gasses work in a closed container. I've seen random motion in the lab and this isn't it!" So, if that's not random, maybe there's something to be learned.

System ideas are testable without any cost except some thinking and labor. You don't have to go into the market and risk money. You can play the game on the old numbers providing you don't use the old numbers for your input.

HOW DO YOU DETERMINE WHETHER A LOSING RUN IS WITHIN NORMAL PARAMETERS OR IF IT'S GONE FAR ENOUGH TO WHERE YOU'RE FORCED TO QUESTION YOUR SYSTEM?

Our answer is, if the drawdown is no worse than what we have seen in the past, then we know in the past those would have been particularly bad times to stand aside. If it's no worse, then we should not be thinking of anything other than what a great investment opportunity this might be.

Today, of course, we have 28 and a half years of experience behind us rather than just a year and a half like when we started. If it should go or did go beyond that, just how far does it have to go before I say there is definitely something wrong? If I were going to come to the conclusion that there was something wrong, it would probably involve more than just loss. I would be looking at the individual things that are causing this and asking whether they are way out of character. Is something really different about either the market or how our models are handling the different markets? But it hasn't happened.

It's a very hard thing to say before you start as to when you should step aside. We have clients who, without consultation with us, have told themselves that if this account loses 25 percent, "We're out of here." Well, they didn't tell me that before they started because I told them otherwise. I told them in the beginning that, "You're going to have to be ready to live through 50 percent losses." Now, if they didn't want to risk a 25 percent loss, they should have told me that and I would have said, "OK, I'll cut your risk by 50 percent as well as the returns and you probably won't ever have to look at a 25 percent loss." But, they weren't that smart or they were too greedy, or something. They're into micromanaging. They're hiring us anyhow—why the hell wouldn't they let us help them?

I can keep that loss from happening if I knew that's was what you wanted to do, but the requirements were conflicting. They wanted to make money at full leverage and they didn't want to have to weather the kind of losses that we've seen several times in the past. Well...then you shouldn't play our game our way.

IS THIS SOMETHING YOU'RE REGULARLY ENCOUNTERING, OR DOES IT REPRESENT MORE OF AN ANOMALY AMONG YOUR CLIENTELE?

We have had very, very few losers. Almost everybody comprehends and accepts what we explain to them, which is, this is a long-term deal. "Don't put any money in here that you can't leave alone—that you don't have any requirements on for five plus years." We tell them it's going to be a rough ride...but it's going to be a good one. "Decide you're going to hang with it...or don't start."

IS THERE AN EXPECTED RATE OF RETURN YOU PITCH THEM?

We give them all the information on what we have accomplished. Our long-term results are above 20 percent for periods longer than five years. A 20 percent compounded annual net return is certainly well within the norm and preponderantly, that is what we have. We've actually accomplished over 23 percent compounded net of everything except taxes.

We make a huge effort to get rid of the weak sisters before they start, and as a result, we don't have them. It's rare indeed when someone has a secret cutoff point and doesn't tell us about it. If we knew what it was, we could advise them that there's a 10, 20 or 80 percent likelihood in the next three years that that will happen. "Is that what you want? Because that means you'll be leaving at the bottom."

HAVE YOU EVER HAD A BAD RUN THAT HAS SHAKEN YOUR CONFIDENCE?

Not enough to make us change anything. When I started without any experience at all, I first adjusted the risk level to where I could withstand a 25 percent loss, and then moved it to 50 percent. A little over a year later, early in 1976, we walked into a really ugly market. We had back-to-back 25 percent losing months. We were off maybe 52 percent from an equity high, and there we were, facing the worst fail-safe we were ever going to have to see. It shook us. I was surprised that it was that ugly for as long as it was, but we didn't change anything. It wound up going almost straight up for us for about a year.

**IN PUTTING TOGETHER SYSTEM PORTFOLIOS, CAN YOU SIGNIFI-
CANTLY IMPROVE ON SYSTEMS NOT PERFORMING STUPENDOUSLY
BY THEMSELVES? CAN THE SUM EVER BE WORTH MORE THAN THE
INDIVIDUAL PARTS?**

Oh, absolutely! This is modern portfolio theory. If you have two
streams of equity, and if they are approximately the same expected
rate of return, but they do it in such a different way that the correlations between the two of them as they go along are modest, being
point five or point four or point three, and you do 50-50 of them, if
you can get the average return, you're going to lower your risk quite a
bit. Or if you move the risk up to where it was for a single equity
stream, you're going to improve your rate of return by 10 or 20 percent.

If on the other hand, they are perfectly correlated, why would you
play with two of them? Take the one that has the higher mean. But
most things are not perfectly correlated. They are something between
high to low.

Our portfolios have zero correlation with S&P and the bond index
and the Russell 500 and the real estate and anything you'd care to
look at. It's a different portfolio and it trades long as well as short and
it just does it completely different. You wouldn't expect it to have any
correlation, and it doesn't.

We bring a huge amount of benefit because of the zero correlation
to somebody's portfolio, and typically, we have a higher rate of return
than the other investments that are in his portfolio. So we can bring
his risk way down and we increase his return. Our biggest clients are
institutions, and I can assure you that we are not their only trading
program. We bring a whole lot to their table when they've got a lot of
other things, because we've got no correlation with them.

IS YOUR SYSTEM APPLIED THE SAME WAY ACROSS ALL MARKETS?

In a way, our strategy is always the same, but we would look at the idiosyncrasies of each market. The same basic strategy would use different parameters accordingly, resulting in such things as different frequency of trading.

At least once every year, we updated our research with another twelve months of data. We tweaked the individual models as we got more data, but the changes were so minor that nobody outside of us could ever tell the difference. The changes would occur in rules and models to build the portfolio and allocate the risk among the different futures markets within it. That's been a constantly evolving thing, and we won't change anything until we think we've got a better idea.

When we'd re-look our models, we'd occasionally find that where before, there were two or three best solutions to the problem, now, there were still two or three best—probably the same ones as before—but now, one is demonstratively better than it had been. We pick that one for the next year.

SO YOU RE-OPTIMIZE ONCE A YEAR?

Yes, minimally. And the kind of markets that will give us more information are bad markets, not good ones. When we have difficulty, that's when we get the most help choosing solutions to the problem.

HOW MUCH DATA DO YOU LOOK AT?

We do not have enough data, ever, to satisfy me.

For whatever model you're trying to use, different markets will have periods of time where they're more friendly to some ideas than others. In that same period, while some market groups are friendly and profitable for this one concept, they'll be unprofitable in others. I think the safe thing to do is look at long market periods that have a number of different kinds of behavior going on so that you don't have

177

the opportunity to fix one part that makes it look really great because it's going to chew you up everywhere else.

We look at long enough periods with enough trades that we can't fool ourselves too easily. Historically, we used a minimum of five years. Now, since we have so much more data, it's more like 12 to 15 years.

We must have sufficient robustness that a single market is good overall and good over all chunks of any of its history. That's how we try to keep from fooling ourselves.

In the end, when you put the portfolio together and you run it through a long number of days where a lot of different things occur...you can have stock market crashes and wars and peace breaking out and contested elections... run it through all that and see if it does OK. When it's dipping and rising, can you point to world events as to the reason 'why?' In our case, you can't. That says something about robustness.

ARE THERE OTHER THINGS ABOUT NORMAL MARKET ACTIVITY THAT NECESSITATES ADDITIONAL ATTENTION?

Some markets tend to dry up and we can't trade them with our volume requirements. Or new markets suddenly become very robust, and we have to determine whether or not to add them.

When we started back in 1974, and up through the early 1980's, we were predominantly trading agricultural futures. Since the mid to late 1980s, over 90 percent of all the money that we are trading is in the financial markets. Those are much newer markets. They're much more broad-based and liquid. We are able to move our accounts in and out easily without upsetting those markets. This would not be the case with the physical commodities, partly because there are position limits imposed on them, but second, they are just not robust enough for the kind of money we would like to move in an out.

HOW IS TRADING LIKE ANYTHING ELSE IN LIFE, AND HOW IS IT DIFFERENT?

For our model and our program and our clients, our trading is very stress-free because we are not responsible for the events that are out there. We're responsible for having done the research and having developed a program that is overwhelmingly likely to do well over the long-term. We don't have to churn our guts when we buy bonds or sell gold. If things turn out poorly, it's the market's fault it's not the model's fault. There's almost nothing new under the sun.

Generally speaking, in real life, when things go well or when they don't, there's a great tendency to say, "I messed that up" or "I was lucky" or "Wasn't I good, I stuck to my guns?" You take a lot more credit and a lot more of getting beaten up in most people's everyday world than what we do in the markets. I go home with a clean conscience and I make a full confession to my clients every month.

HOW DO YOU DECIDE THE PARTICULARS OF YOUR ASSET ALLOCATION?

Well, you could think of something very simple and say, "I'm going to just apply the same number to each thing that I'm trading." That turns out not to be very brilliant, because the value of a contract is vastly different for Eurodollars than it is for soybeans. You have a very skewed bet system there. A better simple idea would be to say, "I'll just risk an equal fraction of my NAV [net asset valuation] in each market that I'm trading." That's a little more sophisticated, but if you have three grains and four meats and one coffee, why would you give grains three times and meats four times the weight of coffee? Maybe that's not very smart.

We're more sophisticated than that. We think we have a better way of getting our risk spread out, which takes into account the different correlations that the different futures have with each other. From that, we can get maximum diversification. This is all testable and we've found that whatever is satisfactory enough in the past is probably going be OK in the future.

The other thing is, we've always had a risk profile target that we were shooting for. We want to adjust the risk so that we expose ourselves to a one percent chance of having to suffer a loss of 20 percent or more in a one-month period. We have had almost 350 months of history and out of that, five actually lost 20 percent or more. While that's a little over the one percent, it's well within the statistics of small numbers.

HAVE YOU EVER VIOLATED YOUR PROGRAMS?

Back in '75-'76, I believe we were short the nearby contract in coffee. The system said that if we got a [reverse] signal in the next week or two, just liquidate the nearby and initiate the new signal in the more deferred contract. If that didn't happen, we'd just switch out of the nearby into the more deferred before delivery notice.

A freeze hit Central America, and the price of coffee started marching up. We got the signal to buy and we were short. The daily allowable price change in the nearby was unlimited because they had to let it work toward the [cash] market, so you could settle the contracts. The more deferred contracts had daily price change limits—they could only go up or down maybe seven or eight cents a day.

The nearby took us out because it was up two or three [would-be] limits, although it was unlimited. So, we went flat waiting for the signal in the deferred. The deferred, however, was limited to its seven or eight cent limit price. By the time it hit the buy stop signal, it had been limit locked for six, seven or eight days. In the meantime, there wasn't any trading available and we were miles away from our actual signal.

I decided that was way more risk to take than the research had ever allowed. It would have been inappropriate to enter, so I didn't until it finally came back down and I took the new short signal. This was a mistake. I should have gone in, but I should have re-evaluated the instantaneous risk and cut back on the contracts as indicated [by the risk control model]. And this was assuming I could have executed on the signal, but I knew I couldn't. [No available sellers in a locked limit up market].

Since that time, we've developed methods that instantly make that new calculation whenever there's the rare but huge move through a signal. We'll still take the signal, realizing that there's more risk now than what had been planned. [And therefore the necessity to cut back on position size].

The second incident occurred at the end of 1979 into the beginning of 1980. We had the Hunt boys playing with the silver and gold. If you'll remember, silver eventually went to over $50 and gold went to over $900 an ounce. This was in January 1980.

We have a rule that when we have to get out of the nearby contract and into the more deferred contract, we recalculate what the risk is in the new position. If it is significantly different than we were in our previous equity, we take a position according to the new risk.

We saw this stuff in the stratosphere and we were within about a week of where we were going to have to move out. I said, "Maybe we should just move a little early." In doing so, we cut our positions by about 80 percent. We had held these positions for three or four months and they had just gone through the roof and the risk was just enormous.

So, we switched from the near-term to the deferred and cut back our position. Most of our profit was now in our pocket—no longer on the table at risk. Then we got the short signals and rode silver down to eight or nine dollars an ounce.

It wasn't exactly a violation of the system. There was a fuzzy area as to what day you actually do the [contract rollover] spread. But I rather maliciously said, "This is just too risky. It's so toppy. Let's do it now."

Other than that, I'm unaware of any deviation in the 28 and a half years.

WHICH CERTAINLY MAKES YOU UNIQUE. EVEN SOME OF THE MOST STAUNCH MECHANICAL SYSTEM ADVOCATES HAVE MAJOR VIOLATION STORIES TO IMPART FROM SOMEWHERE IN THEIR CAREERS.

And often, that's how people wind up getting out of the business. They may do it a few times and maybe it's not too disastrous and they feel better about it. Then, they do it again and pretty soon they're in completely uncharted waters, and it doesn't work.

WHY DO YOU THINK IT IS SO HARD FOR THE AVERAGE PERSON TO FOLLOW SYSTEMS?

First of all, I think that everything we were ever taught in school and in life tells us we're supposed to figure out the future. We're taught to look for cause and effect—things like that. We're supposed to do things like buy bargains and sell when something is too high. We're led to believe that this is all something that ought to be doable. Our nature is that we want to believe we're smart. We have all this baggage going into it.

The second thing is, unless the person who is responsible for executing trades did the research themselves and is aware that what the model says to do today is the distillation of their best effort of researching 10 and 15 years into the past, they're going to be lacking necessary mental convictions. Without the knowledge of "this is the smartest thing I can do, and it's not going to be without losses because there are lots of losses in reality and on paper in the past, but the risk control is such that it won't kill us anyhow"...without the belief that we don't have to be right all the time, in fact, we *know* that we're not going to be right all the time because of our research...if we haven't experienced this directly, we're going to be at a disadvantage.

Follow the system and go with the flow. At least then, you're in charted waters.

We tell employees to follow the system or they won't have a job. They could have all kinds of juices flowing in their stomachs over the trades. It doesn't matter. "Execute these orders. I'm not asking for your opinion."

I used to say that I could publish these signals in The Wall Street Journal and no one would follow them. Either they're too smart and could do it better or they just wouldn't do it because they hadn't done the research. They don't know why those are the right signals for us and our portfolio and why they're right for us right now.

SO A BLACK BOX IDEA IS JUST DOOMED TO FAILURE, RIGHT?

Right, if the person who has it didn't build the box himself.

ARE YOU STILL ACTIVE IN RESEARCH?

Yes. I help evaluate new ideas we look at.

BUT ARE YOU TALKING FINE POINTS? YOU SAY YOU HAVEN'T CHANGED ANYTHING MAJOR IN 28 YEARS.

Well, but we're looking to. One thing we're looking at relates to extreme environments such as Black Monday. There are events that occur and markets change what they're doing and how they're doing it very, very rapidly; in short periods of days—hours sometimes. While we have seen lots of volatility and change and have incorporated corresponding risk control, we'd really like to get better at this. We have just spent about a year of some really heavy thinking and some programming. We have the tools to do some experiments to see if we could get a better handle on managing the risk that we have. That's still a research project. I have to tell you, most research projects don't end up improving anything, in part because we've been doing it a long time and we're not that bad.

This concept is a very hard thing, and I'm not aware of anybody who does it. Certainly, though, if it were doable, it would be wonderful. To lower the risk and increase the rate of return would be a very good thing. I don't know if it's going to happen, and I'm in fact rather skeptical. But the proof is in the pudding and we'll know within a few months whether or not we're on the right track.

I'm very much involved in what to research and what kind of effort to put into it. I am also involved in evaluating the results and deciding to what degree the results should be implemented for existing clients. I don't do the programming and I don't do the research itself anymore. I have a staff that does that. My son [Daniel, Dunn's Executive Vice President] is anticipating taking my job. Probably within two to four years, he will have fulfilled our contract, and I'll be without a job.

HOW ARE YOU GOING TO FEEL ABOUT THAT?

I think I'm going to feel fine.

WILL YOU DABBLE WITH LOOKING AT IDEAS? IS THAT SOMETHING THAT IS IN YOUR BLOOD?

I don't know that I would. I doubt that I will try to reinvent the wheel.

TOM WILLIS

"ONCE YOU HAVE A SYSTEM, THE BIGGEST OBSTACLE IS TRUSTING IT."

Tom Willis is blessed with acute market savvy, a characteristic not shared by your typical mechanical system speculator. Along with mentor-friend Richard Dennis, Tom demonstrated that an exceptional trader could parlay the small resources of the scaled-down, relatively illiquid Mid-America Commodity Exchange markets into a fortune.

Despite his inborn system-contrary skills, he is included in this book for two reasons, aside from the fact that his observations are always well received by trading aspirants. First, although having been on both sides of the fence, Tom is an advocate for the mechanical trading approach. Second, his discretion-history aside, he has always been methodical in his various trading facets, including how he incorporates everything together.

"I had my approach down to where it was almost like a batting average," he stated in a previous interview. Like a mechanical system expert, he would utilize the same stringent historical testing to ascertain the nature of his edges, as opposed to, say, having a self-evident edge like pure scalping. It was comprehensive enough that it became a kind of business plan.

"I took the number of trades I'd make in a day times the average edge in a pit— that being the difference between the bid and offer," he said. "I'd divide that by two because half the time the participants were right, and half the time they were wrong. The number I arrived at, plus or minus ten percent, was very close to what my statement would say the very next morning."

He would frame his individual trades—why he'd take a given profit or loss within that context. He might grab an instant four percent windfall because he'd projected a yearly average of ten trades hitting the two percent profit level. As he describes later, this would make personal sense for him even though it would sometimes mean violating or modifying a trusted methodology and consequently, leaving occasional money on the table.

His technique was cultivated through necessity—the Mid-Am's secondary mini contracts didn't have a lot of volume, so Tom learned ways to compensate in market "breadth" (i.e. diversity) that was unavailable "depth-wise." He scalped some, but knew that his survival in the scant environment would depend upon using his wits as well. Consequently, he held positions; again, in a manner determined by his research.

In short, Tom is systematic and well versed enough in the strict mechanical approach that he can cite it as a preference to 'gut trading.' This puts him in fairly rare company—one who achieved both personal and fund-managing success through judgment, who nevertheless maintains that he would have done even better had he kept his personal spin out of it.

That's quite a validation for mechanical proponents. The standard mechanical story depicts people struggling or even busting out before seeing the emotion-free trading light. Tom represents someone who arrived at the same place from a position of strength; not necessarily better, but encouraging if you're looking for a diverse array of affirming voices.

Tom's trading style centered on the concept of relative market strength. If he wanted to be a buyer in a given complex, say the grains, he would enter the commodity that was outperforming the others. Sometimes that would mean buying a market that wasn't breaking as hard or fast as its neighbors, such as buying corn a cent and a half lower while beans were limit down. The technique would sometimes get him in just off major highs or lows, normally a very tough endeavor. Most mechanical approaches are doing roughly the opposite through momentum or trend following methods. "Top and bottom picking is completely discretionary," Tom observed.

He bought his Mid-Am seat in 1971. Four years later, his combined scalping, position trading and relative strength techniques had served him well enough to buy a full Board of Trade seat. By the early eighties, he was wealthy and respected to the point where people were hounding him to manage money. He recruited his boyhood friend, Bob Jenkins, to become a partner. The two opened one of the very first commodity trading funds, which was largely discretionary.

Throughout its five year existence, the Willis-Jenkins Floor Traders Futures Fund was at or near the top of the performance ratings. Ironically, its hyper-returns may have been a factor in the fund's ultimate dissolution. After enjoying a net asset value jump from $1000 to $4000 in less than five years without a losing quarter, the customers of the fund began regarding double-digit returns as the norm. When the account finally had an eight percent drawdown near the end of 1986, several members reduced their stake or cashed out. According to Tom, the fund finished the year 23 percent up, but that was obscured by the retreat off the 30 percent high.

The second Willis and Jenkins fund faced a similar situation during the late '90s stock market bubble. A million dollar investment at the 1996 inception would have been worth a million and a half four years later. There were, however, phone calls along the lines of "What is wrong with you guys? I can get this kind of return in a day!" Dot com fever was rampant.

Despite frustration with both experiences, Tom is contemplating operating another fund, this time with his 25-year old son, Tom. Tom the Younger, (not a junior—different middle names), got his economics degree from Lake Forrest College. His current full time endeavor is system development. Perhaps more accurately, it could be described as the construction of a multi-faceted trading model. Older Tom is careful not to divulge too much, although he acknowledges that the rules largely reflect the facets of his own market experience.

The Willis' won't need to self-promote—Veteran Tom has made enough contacts with relevant players after all. Unlike the previous two ventures, however, the selling point this time will be the mechanical nature of the program.

DESCRIBE YOUR HISTORICAL INVOLVEMENT WITH RESEARCH AND SYSTEMS.

Back in the Willis-Jenkins days, we did extensive research. We burned up the computers. Most, if not all, of what we were doing was asking "what-if" questions based on our perception of the market, the way we looked at things. The net result was, we created a trading model that kicked out buy and sell signals.

We were viewed as a discretionary group of traders because we wouldn't take the signals as if we had a gun to our head, or as Jenkins said, "We wouldn't just check our brains at the door." Our approach was to trade a model that gave a direction, try to take the buy or sell signal in the corresponding strong or weak market, and then ignore what we considered secondary strength or weakness. Based on where we came from, which was the floor, and given our style and approach, that was right for us. I'm not sure we were capable of doing anything other than that. People were coming to us because of our floor reputations. The perception was we didn't lose, which our money-management performance confirmed.

SO YOU WEREN'T SPREADING, BUT YOU'D ALWAYS TRY TO ENTER AN OUTRIGHT POSITION IN THE CORRESPONDING STRONG OR WEAK PART OF A COMMODITY COMPLEX. YOU'D IGNORE SIGNALS THAT WEREN'T CONFORMING TO THAT CONDITION.

Absolutely. And you can't say it was a bad idea, because in the end, we made money every quarter that we were in business. But if you're discretionary, you have to come in every day and make decisions. If the decision is wrong, that's when emotional damage happens.

I think that's the strength of having a mechanical approach. When the approach doesn't work, you can kind of blame the approach. You can say, "Well, this is fairly predictable, we knew a certain percentage of trades were not going to be any good and this was one of them." Then, you should have a lot of expectations on the next trades that are coming.

HOW COMPATIBLE WITH HUMAN NATURE IS THE MECHANICAL SYSTEM APPROACH?

I think the hardest thing I've ever seen is what Richard Dennis accomplished. This is within the last six or seven years, the day the Japanese yen was up, I think, 1000 points. He came in long. I don't think he'd mind me talking about this because it's really a compliment on how close you can come to harnessing human nature.

I'll ask you—you're long the Japanese yen and it's up 275 on the day. What is your expectation that it should be up 400? Not very high I'd imagine. And I'm getting out well before it's 275 up on the day because I just know myself. I'm hoping I get a 2 percent trade and get ten of them a year. Some of them that I think are going to be 2 percent might actually wind up costing me 5 percent. But on average, if I make 15 trades, I might have 10 winners and two losers and my drawdown might be one percent and it's back to new high ground within 20 trading days. I hope I'm managing 100 million dollars if that happens.

So, I'm selling the yen not even 275 higher because I'm looking at it like, gosh, I'm looking for 2 percent and they just gave me 4 percent. Ok. Two down, eight to go toward my goal, right? Well, Rich not only passes on the 275—and I've got to tell you, I can think of no other time when I've watched the yen and it's up 400...he passes up 275 and he also passes up 575....and he passes up 875! To my knowledge, he doesn't sell any of it. And it closes like 900, 1000 higher. The next morning, it breaks maybe 150 off of that and in the next couple of days, he adds to his position. Now, that's *hard*. That's real hard. For me, that's impossible action.

If it goes 300 higher that night, I'd go home wondering how much they're going to take away from me the next day. Starting at that 2:00 close, I'd be harboring fears that maybe have nothing to do with markets, but you can't really control what you bring to this party in that sense. I'd say 99 percent of the people wouldn't even get the 300 points. I could get that, but like 700? Withstanding that is unnatural. It would involve something superhuman.

Everyone was talking about his great trade—how he made 100 points or whatever. And all I could think of was, it's the hardest thing I've ever seen anybody do. How do you manage to not screw up the last 700 points? How strong do you have to be? How committed to your mechanical approach must you be?

So to what extent have I harnessed my human nature? Within what I'm able to work with, I think I've got a way to eliminate as much of my human element as I can. I've created a form-fitting system—not in the usual sense of where we've optimized the results. I mean form fitting to my psychology, to where I'm at. I've at least got the human element down to grabbing profits on only half the position. I think I can stay systematic up to the point where you get the windfall part of it. Rich, of course, will tell you, that's what you're playing for—the windfall. I don't disagree with that.

ARE THERE OTHER EXAMPLES OF WHERE YOU'D BE DISINCLINED TO COMPLETELY FOLLOW A MECHANICAL APPROACH?

You'll get a problem sometimes when you get on these macro trends, when you'll see everything hitting on the same cylinders. The [impending Iraqi] war scenario is the most recent example—bonds up, stocks down, dollar down, euro currency up, copper down... And you go, "copper, too?" But, there is a correlation throughout. Now we get back to the human element, the problem of can we stomach it? We're really talking, after all, about just one trade being put on five different ways.

IS THERE ANYTHING ELSE THAT THE COLD NUMBERS OF A MECHANICAL SUMMARY MIGHT NOT BE CONSIDERING?

In the old days, there was a tendency to ask a lot of questions and have the computer spit out the answers. You made 20 trades that produced $20,000 profit for a $100,000 account. You say, "Great!" Then, you look at it more closely and find that you bought the yen at 8600 and you had to get out of it the next day at 8350 and you got the buy back again at 8600. Then it went to 9600.

Let me encapsulate the two days. You buy the Yen at 8600 and get out 250 lower. That's dead wrong. You get another buy at the same price two days later. I go, "No problem" and get back in again because, why—I've got nothing behind my eyes? No blood in me? (Laughs).

SO HOW DO YOU GET AROUND THAT?

I think one of the ways people get around it is they just hire someone for $40,000 and tell them, "do whatever it says, or you'll get fired." That's one way to get around the aggravation.

Bob [Jenkins] and I kidded around about it, but we would have been better off had we been on a ten-minute price delay. First of all, we would have saved a lot of money not having to pay for real-time quotes that I'm not convinced do you any favors. The impulse to make a trade based on some feeling or some data that you're processing is minimized because you'd say, "Well, wait a minute, the information's ten minutes old."

I think everybody would be better off if they said, "Here's my approach. I'm going to demand that it be green or red [buy or sell mode]. I'm going to demand that it be in some cycle of retracement. I'm going to demand that it get into this specific area. After I have all that, I'm going to risk some pattern recognition low, or a high if it's a sell."

And then, essentially, turn the machine off or have a rule that says, "And I can only turn the machine on once an hour." That would solve a lot of problems.

IF I HAD YOUR ABILITY TO DISCERN WHEN A SYSTEM WAS ASKING TOO MUCH OF ME, I MIGHT CONSIDER NOT USING ONE AT ALL AND JUST APPLY MY DISCRETION DIRECTLY TO THE MARKET. SYSTEMS AREN'T PERFECT. THEY DO PUT YOU THROUGH PAIN THAT SUCCESSFUL GUT TRADERS SEEMINGLY SIDESTEP. WHY ARE YOU MOVING FURTHER INTO THE SYSTEM REALM?

From a fund-managing perspective, investors want a systematic approach. They don't really trust the discretionary trader at this point. When a fundamentally flawed trend following system doesn't work, you want to be able to go back and say, "We did our due diligence, we did the best we could, we told you about how past performance blah, blah, blah. It just didn't work."

I think fund allocators are worried now that they'll give money to a discretionary account that will blow-up. They can accept somebody losing 10 percent, but not somebody that loses 90 percent and literally blows it up and the customer comes back and says, "Why did you give it to a guy that didn't even have a system?"

From the personal side, I'm not a proponent of making lots of trades and lots of trading decisions. Maybe that's a backlash to when I made so many trading decisions in the discretionary office that I got tired of doing it. The discretion might have helped us because it was the only approach we knew, but it wasn't the right answer. Can you make a lot of money not having the right answer? You bet. But money was left on the table fighting markets because we thought we saw something and wound up taking money off the table before we should have. We could have made a lot more than we actually made.

That aside, doing that grueling decision-making every day—go back and look at that really attractive Willis-Jenkins performance from June 1982 to September 1987....maybe September '88.... I'm going to say flat out, I'm not sure there was a better track record out there. People might ask, "Why aren't you guys managing 500 million?" There's ways of deciding how much you're making as opposed to how much you're risking, too, and that might determine we weren't the best.

What happened? I think we were making ten times the number of decisions a normal trading firm would make. And it just wears you down, because they're generally not right. They're generally emotion-driven or even sometimes anger-driven. In a sense, we wanted to be right and we wanted everyone else to be wrong. We used to pick tops and bottoms. You think you're fooling the rest of the world. Sometimes you can't. It's what do you do with it even once you do fool them. We'd sell a top and it would be right for a day and a half, but it would be wrong three days later.

I would think if an average fund traded a thousand or two thousand contracts per million (invested), in a year, that would be about what you'd see for an average trend follower. We were doing sixteen or seventeen thousand turns per million for the first couple years. We slowed it down.

It wasn't because it was heavy, (highly leveraged) although it was heavy. We'd pile on three or four bonds per hundred thousand. Normal groups would do two and one of the groups would do one. But the real reason the volume was heavy was because of the decisions. Maybe there is only so many decisions you can make in this world. We did it in six years instead of 20.

DESCRIBE THE ENVIRONMENT NEAR THE END OF YOUR FUND.

When the markets changed, we were kind of on the cusp of it. The markets got bigger—well, maybe "bigger" is a bad word. More sophisticated. People with real money started entering, better researched...maybe just overall better.

We would make the same trades in the late 80's that we made in the early to mid eighties, back when we were dead right....*spectacularly* right. Beans would open 30 cents higher and meal would open two dollars higher, we'd sell the meal and it would go limit down in ten minutes and stay there. Then it would be limit down the next day and we'd cover. No heat.

Now, suddenly, crude oil's unchanged, heating oil is up 500, and natural gas is at a 50 percent discount. Our trade might be to sell the crude five dollars higher, and when it was 50 cents lower, sell some more. Well, now we're seeing it go from 50 lower to unchanged and then rally $5.00.

In the late days of the fund, we weren't getting hosed, but we were starting to look at each other like "How did they get away with *that?* How do you buy the crude 50 lower—who's the guy making *that* decision, to be buying the market that's 50 lower when you could be buying the strength—buying something related that's even stronger? I'm not buying this at all!" You would see that sort of thing a lot more, because the money flows were much bigger.

Now I think the markets are doing more heavy lifting than they used to, running further. They trend longer than before, but they also have more vicious counter moves. They will put maximum heat on you. I would think a guy today would have to put on two contracts where he used to do three. Having the position that Willis-Jenkins used to have on in the mid-80's...I'm not sure I'd be at all comfortable with them.

Markets are more open now to the blind shot more often than they used to be. What creates those is anybody's guess. I won't sound purposefully like a conspiracy theorist, but I think there are bigger forces out there now who know when there are people out there who are long, and they can take advantage of it and hammer the market. That's their approach, and that might even be systematic as far as I know. There are definitely forces out there taking runs at big open interest.

ARE TRADERS BORN OR MADE?

That was the essence of the whole Turtle experience. Are turtles grown, or can they be taught? Do they have a magic sixth sense or something? The jury is in, isn't it? They'd be better off having the knowledge implanted than relying on a sixth sense.

SO YOU WEIGH IN ON THE "TRADERS ARE MADE" SIDE.

Yes, that would be my answer. If they're implanted with a non-stupid approach. With just the work that (my son) Tom and I have done recently, which is really a hybrid of all the work that's been done by me and Jenkins and a guy named Dick Nilson to the extent you put handcuffs on human nature, I don't know how much money you could make.

BUT THEN AGAIN—HERE YOU ARE, A PERSON WITH TRADING ABILITIES MOST OF US DON'T HAVE—MOVING FURTHER INTO SOMETHING WE COULD ALL THEORETICALLY DO.

Here's how I put together everything I think I know, have seen—all the things I think I smell maybe just a little bit before the next guy. Stuff that works for a day. This is what I think all that is worth in terms of money management. (Dramatic pause). Nothing.

I think I could take a kid who wasn't my son and say, "Do this, I'll pay you $50,000 a year, or you're fired if you don't exactly follow it." He'd beat me every day, every week, every month and every year.

SO YOU MUST REGRET NOT HAVING BEEN TOTALLY MECHANICAL.

Oh, I think so, yeah. Our money managed accounts would have performed better if we'd had been totally systematic. But that's a little like saying I would have been better if I were seven feet tall though. When I came down here in 1971, a few traders had heard of trend following *maybe*. You were sophisticated if you had charts. It was a big deal when *Commodity Perspective* came out and put them all between a front and a back cover so we didn't have to go out and buy graph paper.

I cut my teeth in the pits with a certain way of approaching markets that keeps you in the game, but also probably keeps you from hitting grand slam home runs. I've never had a blow up. There was a time when I first started when I might have had a thousand and I went to nothing—in a sense, that's a blowup, but overall, it's been an easy ride.

Jenkins has forgotten over the last weekend what a lot of money managers know about the intricacies of how markets work. They're managing a billion dollars and we're not. So, all of those things that I knew, all of those things that helped me...yes, they helped me stay afloat, stay in the business, feel blessed. I don't know if I can get over the hitch in my swing though. I've got some bad habits that are just a part of me.

GIVE US AN OVERVIEW OF YOUR CURRENT TRADING MODEL.

We use three or four very broad indicators that gives a general sense of whether the trend is up or down. All four have to ratchet in. It's very basic—two moving averages one short term and one long term, and two "snapshots" of dates preceding us. It gives us a good picture of whether the market's going up or down. It'll either flash green [buy] or red [sell]. Eighty percent of the time, it's doing neither.

So, now we've got our direction. We've eliminated half our potential trades; if it's a green, we never sell. Within that, we have signals that must point in the direction of the macro trend. Because it has to buy within green time frames, we get green or red signals only about 20 percent of the time. Again, by definition, it spends a lot of time gray [neutral].

When it turns green or red and stays there for four or five days, it has a great tendency to stay green or red for a very long time, which means you should be able to take advantage of it. Once in, it's hard to turn the 'Queen Mary' around.

We enter by buying bull markets on retracements, and selling bear markets off rallies. We get specific with timing using the 30-minute Market Profile. We massage it a little differently than normal. Again, it's very specific, like within a hundred dollars a contract. Two ticks in bonds, a couple cents in beans, a half a buck in meal....

Hopefully, I think we've constructed a trading model that can't trip over itself. It can't sell when you should be buying. It can't pick tops and bottoms. It's going to be content with grabbing pieces out of macro trends. Can you identify macro trends and not get caught in the chop suey stuff? Yeah, I think you can. Not 100 percent, nothing can be that way, but to a really large percent—a very high hit ratio. Sixty-five to 70 percent of the trades are going to be winners and I think the losers are going to be very acceptable. Very minimal.

AT WHAT POINT WOULD YOU REGARD A LOSING STREAK AS EXCESSIVE RELATIVE TO EXPECTED DRAWDOWN PARAMETERS? WHEN, IN OTHER WORDS, WOULD YOUR FAITH IN THE SYSTEM BE SHAKEN?

Well, in my case, in order for the approach to not be viable any more, you'd have to in a sense change the way the game is played. I'm not saying that can't happen. But at that level, my approach is very demanding and very broad. I don't see potential buy areas on a green chart being consistently bad for days upon months unless they change the nature of the game. If, in a market that is going to be directionless 80 percent of the time anyway, you demand that it declare itself, declare a direction, declare that a timing issue also be in place, and then be very specific on an area of retracement, then by definition, they've already done some damage to price if it's a buy, and some rallying if it's a sell. So there is some cushion already on the approach.

ARE THERE ANY OTHER GENERAL OBSERVATIONS ABOUT SYSTEMS YOU'D CARE TO MAKE?

I think the simpler they are, the better. You don't need 'quantum physics' to make them work. There isn't "an answer" out there to find in that sense.

By definition, there's discipline in creating buy, sell and exit signals. There's a game plan that incorporates a strategy that works and there's discipline applied with that. Maybe most importantly, psychologically, when it goes through its inevitable periods that are slack if not slumping, you can disassociate yourself from it. You can say it's the thing and not you.

This allows you to come in day-by-day without having to re-create the wheel or pull a rabbit out of the hat. You don't have to make a decision under stress that has to be right again and again. It presumably would have the what-if questions answered before you walked in the door. It takes you off the hook emotionally, which in the end will just grind you down. Let's face it, most of the time when we're asked to make decisions we're under great stress, either with huge profits or potentially scary losses.

BUT SYSTEMS ALSO DEMAND YOU DO SOME PRETTY NERVE-WRACKING THINGS ON OCCASION. INVENTING A SOUND MONEY MACHINE IS ONE THING—FOLLOWING IT IS SOMETHING ELSE. THE INDUSTRY IS RIFE WITH STORIES ABOUT SYSTEM OPERATORS WHO MELT DOWN AND FUDGE OR SIDESTEP THEIR APPROACHES COMPLETELY.

Even following systems can grind you up, no question about it. Once you have a system, the biggest obstacle is trusting it. I can only reiterate, people ought to consider hiring someone for 30 or 40 thousand dollars—whatever the going rate is—to do the trades for them.

WHAT IS IT ABOUT HUMAN NATURE THAT'S AT ODDS WITH TRADING?

I think you can broaden the scope. There's something about human nature at odds with happiness—joy. As a Christian, I'd say you experience those not because of your human nature, but in spite of it. You achieve them after finding a higher calling...a higher order. Christianity gives order to a chaotic world and I'd suggest that other religions try to do the same.

I think Paul best addresses flawed human nature in Romans. "I do those things that I don't want to do, and I don't do those things that I do want to do."

The Ten Commandments and the Sermon on the Mount were guidelines to keep us in bounds, to keep us out of harm's way, not to restrict us from having fun. I suppose if you continue on a path of adultery, stealing or killing people, eventually your life is going to be lousy.

What was heralded 2000 years ago is as pertinent today on this subject as any other. When we're talking about trading models, we're talking about handcuffing our human nature. It's the best chance we've got.

JOHN HILL

"**W**HAT **I** HAVE FOUND IS, IT'S GOOD TO MAKE IT EXCEEDINGLY
DIFFICULT TO ENTER THE MARKET BUT VERY EASY TO GET OUT."

*John Hill is one of the most prominent people in the field of
technical trading analysis. Nearly three decades ago, when I was
first starting my futures education, his book,* "Stock and Commodity Market Trend Trading" *was one of the primers routinely
referenced by my instructors, and remains a technical trading
staple to this day.*

More recently, John has co-authored "The Ultimate Trading
Guide" *with fellow technical analysis experts Lundy Hill (his son)
and George Pruitt. The book delves extensively into how widely-
recognized trading principles, as well as some less considered
axioms, can be applied in unique and pragmatic ways. In 2002,
he and Pruitt released* "Building Winning Systems With TradeStation."

*Perhaps the height of John's fame, however, resides in his bi-
monthly publication,* Futures Truth Magazine. *Industry insiders
regard it as a sort of consumer advocacy bible and system vendors vie for the potential profitability associated with the
periodical's endorsement. Its centerpiece is the Top Ten Table
where publicly offered trading systems are rated every other
month. There is a virtual avalanche of systems John and company are asked to consider. They respond with stringent controlled methods of tracking real-time performance. Maybe not*

201

surprisingly, most would-be grails are shown to be worthless early on. There's a self-evident prestige and commercial viability to surviving the weeding out process and making it into the top ten.

I interviewed John at the Sheraton Hotel, Chicago, host of the 'Chicago Online Trading Expo.' John was one of the featured speakers. He has a homespun, dry Mark Twain type wit, and a southern vocal delivery reminiscent of Strother Martin in Cool Hand Luke. ("What we have here is a failure to communicate!") At the end of an extensive conversation where he provided a mostly upbeat outlook for serious technical analysis devotees, I asked him if he had anything to add. "Yeah," he replied deadpan. "A speculator who dies rich dies before his time." As I recoiled a bit, he gave me a sort of knowing laugh—one of several "gotchas" of the afternoon. At 77, he is showing no signs of slowing down.

FILL THIS IN—JOHN HILL IS....

Primarily a trader. I trade for myself. If you want to go back, I've got a couple of degrees in engineering. I worked in the chemical industry for a long period of time. I started fooling around with the markets. I ended up making more money in the markets than I did playing with chemicals, so an avocation became a profession. I resigned from the chemical industry when I was 45 years old.

IT'S INTERESTING HOW MANY PEOPLE I'VE TALKED TO IN THE COURSE OF THIS PROJECT HAVE COME FROM A SCIENCE OR ENGINEERING BACKGROUND AS OPPOSED TO A BUSINESS BACKGROUND.

I've also found that. A lot of engineers come to the financial profession. Engineers basically think they're smarter than most people because they took the toughest courses in college. They're analytical by nature. They're of the impression that they can beat the markets.

DID YOUR MARKET CAREER START OUT LIKE MOST—PRIMARILY SEAT OF THE PANTS GUT TRADING?

When I started trading, I had a wife, three kids and a thousand dollars. I started trading the sugar market. Within a couple months, my account was up to $18,000. So I said, "Where's the next market opportunity?"

They were having a big drought in the Midwest, the likes of which the world had never seen. I started buying soybeans and I was inverse pyramiding or buying in ever- increasing increments as the market went higher. There was a front developing and I was calling the weather bureau every hour on the hour. Still, there was nothing but drought.

But then on a Saturday night, they had a weather phenomenon that hadn't occurred in a hundred years. A front moved through the Midwest and by Monday morning, instead of this great drought, we suddenly had perfect growing conditions with a predicted huge surplus of soybeans. I'm sitting there with two hundred contracts, which on Friday were worth $80,000. I had a big meeting with top executives of Procter and Gamble on that day, so I told my broker, "It's in your hands. I'll be busy in a meeting all day."

I ended up with $5,000. Running one thousand up to five isn't bad, but I decided there were two elements at play. One is that I committed a great stupidity and I had to get some smarts. The other was that if a spectacular account run-up could be done once, it could be done again.

For the next half-dozen years, I was traveling a lot for the chemical industry and I'd end up in Washington D.C. on Friday nights. I'd spend my weekends in the Library of Congress learning everything that I could about technical trading.

WHEN WAS THIS? I ASSUME IT WAS DURING A PERIOD WHEN THERE WASN'T A LOT OF TECHNICAL ANALYSIS LITERATURE AVAILABLE.

It was somewhere around 1956-58. There were a few books. One of them was by Richard D. Wyckoff. Among technical traders, his name is pretty well known. I spent $500 on his course. It was the best $500 I ever spent. I learned what moves the markets. In the long-term, fundamentals move the markets. Short-term price action is tied into human psychology.

YOU'VE BEEN QUOTED AS SAYING THAT EVERYTHING YOU NEEDED TO KNOW ABOUT THE MARKET CAN BE SEEN IN A BAR CHART.

All the news is factored into the latest price. Also, markets do not support the random walk theory. If they did, Warren Buffet wouldn't be as rich as he is, nor would a lot of other people who have made large sums of money through technical trading. Of course, fundamentalists make money in the markets, too. The problem with that approach for 95 percent of us is, by the time we know what the fundamentals are, it's too late.

The bar chart will show you supply and demand....fear and greed. I don't mean to say that it's easy. But what you're working toward is learning how to interpret who's in charge of the market—the bulls or the bears. You try to capture that edge.

HOW DID YOUR WRITING CAREER COME ABOUT?

My first book [*Stock and Commodity Market Trend Trading*] came about because engineers by nature keep very prolific notes. I'd ask, "What do you see in a bar chart?" When you make a trade, "Why did it go right or wrong?" What had I not seen in the market? I would encourage that sort of approach to anyone.

I'm a people-oriented person. I was very involved in anything people-related during my tenure at Effron Corporation. So, when I resigned from that company, Payne-Webber approached me to write their market letter, which I did for several years on the futures markets. It was those ideas that became the content of my first book.

My second book was *Scientific Interpretation of Bar Chart*. After the first book, people kept coming up to me saying, "Have you got anything else, John?" I said, "Well, I've got a bunch of notes here, so I'll send them to you and charge you fifty bucks. If you like it, fine, if you don't, send it back and I'll send your money back." I put a title on it and published it.

It was about 1975-77 when I published these books. I had left the chemical industry in 1973.

WAS THIS THE POINT WHERE YOU STARTED GETTING RECOGNITION?

I don't know that I'd say I've had a lot of notoriety in the industry. I used to get invited to speak at *Futures Magazine* seminars. I was noted in *The Wall Street Journal* and *Barrons*. I would give weekly commentaries on CNBC.

DOES MOST OF YOUR INCOME COME FROM YOUR PERSONAL TRADING OR FROM YOUR POSITION AS AUTHOR-ADVISOR?

It all comes from trading. You don't make any money selling books! [Laughs]. Well, I will add that I organized a CTA that I gave to my kids in 1992.

In the early years, I made a tremendous amount. I was able to leave the chemical industry largely because of the silver and gold markets of the early '70s. I'm not saying I've always made money trading. I have not. I survived in this business by writing a market letter and a couple books. You don't make money speaking, although that does bring you clients.

Today, I seldom go out to speak and there's no money in selling books. I don't sell how-to video tapes. I make my money trading.

MY EARLY EXPOSURE TO JOHN HILL WAS YOUR BOOK ON TECHNICAL SIGNALS. TODAY, YOU'RE COMPARING AND RATING TOTALLY MECHANICAL SYSTEMS IN YOUR PUBLICATION, *FUTURES TRUTH*. BETWEEN THEN AND NOW, HAVE YOU PURSUED A TOTALLY MECHANICAL APPROACH IN YOUR OWN TRADING?

I have not.

DO YOU ADVOCATE THAT APPROACH, WHICH AGAIN, YOU'RE ROUTINELY EXAMINING IN YOUR MAGAZINE?

Mechanical systems *should* be used by eighty to ninety percent of the population. But I'm a discretionary trader. The human mind is the greatest computer of all and it can see things that a computer can't. Still, I do trade real money in real systems.

TOTALLY MECHANICAL?

Oh yes. I separate my discretionary and system accounts. Also, if you're trading with enough ideas, your discretionary approach is going to be almost mechanical. The guy who's going to survive is the one who approaches this as a business—who does the research that convinces him why he should be trading in certain ways. For example, I determined that the first hour [of a trading day] is Amateur Hour. I did a study showing that if you did an opening range breakout on the first hour, you will get some of your best moves as is popularly believed. But it also happens to be the biggest area of unpredictability.

If you trade after the first hour, you make the most amount of money with the least amount of drawdown. But don't just believe me. That's the sort of thing any serious trader ought to be willing to prove to himself.

Compare the opening breakout trades in the first hour to those that happen after. You can also restrict it to later afternoon, say one o'clock. You can have a rule that gets in after one o'clock or a rule that gets in between the end of the first hour and one. You'll find that among those three different sets of numbers, the latest one is the most profitable.

I did another study showing the percentage of times that a market would close above and below the breakout point. These kinds of studies can help with discretionary trading in that when you combine them as filters, you're almost trading them mechanically. Opening range breakout would be one filter. A second filter could be where the price is relative to a 40 day moving average. Here's another one; compare whether yesterday's close is above or below the midpoint of a ten-day average range. The numbers show that you want to be a buyer when the close is above that point.

This is how, as a discretionary trader you begin to stack up filters to the point where your trade becomes almost mechanical. You decide that you must take a trade because you have four filters in your favor.

LIKE MANY PEOPLE, WHENEVER I'VE TRIED TO DO MARRY DISCRETIONARY JUDGMENT AND MY SYSTEMS, I'VE WOUND UP WITH THE WORST OF BOTH WORLDS.

Well, the markets are designed to defeat you. Just when you think something is going up, it goes down and vice versa. That's because of the herd instinct. Primarily what you exhibited with trading mishaps is that you're comfortable with the crowd. The guy who really makes money is the guy who makes his move as the crowd is getting uncomfortable.

COULD WE THEN SAY THAT CONTRARIANISM IS A BIG PART OF YOUR TRADING SUCCESS? AND IF SO, HOW DO YOU ACCESS THE NECESSARY INFORMATION?

No, actually I try not to read anything. News will mess you up. All you need to know is in the charts.

CAN YOU GIVE AN EXAMPLE OF HOW A CHART PROVIDED A MAJOR TIP-OFF OF AN IMPENDING MOVE?

I'll give you two. Take a look at today's date [July 25, 2003]. Look at Euro currencies about three weeks ago. Based on the news, there was no way you could go short that market. People were predicting the Euro would go to 140 to 150 versus the dollar—that the dollar would sink into the ocean. There were huge budget deficits, the situation in Iraq, and so on.

It would have been exceedingly hard to short that market. But look at what happened in the last three weeks. You had a tremendous down move. The technicians could have seen the warning signs in the charts. You had what the candlestick followers would call an 'engulfing pattern.' You had two sharp down days in an uptrending market. That doesn't necessarily indicate that the market is about to go down, but it does say that the upmove is over for the present. It has found supply in the market. Until that supply is absorbed, the market is not going up. When people ask me, I'd tell them [the upmove] was all over for at least ten days.

All long-term systems are pretty much the same. Maybe some who follow them have hung on and maybe the Euro eventually *will* go to 150. Two days ago, the market did give a signal to get back long. I question, though, whether the average retail trader could have withstood the pain he would have had to endure staying long that whole move.

SO HOW WOULD YOUR STOPS HAVE APPLIED IN THIS SITUATION? ARE YOURS RELATIVELY TIGHT? LOOSE?

What I have found is, it's good to make it exceedingly difficult to enter the market but very easy to get out. When you design a system, three things have to be synchronized—entries, where to take profits and where to take losses. They have to be very compatible.

For instance, say that you're trading an 80-day breakout system. You don't exit that type of system on a two-day reversal. You need them to be compatible. You can trade a short-term system that keys off 10 or 15 days of data that's hard to get in, but once you get in, you can use a quick exit signal. You can use a momentum filter, for example. If the close of today is greater than the close 40 or 50 days ago, the momentum is up, so you'd only trade the long side. You can combine that with other filters, such as the opening range breakout. You can look at the last three or four day's action to apply your entry. On the exit, you throw out the momentum filter making it a lot easier to come out of the trade than it was to enter.

We've always found that it's best to come out on some kind of reversal rather than coming out on a profit objective. We also do not like a dollar amount [fixed money management] stop. We believe that all systems should have a stop, but they should be based on a function of the market—something dynamically related to market action. A dollar stop has no relationship to market conditions. People will just put up a straight $1000 stop, for example.

ALTHOUGH THAT'S BETTER THAN THEM NOT USING ANY STOP AT ALL, RIGHT?

Oh, yeah, you'd better have one. If you don't, sooner or later, you're dead.

WHAT'S THE SECOND RECENT CHART SIGNAL YOU WERE GOING TO MENTION?

The bond market, which topped at just over 123-00. You were hearing that interest rates were going to zero and Alan Greenspan was going to cut rates again. How in the world can you short that kind of news? If you hadn't been reading anything though and were just looking at the bar charts, you had a key reversal day at the very top. Now, you see where bonds are [109-21] and they are beginning to talk a different story. It could be time to buy on a technical rally, but this big thrust down to me means that the bull move is over for at least the next three or four months.

LET'S TALK ABOUT *FUTURES TRUTH*, OBVIOUSLY A HIGH POINT OF INTEREST TO MANY SYSTEM DEVELOPERS.

Let me tell you how *Futures Truth* got started. At one time, I thought there was 'an answer' to the markets. People had trading systems for sale and I bought a number of them—$1500, $3000.... Most of them turned out to be completely worthless.

So, I got angry one day and said, "Enough is enough. I'm going to start revealing the truth about these cats." So in effect, *Futures Truth* got started in a sort of negative vein.

I've been threatened with lawsuits so many times I've lost count. I've been sued once and the judge threw it out. I'm just a small fellow in North Carolina, but I was meddling in a gigantic business. We actually helped put people in jail.

Give an example of what would have typified a fraudulent claim.

A fellow copied two pages out of my book that I had been selling for fifty bucks. He started selling it for one hundred dollars, claiming it was the greatest system that he had ever developed. I knew the system wouldn't work by itself because you had to add other things to it. I called him up and said, "I believe you're violating a copyright." He was a big shot and he said, "Who are you to question *me?*"

Did you ever hear of the Battle of the Bulge—General McColloch? The Germans asked him to surrender and he wrote, "Nuts" and sent the note to them. The Germans didn't know what that meant, so they had to get an interpreter. That's what I did to this guy. I wrote him a note back that said, "Nuts."

I probably have more larceny in my soul than you do, but again, this was down to the anger that I was feeling. I never made money on *Futures Truth*. What really got me involved with it was just how much this kind of thing was bugging me. One night, I poured myself a tall glass of whiskey and had a discussion with myself. I decided I was going to go through with it come hell or high water. I put some money aside and said, "Any of you cats want to sue me, come on!"

Eventually though, people with good systems started coming to us. I tell people we have a better research department than Merrill Lynch. The best ideas we get come from individuals. They don't come from the big corporate enterprises. We've launched some very successful people who have made millions of dollars and have gone on to manage huge amounts of money.

But presumably in your encounters, the person who provides the viable system is the relative rarity. Are you mainly in the position of having to disillusion people?

We have people who come into our office and feel that they do indeed have 'The Secret.' They're in agony because for us to test it, they've got to tell us what it is. That's not completely true any longer because people do submit black boxes to us.

I tell them two things. One, you know darned well that if it's the greatest thing in the world, I will trade it with my own money. I won't do so with managed money. Two, the chances of you bringing in anything I'm remotely interested in is about that much. [Makes miniscule finger gesture] Three, you show me data for 18 months— about 60 to 70 trades. I'll give you five to one odds that when we program this and test it back 20 years, it won't work.

We can do portfolio analysis. We can merge equity curves from one system to another to see the correlations. George is my one full-time programmer and we call him 'the bubble-burster.' I'm a pretty good programmer myself, although I'll admit to being computer illiterate. George has certainly busted my bubble a number of times.

ARE THERE OBVIOUS DIFFERENCES BETWEEN THE INDIVIDUAL VERSUS THE MORE PROFESSIONAL AND OR BUSINESS-ORIENTED TRADING HOPEFULS YOU ENCOUNTER?

The advantage the big traders have is capitalization. They diversify into different systems and they make more effective use of money management. Also, they don't believe all the bull about how you can make 50 to 100 percent on your money.

BASED ON THE CONSTANT SOLICITATIONS THAT YOU RECEIVE AS WELL AS YOUR OWN PERSONAL EXPERIENCES, WHAT OTHER GENERALIZATIONS CAN YOU MAKE ABOUT SYSTEM DEVELOPMENT?

You have to be conscious of the element of slippage and commission. A short-term system that makes money in soybeans will probably bomb out in corn. The volatility simply doesn't exist in corn to take care of commission and slippage. It would be a different story with a long-term system.

If you're going to be a systematic trader, you have to take chances [on your signals] even when it seems like you're throwing your money away. A risk-adverse person won't do that. I don't mind risks. I've been taking them all my life.

You've got to give up on the 50-to-100 percent system return bull. You might get *lucky* and do that—perhaps you'll catch a great market every now and then. Most of the time, you shouldn't chase a running market, but you could develop techniques for getting aboard a market with a move that is likely to persist.

AND EVEN AFTER DEVELOPING SOMETHING IN WHICH YOU HAVE FAITH, THERE IS STILL THE OCCASIONAL TEMPTATION TO VIOLATE.

You mean override the system. Well, but then you're not trading that system. You're trading something else.

WHAT IS THAT ABOUT HUMAN NATURE—THAT DESIRE TO BE SMARTER THAN A SYSTEM?

Ego! [Laughs]. Also, fear and pain. And greed. You've got to know who you are.

I tell people, for instance, I can only tolerate so much profit.

SWEATING PROFITS IS HARDER FOR YOU THAN SWEATING A LOSS?

Well, I just came out of a loss. I think that goes back to the mentality of being a child of the Great Depression. I know what it is to be hungry. Also, my trading history—I've been up on the mountain and down in the valley quite a number of times. I made myself a promise that if I ever made it halfway back up that mountain again I wasn't ever going to come back down.

I talk to people all the time and I tell them that when you're under forty, you probably can and should take bigger risks. I traded 200 contracts of silver at one time and sat through huge swings. But I've seen people my age go broke and it's pitiful.

It's how you look at money. Money is only freedom. If you've got three squares a day taken care of, you've got your house payment handled and you've got your kids educated, how many fancy resorts can you go to?

If your main goal is making money, you've got a problem. You've got your priorities screwed up and I doubt that you'll achieve that goal. Also, if you're not happy with yourself, I question whether you're going to make much money.

ARE YOU A BETTER TRADER THAN YOU USED TO BE?

Overall yes. I love the game. I'm a trading addict. I learn something new every day. I have a tremendous curiosity as to what moves the markets, which I think contributes to my success.

I've had streaks where I've netted millions and I've had streaks where I couldn't buy a trade if I had next week's *Wall Street Journal.* Why is that? I'm human. I let news influence me when I shouldn't. At times, I don't have the necessary patience, such as when I'm afraid I'm going to miss a move.

There are two kinds of people—those who can pull the trigger, and those who can't. I'm the kind of guy who can. This is a big part of finding out whether or not you're going to be a successful trader. If you're very risk-adverse, you're going to have a hard time making money in these markets unless you find a system and turn it over to someone and say, "Do it!"

WHAT WOULD SUCH A METHOD ENTAIL ROUGHLY?

In part, restricting the times you check a market to three times a day. I think day trading is a bit of an exercise in futility. A market will beat you to death if you're going off one, three or five minute charts. In my judgment, the most money to be made is to be found in three to five day moves.

I also think it's important to study the Elliott Wave. Do so in its simplest fashion. Don't get hung up on Elliott's intricate fine points. There is more money to be made in A-B-C [Elliott Wave primary moves and corrections] than anything else. A-B-C sell, A-B-C, buy. That's the primary Elliott Wave characteristic. But if you try to get into all these extensions and extensions of extensions, you will get lost in the fog.

DO YOU APPLY THE SAME METHODOLOGY TO EVERY MARKET?

Oh yes. If a methodology with the exact same parameters does not work in a lot of different markets, then I question whether you have a viable system.

The one exception is the stock market indexes. I guess it's because there's just so much more noise in those markets.

Some things do work just as well there too, however, such as the opening range breakout. But you do get whiplashes in the S&P's. Trade the currencies if you're looking for less intra-day whiplash.

HOW IS TRADING LIKE EVERYTHING ELSE IN LIFE AND HOW IS IT DIFFERENT?

Trading offers a greater degree of freedom than other structured aspects of life. That's why so many try to get into it and also why so many fail.

WE ALL KNOW THERE IS NO HOLY GRAIL, BUT WHAT WOULD COME CLOSEST TO REPRESENTING ONE FOR YOU? WHAT RETURN ON ACCOUNT LEVEL, FOR EXAMPLE, COULD YOU IDEALLY SEE YOUR-SELF REACHING SOMEDAY?

There *is* a Holy Grail.

[MOMENTARY CONFUSED SILENCE]. OK, I'LL BITE. WHAT IS THE HOLY GRAIL?

The realization that there is no Holy Grail. [Laughs]. The top money managers in the world only produce 20 to 25 percent returns.

There are so many rainbow merchants out there. People are gullible. They start their own businesses and study and work for years and years. Then, they come to a seminar, thinking, "This guy knows the answer and he's going to give it to me in three days." Two or three thousand [seminar fee] and three days, and they think they're going to have the answer.

I could sit here and tell you exactly how I trade, but you would never make any money with it. I could give you a trading idea, but it belongs to me. If you look at a hundred or two hundred charts, you'd say, "Well, John had an idea here but it works better this way." At that point, it's *your* idea and you might be able to make money with it. You couldn't make it with mine. You wouldn't have the faith to keep following it. You haven't done your homework. You'd get into trouble and you'd start thinking, "Well, maybe John was full of bull."

It's not easy. It's hard work. You can't even make money with a system unless you have studied the system. You have looked at 20 years of an equity curve on the system and you have looked at the various buy and sell signals that the system generates. You've seen things like, "Well, this went for twelve months without making a dime. This had 'x' amount of drawdown." Until you can get comfortable with all of those elements, I doubt you can make money trading a system.

Murray Ruggiero

"If you don't like the neighboring numbers, you've got a problem, because odds are, you *will* wind up with the results of the neighboring set of parameters."

Murray A. Ruggiero Jr. is one of the investment industry's premier hired guns. Aside from money earned through trading, most of Murray's professional income is derived from developing systems for others, which he does independently for the most part.

For a couple of years in the mid-1990's he received a regular paycheck from Larry Williams. "He paid me every month to come up with new ideas," said Murray, "enough to keep me going so I could turn my attention to research. Then, he'd decide what research he wanted to keep proprietary and what he'd let me put into articles or sell."

Murray also developed the trading system, I-master, for Keith Fitschen's TradeSystem Inc. His firm, Ruggiero Associates, develops market-timing systems and publishes a newsletter called "Inside Advantage," featuring fully disclosed trading systems.

Murray has also authored three books including "Cybernetic Trading Strategies." *He has contributed numerous articles to* Futures Magazine, *the content of which was compiled for his book,* "Trading and Technology For the New Millennium."

Currently, he is consulting with TradersStudio ™, a company that is looking to challenge today's widely-used trading software. Among the advantages that Murray regards as crucial to prudent analysis, TradersStudio ™ will provide a readily accessible portfolio testing capability.

"If you're looking at 20 markets," said Murray, "6 might be the best parameter number in cotton and 20 might work best in the yen, but you also want the one that produces the best risk-adjusted return across all 20 markets. You want to trade on one number to maximize the number of trials in your data, which gives you confidence that your system will continue to work in the future." According to Murray, the only way you can access the same information on today's platforms is by exporting and combining your individual results into spreadsheets.

Probably paramount among Murray's abundant reflections was the importance of understanding one's trading drivers—the behavior and characteristics of markets that would impact a given system's credibility. Impressive data results by themselves don't mean much. They only have relevance after confirming a well-laid out trading driver theory.

A second recurring theme was the fact that, any trading arena is a potential source of new system ideas for Murray Ruggiero. Whether he's mechanizing widely held discretionary concepts or converting market fundamentals into technical signals, Murray's approach is pretty much uniform. He is perhaps one of the last people likely to debunk anything out-of-hand. As he said in the interview, tools work—it's just a matter of discovering how they work in the framework of the marketplace.

YOU WILL BE HAPPY TO KNOW THAT I DID GET A CHANCE TO READ SEVERAL OF YOUR *FUTURES MAGAZINE* ARTICLES. I ACTUALLY CONFIRMED ONE OF YOUR FINDINGS IN MY OWN TESTING—THE IDEA OF FADING FINANCIAL MARKETS AFTER THE 7:30 A.M. GOVERNMENT REPORT NUMBERS HAVE BEEN RELEASED. [ON THE DAY OF A 7:30 A.M. REPORT, GO OPPOSITE THE DIRECTION OF THE RESULTING MARKET MOVE IMMEDIATELY FOLLOWING THE RELEASE OF A REPORT. SPECIFICALLY, GO LONG IF THE 7:40 A.M. PRICE IS AT LEAST NINE TICKS LOWER THAN WHERE THE TEN-MINUTE BAR OPENED AT 7:30 A.M., AND VICE VERSA FOLLOWING A NINE TICK OR MORE UP MOVE].

Do you see how a premise gets built there? That idea started with the premise that people overreact. Everything else in the system gets built on top of that.

WHICH AFFIRMS WHAT I'VE BEEN HEARING ELSEWHERE. MECHANICAL TRADERS WANT TO UNDERSTAND THEIR TRADING DRIVERS.

Exactly. That's really the underlying issue—understanding the reason(s) why something works. Your model should be representative of your driver. Once you have that, you can start to work with it.

Let's consider this bond number idea and the premise that people tend to overreact. Whatever their fears are, they're going to overreact because nothing is as bad as they initially think it's going to be. Say they sell off bonds going into a report. With any given report, one of three things can happen.

First, the number is going to be more bearish than expected in which case the bonds will keep going down. That's our one losing scenario. In the second case, the report comes out as expected. Based on the fact that people overreact, we're going to get a little bounce that'll maybe last a day or two. In the third case, the report comes out much more bullish or less bearish than expected, which means the market takes off.

So in two of the three scenarios, you win.

HAVE YOU DETERMINED THAT THE THREE SCENARIOS ARE PRETTY EVENLY DISTRIBUTED—THAT THEY EACH OCCUR ROUGHLY A THIRD OF THE TIME?

They're close enough that you can make an estimate that, yes, you should win—maybe not quite two out of three times, but somewhere near the sixty percent range, perhaps in the 58 percent to 62 percent range. The theoretical winning percentage is pretty close to what actually happens in the data, which helps to support the theory.

Another issue is people might be doing nothing before the report, and all of the [post-report] movement is noise. What research shows is that volume does not dry up before the reports as much as you might think it would.

WHICH KIND OF SURPRISED ME WHEN I READ THAT IN YOUR ARTICLE. SO PEOPLE ARE ACTUALLY PLACING BETS AHEAD OF THE NUMBERS MORE THAN WE THINK?

Right, because they're looking for the 'home run.' They're making bets that don't necessarily make sense because again, people tend to be on the wrong side of the market.

Those are examples for the kind of methodologies you need for building a system. You have to know why it works, and then you have to start to build around those pieces.

**YOU OBVIOUSLY GO TO SOME UNIQUE AREAS FOR YOUR METHOD-
OLOGIES. YOUR ENTIRE APPROACH TO MECHANICAL TRADING
SEEMS UNORTHODOX.**

That's because traditional approaches don't really work that well.

HOW DID YOU COME TO DISCOVER THAT?

Back in 1988, I co-founded a company called Promised Land
Technologies, which developed neural network software. Many of
our customers wanted to use neural networks to forecast the markets. So, to help them, I got involved in the research. We developed
an add-in for Excel, which was released in 1991.

Neural networking is a form of artificial intelligence. Through it,
you learn based on the data to develop a model. You don't have to
know what the rules are. You put in the data and it makes a predic-
tion. It's actually a fancy multiple non-linear regression.

At the time, everyone wanted to use neural nets for financial forecasting. I was dealing with customers who wanted to predict the
market. At that point, circa 1990-1991, I knew very little about the
market. My undergraduate educational background is in physics
and computer science. So, I treated the research like a signal processing problem; in other words, I treated it like I was an engineer.

I found out that the approach wasn't really applicable to the problem at hand. When you treat the problem as a signal-processing problem, it works wonderfully in the past, but you can't trade the past.

The main method that we used was predicting technical indicators.
For example, using a neural network to predict a moving average and
using the predictive moving average in the system. The work got me
enough attention that I was featured in *Business Week* in November
1992. I left Promised Land Technologies in 1993 and became a
contributing editor for *Futures Magazine* in July 1994.

I decided that I wasn't going to get anywhere with the markets, even with neural nets, unless I understood what makes a successful trading method and the reasons why some people have successful methodologies. Again, the engineering approach didn't seem to work that well.

So I went back and re-learned everything that I needed to know about the markets. I studied the classic indicators with all of the rules that you find published in books and found that none of it worked. Things like "Buy" when the stochastics indicator crosses below 80, although there are some things you *can* do with stochastics; divergence signals are very good, for example. The classic approaches that you see in book after book never worked though.

I then started studying John Murphy's intermarket book. [*Intermarket Technical Analysis: Trading Strategies For The Global Stock, Bond, Commodity And Currency Markets*]. He detailed how the major markets interact. Suddenly, I was sensing a fundamental reason why things in the markets work—something that actually made sense.

Then, I discovered the Donchian Channel Breakout—buying the highest high and selling the lowest low of the past month. I studied Larry Williams' 'Oops' pattern. [When a market gaps open above a previous high, short it when it gets back down to that high. Vice versa for lower gap openings]. These are market ideas that are classic and simple.

I began combining things that worked in markets, which again, does not include the classic engineering approach. I discovered in my research that among most successful methodologies, there is one of two things behind them. First, there is a strong fundamental reason that they work which goes to the basic model of how their prices are derived. In the other case, it's because something is happening in the marketplace that is contrary to human nature.

The underlying premise is, "What are the markets?" The markets are a mechanism to take money from the masses and give it to the top five percent. Ninety five percent of people lose money because of their natural psychology.

Again, you can trace what is working to either the fundamental or psychological aspects of the markets. For example, what is behind the Donchian Channel Breakout—why is it effective? The reason is that it is hard to implement this strategy because prices are already at a one-month high. Psychologically, that fact deters you from getting in. You say, "Well, what will happen if prices go back down?" It works against human nature.

The 'Oops' pattern works because there is some pre-released news that causes the market to gap on the open and then people realize that the news isn't what they thought. When the market starts to fill the gap, everyone panics. Everyone who bought—the weak hands who caused the gap opening in the morning—are the first to puke it. As soon as they give up the position, you have selling, which triggers other selling to come in. The intermarket stuff works because of fundamental reasons.

SO IN A SENSE, YOU'RE WORKING BACKWARD FROM THE APPROACH OF RANDOMLY CHURNING OUT GREAT NUMBERS AND THEN TRYING TO DETERMINE WHAT FUNDAMENTALS MIGHT BE BEHIND THEM LATER.

Right. We want to know [from the onset] why something works. Now, it's OK to churn numbers out, but then once you've got the system, you've got to ask, "OK, why does this work?" If you can't discover why it works, then you can't use it because it's going to fall apart in the future.

TO BACK UP FOR A SECOND, WHAT WOULD DEFINE THE ENGINEER-
ING METHOD OF ANALYZING MARKETS?

When I was doing neural nets, you'd use classic signal processing data, like cycles. You'd use MEM, [Maximum Entropy Method, a cycle-finding technique] which is used to find the current cycle and make linear predictions based on a regression to fit the data to a sine wave.

You'd take a market and run it through something like MEM or FFT [Fast Fourier Transform, an advanced signal processor] and predict where the tops and the bottoms should occur. It's based on pure cycles. It doesn't work because the markets don't stay in cycle modes for that long. Cycles tend to change.

If you treat [market research] like it's a signal-processing problem with noise, you will find out it doesn't quite work like that. I guess that's the point. A lot of engineers had to find out that they actually had to learn about the markets. They had to find out about mass psychology and/or the fundamental issues as to why things work. With everything that works, you can develop a premise that makes sense, is logical, and can be validated.

ARE YOU SAYING THAT ENGINEERING METHODS DON'T WORK AT
ALL IN MARKET ANALYSIS?

No, not exactly. What I am saying is that you cannot use engineering type methods as the core premise of a system. A trading system must be based on a solid premise. The engineering approach can be used to enhance an existing strategy, but it should not be used as a stand-alone system by itself. One example that I can think of is a method discussed in several of my *Futures Magazine* articles called 'Adaptive Channel Breakout.' This method is based on the classic Channel Breakout system except instead of using a 20-day breakout, the length of the breakout was determined using the current dominant cycle as calculated by my MEM. This is a perfect example because the engineering method was trying to solve the problem of whether the market had moved too far and was trending.

The 20-day high is a simple estimate whether the market is trending or not. A better estimate is the current cycle length because if the market has a 30-day cycle, it should go up for 15 days and down for 15 days. If the market makes a 30-day high, it is trending. You can also see that if you have a 40-day cycle, the classic system would be losing since the market would set many 20-day highs and be on the wrong side of a trade. This should not happen with the MEM adaptive version. It should not get whipsawed like the classic approach.

HOW DO YOU GUARD AGAINST GETTING SO CREATIVE AND WIDE OPEN WITH YOUR THINKING THAT YOU'RE JUST RETROFITTING ANY EXCUSE BEHIND A SYSTEM?

If you really understand your premise, you will have to figure out what the accuracy should be based on that premise. You should also determine what the average trade [yield] should be, etc. There are too many pieces that are required if you thoroughly go through the logic to retrofit a system.

With something like 'Oops,' you might not be able to figure out what your average trade should be. But still, it's a solid premise and is not that creative. The Channel Breakout idea that we discussed works because people are afraid to buy as prices go higher.

ALSO, THERE IS CLEARLY MOMENTUM IN MARKETS, RIGHT? A LOT OF THOSE "BUY THE HIGHEST HIGHS, SELL THE LOWEST LOWS" METHODS DO WORK EVEN IN THEIR SIMPLEST FORMS.

Right, that's the point. The Channel Breakout works even in its simplest form, but the reason it works is because it's hard for people to do.

Let's talk about seasonals as another example of "if there's a reason behind it, it's fine." It's been long accepted that there is a time, from February until the middle of April, when T-bonds sell off. That's due to tax selling. Or, consider the stock market problems in September and October. That's due to repatriation of funds in Japan that are the U.S. stock market and also due to the September 30 end of the fiscal year for many mutual funds. So, there are underlying reasons for these moves.

The problem with seasonals is that people will pull numbers. They'll say, "OK, let's try buying between the third and fourth trading day of the year, the fifth and tenth trading day, the twentieth and thirty first...." They'll try every combination of buys and sells. And they'll find something. Statistically, if you do something like that with a Poisson distribution (the classic bell shape curve) and try enough combinations, you will find a handful that pass the statistical test of whether they're significant. That's why the significant levels are at the 99 and 95 percentiles. It's because those one and five percents exist. But they *could* be random.

If you look at a whole year and allow that your seasonals could be between any days no matter how far apart, you've got millions of combinations you could try. So, out of millions of trials, you're going to find at least several hundred that look like they are statistically valid. If it's random like that, it's a problem, but if the seasonal is based on a reason—say, "OK, this seasonal exists because it's based on the September mutual fund selling at the end of the tax year or Japanese fund repatriation," then it's not a problem.

SO YOU'RE COGNIZANT OF FUNDAMENTALS, AT LEAST AS FAR AS THEY RELATE TO UNDERSTANDING YOUR DRIVERS. IS THERE ALSO SOME WAY YOU ACTUALLY MECHANIZE THEM INTO YOUR SYSTEMS?

Yes, for example, if the CRB (Commodity Research Bureau) Index is above its moving average, that's the same thing as saying the current view of inflation is higher. You're using the CRB Index as a proxy for inflation. You can mechanically apply it against other markets. The classic bond system that I've published is trade the 30-year bond verses the CRB [Commodity Research Bureau] Index. The rule is, take the current value of the CRB futures and bond futures, and a moving average of each. The CRB Index and bonds should be negatively correlated so if the CRB Index is going up—meaning it's above its moving average—and bonds are going up, then it's a divergence from what we expect and then we want to sell bonds. The CRB Index leads the bonds because you have inflation—that's what the CRB Index is signaling.

Other things besides the CRB Index would work, by the way. You could look for any market that would be price driven—a physical commodity that people can actually buy. If it's a commodity and prices on that commodity are going up, that's inflation.

So you would test that type of model. If the intermarket is going up and the bonds are going up, you sell bonds. If the intermarket is going down and bonds are going down, you buy bonds.

You could use things like leading economic indicators and Gross Domestic Product in your research. You just have to be careful about knowing when they were released—line them up with the dates right. A lot of data vendors stick the reports in the last day of the month even though that's not actually when they were released.

YOU OBVIOUSLY HAVE A WIDE ARRAY OF APPROACHES—PROBABLY MORE THAN THE AVERAGE MECHANICAL TRADER. ASIDE FROM ALWAYS WANTING TO BUILD OFF THE CONCEPT OF UNDERSTANDING YOUR DRIVERS, ARE THERE OTHER COMMONALITIES IN YOUR VARIED MARKET METHODOLOGIES?

One of the issues is to make sure that you have enough trades in a sample. If the premise is rock-solid firm, then the number of trades don't mean as much. The number in the sample can be less. For example, if your premise is that when the Fed increases rates by a half point, Eurodollars go down, you don't need a ton of trades. It's a solid concept that makes sense.

But in general, the more trades you have, the more likely it is that the parameters are not on the edge. You don't want a system where a parameter of ten produces a half million dollars and eight produces twenty thousand. The markets are shifting underneath you. You have to assume that [your chosen] parameters are going to act like the neighboring ones as the system's trading. If you don't like the neighboring numbers, you've got a problem, because odds are, you *will* wind up with the results of the neighboring set of parameters.

The problem with a lot of people is that they build their system on one market. Then, they filter out the couple [most severe] drawdowns. They're not even filtering the drawdowns against the basket, but against just that one market. Suddenly, they're picking up some artifact. They're going "OK, if the market opens below the 12-day low, but yesterday's low was above..." and they come up with this arcane pattern just to filter out a single $14,000 losing trade. Now, they don't get in until two days later.

MORE RULES BAD, LESS RULES GOOD, TO PARAPHRASE ORWELL.

It's not that more rules are bad, but rather, how many supporting cases do you have for each rule? Let's say we're trading commodities with a system that has two rules—one to go long and one to go short. It has a huge drawdown coming from one trade—in the coffee market, let's say. If you prefer, we could make it one trade in oil when it spiked to over thirty dollars a barrel or the collapse in natural gas or whatever.

So, you develop a filter that handles that one trade—that is, just keeps you out of that one loser. Suddenly, your results are much, much better. If you end up getting short natural gas instead of staying long the whole time and letting a $50,000 profit go to zero, you get out with a $40,000 profit on the long. But now, you're also figuring you're short at that level, and you're showing another $30,000 in profits. You've just changed the whole system. You've made $70,000 instead of zero. Now, you're right because you added one trade; one rule to handle that one particular trade. You've changed the equity curve by \$70,000 and eliminated the \$40,000 drawdown. Now, maybe your drawdown is \$12,000. All this, and yet all you've really done is filter out one trade.

That's bad. It's not valid, but it isn't about having too many rules. You could have a system with six or eight rules. If each rule handles fifty or a hundred trades, that's potentially OK.

PROVIDED THAT YOUR UNDERSTANDING OF YOUR DRIVER TELLS YOU FIFTY IS ENOUGH.

Right, as long the rule makes sense and there's reason that it's there, or even if the rule is just an accepted technical measurement. If you say "I'm going to get out at a 20-day low on a stop to protect myself," that's probably valid because now you're robbing the concept from Channel Breakout. Even if that stop only gets hit half a dozen times, protecting yourself is valid.

BUT AGAIN, YOU PREFER TO GENERATE MORE RATHER THAN LESS TRADES IN YOUR DATA, RIGHT? ARE THERE TECHNIQUES THAT YOU CAN USE TO BUMP UP THE SIZE OF YOUR SAMPLE?

Well, take I-Master, for example. The average trade is three to four days. But when we developed that system, we tested it against a basket of seven different stock indexes and we used the exact same rules and parameters against all seven. So we were able to generate about 5000 trades. A sample size that large gives you confidence.

Other than trend rules such as saying "get out if the market hits an n-day low after buying," you have to make sure the rules have enough supporting cases. Then you're not just filtering out one trade. On the other hand, if you have dozens or even hundreds of supporting cases, you have to make sure that the rule makes sense—is valid. The whole point is, what is the premise? You always have to ask yourself, why does this work? Why *should* it work?

AFTER YOU GET A SYSTEM IN PLACE THAT YOU'RE HAPPY WITH, DO YOU RE-OPTIMIZE PERIODICALLY?

If the system is built right, it should work unless something fundamentally changes. For example, when they cut the S&P 500 contract from $500 a point to $250 a point. That would give you a valid reason for re-evaluating a system. The introduction of Globex hours would be another example. Another would be the change in [interest rate futures] market hours relative to the 7:30 a.m. release of reports. At one point, they released the numbers before the market opened [at a prior 8:00 start time].

I HAD A SYSTEM THAT TRADED WELL DURING THE TIME OF THE OLD OPENINGS AND THEN FELL APART ONCE THE REPORTS STARTED HITTING DURING MARKET HOURS. SUDDENLY, I WAS GETTING RIPPED HORRIFICALLY ON THE FILLS.

That's what happened to most systems that used Opening Range Breakouts. Larry Williams and Sheldon Knight made fortunes [prior to the change]. Sheldon Knight is one of the few people who more or less duplicated Larry's feat (of running a small amount of money into a fortune], but he did it by running $50,000 to over a million. He did it before Larry—in 1986-1987.

Getting back to your re-optimization question, there might be a point in which the system has a different market condition that you hadn't noticed. One of the problems with systems is that nobody notices the flat periods unless they're trading them. You don't notice it in the data and suddenly in the future, you've got six months of a flat equity curve. Now, you're living with it. You might go back in and make a modification—say you finally figured out what kind of market condition it really is. It meant nothing in the data run, but now you're watching it. You're living it. You might be getting insights based on what almost amounts to a discretionary look at the market. You might come up with a new version of your system. You need a [tangible reason] to re-optimize, otherwise it's not a good idea.

DO YOU HOLD OUT MUCH HOPE FOR PEOPLE WHO WISH TO MARRY DISCRETIONARY IDEAS AND MECHANICAL SYSTEMS?

It depends on what you mean by discretionary. Anything, even if it's, quote-unquote, discretionary trading, should have rules, some reason you're doing it. Let's say that you have a trading system that's going to go long at the open. Let's also say you've got a gap down day and they've just raised the terrorist alert level. You might decide not to take that trade until after the market moves above yesterday's low even though your system would have gotten you in long at the open.

WHY COULDN'T YOUR SYSTEM HAVE BEEN DEVELOPED TO INCORPORATE THOSE KINDS OF THINGS INTO IT?

The truth is, you probably just gave up two or three thousand dollars worth of profit by not getting in at the open. But, you were afraid to get in at the open because what happens if there's another terrorist attack?

SO IT'S VALID TO DO SOMETHING OUTSIDE STRICT SYSTEM RULES IN THE CASE OF EXTRAORDINARY EVENTS THAT COULD BECOME LIKELY DATA OUTLIERS?

Right. Otherwise, discretionary trading is a good tool for developing the fruits of our mechanical systems.

THAT DOES SEEM TO BE A GOOD WAY OF STAYING PSYCHOLOGICALLY ENGAGED IN MARKETS, WHICH SOMETIMES DOES LEAD TO SYSTEM INSPIRATION.

Yes, and also, there are times when discretionary trading is really mechanical trading that the trader has been unable to make totally mechanical. For example, the most recognized trading pattern in stochastics—the cross over 80, cross over 20 indicator —doesn't work. The only thing that works with stochastics is divergence. What is divergence? [Pause].

A COMPARISON BETWEEN...

[Interrupting]. Right, but there are different types of divergence. There's divergence where the human eye picks up a pattern. You see that the top might not even be a true lower top, but it is a weaker top that your eye picks up. Even though it was a slightly higher top, the slope reveals a two-degree angle and the price top was at a 60 degree angle. That's angle divergence that your eye picks up. It's hard to program some of these concepts. You can come up with an Elliott Wave pattern and know you're probably in a four or x wave [sideways wave—neither dominant nor counter trending]. You're not sure—that's why it's a discretionary trade.

In 1994, that's what the market did all year. ABCX, ABCX. We bounced plus or minus 460 on the S&P forever.

You don't know where you are in the count it is most likely an X wave, which is a sideways sort of junk wave, or if it's a four. An ABC could be a one, two, three. It depends on what happens to three. Whether it's an ABC or if C is actually a three is determined by where C stops. This is all discretionary type of stuff, but it's a valid method. Once you see that you've got divergence, which is how you pick a Four Wave up, you get out of your position. That's a discretionary concept because you don't have a 100 percent mechanical Elliott Wave here. *You're* counting the wave based on *your* expertise.

Discretionary trading [should be allowable] when the concept you're expressing requires human pattern recognition qualities that you can't figure out how to make 100 percent objective. Also, it's OK to use in dealing with big event outliers.

SOME MECHANICAL TRADERS WOULD SAY THAT THOSE ARE THE KINDS OF CONCEPTS THEY'RE HAPPY TO THROW OUT.

But some of that stuff, if you could make it mechanical, probably will back-test and make money. In my book, *Cybernetic Trading,* I did an Elliott Wave analysis that Tom Joseph helped me with. We showed that Elliott Wave actually back-tested profitably. Triangles [a type of congestion area] are really powerful patterns. The problem is, when you start looking with your eye, you start imagining that are triangles that aren't really triangles.

THAT'S THE PROBLEM WITH GIVING YOURSELF LATITUDE, ISN'T IT? A LOT OF PEOPLE, MYSELF INCLUDED, WOULD BE AFRAID TO OPEN THAT DOOR EVEN A TINY BIT.

The current set of articles that I'm doing for *Futures Magazine* is called "Case-Based Reasoning." You're quantifying by saying, "OK, I'm going to take the current market pattern and analyze it in the past 20-day window. I'm going to look back in history and find all the similar 20-day windows and see what happened in the next five days after that." You can use that idea to identify the wedges and triangles and head and shoulders and so on. There's nothing wrong with that type of trading. The problem is, you've got to make sure you're being true to yourself.

One of the problems with discretionary traders is they say they trade that way because it makes their drawdowns less than with mechanical systems. All that means is that they haven't traded long enough. Going to the casino once and saying "My method for playing blackjack is good because I was never down more than $500" wouldn't hold up if they went back to the casino one thousand times. If they were the best blackjack player in the world, they would figure out that they're going to blow out, say, 250 betting units. The problem is, if you're using discretionary methods, you're doing it forward. The most you ever had to look back on was, say, a year or two.

Even if you've been trading for ten years, you have more to fortify yourself with when using a mechanical system. You'd have your actual trading time, plus at least another ten years of data before that. Otherwise, you wouldn't have been interested in that market in the first place. You have 20 years total. Whatever you're doing, you always have less data on your discretionary trading that makes your drawdown number more suspect. It just means your disaster hasn't occurred yet.

HOW DO YOU KNOW WHEN A SYSTEM HAS GONE BAD?

If the premise is good, your definition [of a system going bad] will be, "Is there a reason it should have changed?"

SO IF YOUR PREMISE IS GOOD, YOU'LL POTENTIALLY RIDE OUT A SYSTEM PAST HISTORIC DRAWDOWNS?

You should normalize your drawdowns based on volatility. That will give you an idea as to whether you're still on the pathway.

Of course, if you have a system that suddenly loses 23 trades in a row and the drawdown is three times its historical number, you probably have a problem. On the other hand, on I-Master, we saw something like a $12,000 drawdown on a mini NASDAQ contract and $10,000 on a mini S&P contract. I think the combined drawdown was around $13,000. We never actually hit those numbers, but when we hit a $6,000 drawdown, people panicked and started calling us.

THAT SORT OF THING IS WELL KNOWN IN OUR INDUSTRY. DID IT EVER MAKE YOU QUESTION WHETHER DEALING WITH THE PUBLIC WAS WORTH IT?

We sell systems, and so yes, it creates problems to a point. On the other hand, we'll take the money for selling systems because if it's not going to affect our trading, why not?

People always ask, "Well, if the system's so good, why are you selling it?" That's one of the reasons Keith and I pulled I-Master from the market. Enough people were trading the system that we wanted to protect the fills for our trading and our customers. All the copies we had sold prior to that time didn't affect our trading, and we, in effect, stopped selling it before it did. If you have a good system that you are happy trading your money, and if you can sell some copies of it without affecting your trading, that gives you more capital to trade with.

CAN AN INTEGRATED COMBINATION OF SYSTEMS EXCEED THE COMBINED PERFORMANCE OF EACH INDIVIDUAL PART?

That brings us to another concept that we have developed in TradersStudio ™. We call it the Trading Plan. A trading plan combines different sessions. A session is one system on one or more markets.

TradersStudio ™ allows you to test, say, Channel Breakouts on trending markets and I-Master on the indexes. You can develop a trading plan based on those systems, see what the drawdown is across both methodologies and add a money management strategy. You could say, "OK, I have $100,000 to trade. I'm going to trade this basket of currencies, corn, etc. and I'm going to trade a mini S&P. I'm going to risk five percent of my account on any trade. This is what my number is going to look like—here is my max drawdown, my return, etc." You can actually see whether or not the drawdown is going to be less by combining various methods.

SO YOU'RE SAYING SOMETIMES YOU CAN GET BETTER RESULTS MERELY BY COMBINING STRATEGIES?

Yes, if they're uncorrelated. For example, Channel Breakout and a counter-trend stock index system should be uncorrelated. On the other hand, if you combined the *Aberration* system with Channel Breakout, you could wind up with an even bigger drawdown because they're doing pretty much the same thing.

Here's something that people don't realize. Do you know That the trade correlation between the S&P and NASDAQ is 0.18? These markets are more correlated than that but the trades, when applying the same rules on each market, are not. For that reason, you have a $10,000 drawdown on a mini S&P, a $12,000 drawdown on a mini NASDAQ, and your combined drawdown is only $13,000. You're increasing your drawdown by only $1,000 but you're getting the combined profit on both. That's on the same system, the same rules and the same parameters.

So you have a surprisingly low correlation.

The point is: the little fine points that make the systems work aren't that correlated. Maybe a third of the time, you're long the S&P and short the NASDAQ or vice versa. That's what hedges a portfolio. When the market's really moving—a big up or down trend—they're on the same side. But when you have the market going sideways doing nothing, which is where you get chopped up by one while you're making money on the other.

Some of that is randomness. Suppose you have a breakout system where you buy at the opening plus 30 percent of the past three-day average range. Let's say that comes to three points in the S&P and five in the NASDAQ. You might get in on the NASDAQ at five points, but the S&P might have never moved more than two and a half off the open. You'd stay short there. You're long one, short the other. That's an example of how, when the market isn't really moving and is indecisive, you're hedged.

That's how you keep the drawdown small. People wouldn't think you could do that using the same system, with the same rules in sister markets. You can find this relationship in silver and gold and a lot of other markets. When we test equities, we'll put the NYFE in there, too. We wouldn't trade it [due to low volatility], but we'd want it in the data sample just to help set the parameters based on a variety of markets. Now you're more convinced that your trading results are robust. Adding a [nominal] market like that is almost like having out-of-sample data.

Speaking of that, do you recommend withholding sample periods for the purpose of forward testing in virgin data?

If you have enough data and enough trades, it is a good idea. It's more of a problem when you don't have a lot of data and/or trades and when you don't know the fundamental reason why something ought to work. If you were keying off of a strong fundamental idea, such as what happens when the Fed increases interest rates, you're in safer waters.

Marty Zweig did a model of the stock market based on the prime rate, how many moves the Fed had made, etc. The average trade lasted two years, so there weren't a lot of them in the sample. In that case, it's hard to hold out-of-sample data because what are you going to hold? Another issue is, if the out-of-sample period has only six months and the system performs badly, what does that mean? You might even find a similar six-month flat period in the data that is used to develop the rules.

The point is, the idea was a fundamentally sound concept. There is no reason it shouldn't have worked, so you don't need a lot of trades to be fortified.

DISCUSS YOUR APPROACH TO MONEY MANAGEMENT.

You calculate, "What's the risk of this trade?" If you're long in a Channel Breakout system, it could be the entry price minus, say, the lowest low of the last 20-days. That's the risk of the trade. Then, you want to know, what percentage of your account does that fixed-risk represent? Is it two, three percent or what? That is fixed-risk. Then, you've got dollars per contract, which is sort of a simplified way of dealing with optimal F (fixed fraction of an account) type money management. For example, you could say, "I want to trade one bond contract for every ten thousand dollars that I have in my account."

You also could trade one bond contract for every $10,000 of *new* money that you have. Let's say that you build a system and you're trading a 30-year, a 10-year and a 5-year bond. You could say, "I want to trade a five-year for every five thousand I have, a ten-year for every ten thousand and a thirty-year for every twenty thousand." That's thirty-five thousand dollars to trade multiple markets.

So, we start with $40,000 in our account. We're going to trade a one lot on each market. When we have $70,000 in our account, we can trade two units on each. It's dollars per contract and we monitor how much margin money we have. We don't want to be margined more than 50 percent.

But another thing you could do is start with one hundred thousand in the account. Let's assume that the money is more dear than before—it's your retirement money. You're still trading one-lots [lowering fixed risk]. But for new money over the hundred grand, you want to be very aggressive. You want to trade a bond for every two thousand on the five-year, every five thousand on the ten-year and every ten thousand on the 30-year. That would be too aggressive as a percentage of the whole capital, but if you take it only off your profit, it might be worth a shot.

You can test that concept. "I'm going to trade only a one lot on my initial money, and trade very aggressively on my profits."

YOU'VE PROVIDED A LOT OF INTRIGUING IDEAS ON HOW YOU INITIATE POSITIONS. HOW DO YOU MANAGE TRADES ONCE YOU'RE IN THEM?

As an example, let's say we were looking at Channel Breakouts. Again, a key issue is, you need a lot of trades. If you work in TradeStation®, you have to test each panel separately. You want to try to build a system where you have lots of trades, but you want them with the same parameters. You can't test one market with a parameter of 10 and another with a parameter of 50. Ideally, when you build a trading methodology, you want your code to be smart enough that the parameters are actually folding out of the price data itself.

I'M NOT FOLLOWING THAT.

Okay. On an Opening Range Breakout, buy at [the open plus] 30 percent of the three-day average true range on a stop. That's folding out of price data, whether you're buying the NASDAQ with its daily movement, or whether you're buying the Value Line Index with its daily movement.

OKAY, SO IT'S LINKED TO THE INTERNALS OF THE MARKET RATHER THAN SOMETHING ARBITRARY SUCH AS A FLAT $2,000 STOP ACROSS ALL MARKETS.

Right. Another example: one of the other systems I built is something I call the Adaptive Channel Breakout. On that, I actually used an engineering model, which was the Maximum Entropy Spectral Analysis to get the dominant cycle of the market. Then, I took the channel breakout, which is buy at the highest high of the past 20 days, and replaced that number with whatever the dominant cycle was.

The logic behind that is, if the market is in cycle mode—let's say the correct cycle is 20 days—it should go up for 10 days and down for 10 days. So if it goes up for 20 days, that's a violation of a random walk, meaning you're in trend mode.

That's another example of [techniques] falling out of the price action. You could test that system across all the markets with the same parameters. Even with buying the highest high of the past 20 days, that physical number adjusts based on the number you're trading. How far the highest high of the past 20 days is from the current price is different based on the market that you are trading. So, there's a chance a system like that *will* work across a broad scope of markets because the actual parameters are adjusting based on the price action of that market at that moment.

YOU LIKE THINGS TO BE DYNAMIC.

I like things to be dynamic, yes.

IS THERE ANYTHING ELSE YOU'D LIKE TO ADD?

I did an article a while back for *Futures Magazine* on technical indicators. I had a concept that I used in intermarket analysis called "Predictive Correlation." You take the value of the market that you think is predictive today versus ten days ago. Effectively, you look into the future by saying, how does this idea affect price ten days in the future minus today? Guess what the predictive correlation of all technical indicators is. Zero!

So you say, "OK, what can I do with that?" I came up with a concept called over-predictive and under-predictive. You know that the historic correlation is zero. If it approaches one, what do you do with it?

FADE IT?

Right! I then wrote an article to that effect on the RSI (Relative Strength Indicator). It basically stated whether you'd fade or follow the indicator depending on what the predictive nature of the indicator was.

We also studied [Richard] Wyckoff's methods. To a lot of people, the Wyckoff method is discretionary—there are no hard mechanics. But if you look at the charts, you can verify that when both price and volume go up, it's bullish, and when volume and price go down, that's also bullish. You get bearishness when volume and price are moving in opposite directions. A Pearson's Correlation [measuring the strength of the linear relationship between two variables] actually maps out the correlation.

I normalized Pearson's Correlation over a year window and determined that a 0.3 [ratio between price and volume] in coffee means the same thing as a 0.3 in the S&P. That's what I determined the correlation had been over the past year.

The result was the Ruggiero Smart Money Index—a price-volume relationship determining whether the market is bearish or bullish. I had something mechanical out of Wyckoff's [methodology], which again, is not normally used in a mechanical way. I've written a whole series of articles on how I've converted discretionary trading methods into something mechanical.

In summing it up, there are many methods that work, but discovering them takes an understanding of human psychology, statistics and economics. The market's goal is to take money from 95% of the people and give it to the other 5% who don't follow the crowd. To paraphrase Frank Sinatra, let the record show that I traded it my way.

DR. GARY HIRST

"THERE IS NO ONE THING THAT WILL LET YOU SAY, 'THIS WORKS IN ALL MARKETS AND IT ALWAYS WILL'."

Dr. Gary Hirst is the founder and chairman of Hirst Investment Management as well as a partner in Margate Management L P. The latter is based on the island of St. Thomas in the United States Virgin Islands, where Dr. Hirst resides. He is also a director of several funds and companies in Europe and America. He was one of ten industry specialists to co-author the prestigious "Hedge Funds: Definitive Strategies and Techniques," *a book released in August 2003 by John Wiley and Sons.*

All potential investment arenas are fair game to Dr. Hirst, from basic stock and commodity trading to complex hedge fund strategies and allocation approaches. The common thread is that the methodologies are all totally mechanical and tend to be unorthodox. ("Alternative investments" is how his companies define them).

More than anyone else I interviewed, Dr. Hirst is guarded about his methodologies to the point where he won't even discuss certain aspects that merely hint at what he does. Even his investing clientele, though reaping the benefits of his work, are not privy to the mathematics behind it. As he stated in different ways during the interview, a widely held idea is doomed to failure and conversely, that which runs counter to the majority is the most likely pathway to trading success. As a corollary of this belief, Dr. Hirst trusts absolutely nothing that is readily accessible to the public.

He began trading in college. One of his first transactions, made while he was an undergraduate, was a profitable Swiss franc long position where he actually took delivery.

Unlike most people, he did not endure the usual money losing learning curve. As he would consistently do in the nearly three decades of investment activity to follow, he would scrupulously analyze any trade before committing funds. It was a habit imparted to him by his father, an ophthalmologist who became wealthy via the establishment of an eye-care chain.

Since his father's death in 1976, Dr. Hirst has also continued to oversee the family office in addition to his other enterprises.

He has honors degrees in computer science and physics from the University of Miami and doctorates in law and medicine. He is a member of the Florida Bar.

His intelligence borders on the intimidating. It was a relief to learn that he can enjoy down-to-earth activities such as watching "Survivor." Of course, with him, it's more than mindless frivolity. There are many attendant sociological aspects to the program.

Jack Schwager, the author of the celebrated "Market Wizards" book series, referred him to me. Jack asserted that Dr. Hirst is the best mechanical trader he has personally encountered.

WHAT MAKES YOUR INVESTMENT APPROACH ALTERNATIVE?

Traditional investments are by definition being long stocks and bonds. So any program that isn't just long stocks and bonds is alternative. Any time you trade futures or you hedge things or trade derivatives or, for that matter, you're short as well as long, that's alternative. It sounds exotic and perhaps not as safe, but actually, many alternative strategies are less volatile than the non-alternative ones.

A BIG PART OF YOUR APPROACH MUST BE IN THE WAY YOU ALLOCATE.

Right, it's extremely important to combine strategies in a way that reduces the overall drawdown and volatility. One of the major tools that we use for allocating and combining the different strategies and methodologies, styles and instruments is a genetic algorithm, which is basically an evolutionary strategy. It evolves. You start out with maybe ten thousand portfolios. You run them and observe the results of combining the different strategies within the portfolios. Then, you breed the best of them together and allow the worst ones to die off.

When they breed, you have all their normal evolutionary components such as crossover between the chromosomes and genes of the parents. You also get point mutations, which are the random changes within genes.

So, these normal evolutionary mechanisms are used. Typically, we use about ten thousand generations. In the end, you have a portfolio that has evolved to produce the best possible combination of strategies and the lowest possible risk.

Genetic algorithms have several advantages over a neural net approach. The good thing about evolutionary strategies is that you can apply a lot of real world phenomena and get a lot of feedback on how it applies to markets. The actual evolutionary process can also feedback into itself. You can look at how life cycles progress, and that can become part of the end result. If a typical allocation goes through a life cycle, then the evolutionary genetic algorithm will actually incorporate that normal life cycle into the final evolved product(s).

Another advantage of genetic algorithms is that you can be much more confident that you've achieved a global rather than a merely local result. An evolutionary strategy can be used for many things. It can be used to combine a futures market with a futures portfolio or a hedge fund with a portfolio of hedge funds. It can be used to combine different strategies into a combined portfolio. Whatever level you are working at, you can apply genetic algorithms.

If you're looking at hedge funds, you might be looking at up to six thousand hedge funds together. If you're looking at futures markets, there are probably only eighty or so markets that you can combine in a portfolio. If you are looking at strategies, it would depend on how many you have. You might have a dozen or so that you'd want to combine together in the best possible way. The numbers vary depending on the actual application, but it's an algorithm of broad application that can be used in many ways.

PLEASE DEFINE 'ALGORITHM.'

An algorithm is a step-by-step procedure for solving a problem, named after the ninth century mathematician Al-Khawarizmi. All computer programs are algorithms, but they also apply to the real world tasks such as how you go about making a cup of tea. How do you achieve this end result? 'Go to the kitchen. Turn on the kettle. Take a tea bag out of the box. Put the tea bag in a pot. Wait for the kettle to boil. Pour in boiling water.' It's a finite procedure for achieving an objective and a very common term in computer science.

IS EVERYTHING IN YOUR APPROACH TECHNICAL OR HAVE YOU ALSO FOUND WAYS TO SYSTEMIZE THE FUNDAMENTALS?

We use *no* technical trading if that is defined in terms of things like stochastics and RSI and head and shoulders and Elliott Waves. Those are not methodologies that work. All of our trading is quantitative [mathematically measurable]. The quantitative inputs we apply could be fundamental. They could be company earnings or economic data. They could be price-based, but regardless of what they are, they are quantitative.

Even our macro-economic models are quantitative. They look at world-wide macro economic variables and combine those into an analysis of the current environment.

We're all quantitative. We define genetic algorithms as quantitative.

BUT AREN'T THEY BASED AT LEAST SOMEWHAT ON WHAT THE MARKETS HAVE DONE IN THE PAST?

There are some price-based inputs into some of our algorithms. Not all of them. The actual past prices are not always relevant.

WHAT OTHER WIDELY REGARDED METHODOLOGIES HAVE YOU FOUND TO BE FALLACIOUS?

Anything you can buy as a trading system for $3000 probably won't work. Anything that is published in a technical analysis journal probably doesn't work. The things that do work are not published, not available to the public and very closely guarded. It's extremely important for people to realize that if you can buy it, then why would the person be selling it if they knew how to make money by trading it? The answer is most likely that they only know how to make money by selling it.

SO OBVIOUSLY, YOU'RE NOT DISCLOSING METHODOLOGIES TO YOUR CUSTOMERS.

Correct. We are very proprietary about exactly what we do.

YOU'RE WORKING PRIMARILY WITH CORPORATIONS, RIGHT?

Right. Our clients include European banks, European pension funds, insurance companies and family offices.

GETTING BACK TO YOUR METHODOLOGIES: DO YOU AGREE WITH THE COMMONLY STATED AXIOM THAT SIMPLE WORKS BEST?

Not necessarily, no. Things have to be conceptually simple, I guess. If you don't have a basic theorem about why something works, then you're probably not using the scientific method.

SO YOU WANT TO UNDERSTAND YOUR DRIVERS BEFORE YOU START COMING UP WITH NUMBERS?

Yes. If you look at the markets and work backwards, and determine that if you had done this or this and you traded this and got out over here, then you would have made a lot of money, so that's how you're going to trade... well, that's not going to work. You've data-mined. The markets are much too smart to let people trade like that.

What you need to do is to follow the scientific method. Start out with a hypothesis about how the markets work and then develop a system based on that hypothesis and test it. If it works, your hypothesis is true and now you have a trading methodology.

You have to work forward, not backwards. If you're working forward, you'll obviously have a generally simple idea—a hypothesis—that you're keying off. The implementation, though, can often be fairly complex. That could result in years of programming and development. But again, the core idea can and will likely be very simple.

You cannot start with the market and work backwards to develop a trading system. You've got to come up with a theory or hypothesis as to how the market works, and then come up with a way to test it. That's how you develop things that work.

CAN YOU MAKE A GENERALIZATION ABOUT WHAT WORKS IN A MARKET?

There's really no general rule.

ANYTHING ALONG THE LINES OF "MOMENTUM PERSISTS," SAY?

Certainly the distribution of price movements is not Gaussian. [Normal distribution, often described as a bell shaped curve]. That could indicate that you do have trends. There's nothing simple, though; no magic way. Maybe something works now in some market because of the way the market is structured and the psychology of the people behind it. But maybe it won't work tomorrow in that market...or any market. There is no one thing that will let you say, "This works in all markets and it always will." Besides, the things that are absurdly obvious are generally arbitraged out because so many people will be doing them. When many people start using a trading system, returns diminish to the natural arbitrage point of barely break-even.

DOES THIS MEAN YOU HAVE TO PERIODICALLY RE-EXAMINE EVERYTHING?

If other people develop the same trading methodologies as you, then your opportunities can go away. As long as something remains essentially secret, it could theoretically work forever.

FORGIVE ME FOR HAMMERING ON THIS MARKET CHARACTERISTIC IDEA, BUT OBVIOUSLY, SOMEONE STUDYING MARKETS AS THOROUGHLY AS YOU MUST HAVE FORMED SOME GENERALIZATIONS. IF MARKETS AREN'T RANDOM, FOR EXAMPLE, WHAT ARE THEY?

They are chaotic. They have a fractal dimension. If you measure it, you will find that the fractal dimension is not commensurate with random behavior. I'll leave it at that. Anything else about it, people are going to have to figure out on their own.

DO MARKETS HAVE A TENDENCY TO DRIFT?

Obviously anything is subject to change. You can never assume anything will work the same tomorrow as it worked yesterday. When you develop a system, you also have to develop a way to evaluate whether it's going to work or not on a continual basis. That has to be part of the system.

The most important thing in any kind of systematic trading is to have everything planned out ahead of time. If the markets are closed for several days because there was a terrorist attack in New York, is that going to be a surprise and something that you can't deal with because you never anticipated the markets being closed for that reason? Well, it shouldn't be. A perfect system will incorporate every possibility. It will constantly be aware of its own failure modes.

With everything we develop, we also do a failure mode analysis in which we look at every possible mode of failure. If such and such happens, what will happen to every other part of the system and the portfolio? What would be different if more than one thing failed at the same time? What would the combined effect be on the overall portfolio? You have to look at the worst-case scenario.

HOW DOES THE ISSUE OF CORRELATION PLAY INTO THAT?

Correlation is also a dangerous tool. It's a statistical tool and statistics in themselves are not really quite correct for the market. The market is not necessarily random in any aspect. If you use statistics, you will always underestimate risk. We have tools that are much more accurate in measuring risk than statistics.

Correlation doesn't necessarily tell you anything about interrelationships. It's fairly dangerous in that it just fits to the past. When you're doing multiple correlations and combining them together, you're losing a lot of data in the process before you reach your end result. That's also something that we don't like to do. We like to use techniques that keep all the richness of the interrelationships of that data until the final result is determined, which most statistical analyses will not do.

Why are markets so incompatible with human psychology?

I think psychology is a wonderful tool. Using psychology, I can pretty much predict what people are going to do.

Generally, people go crazy long or crazy short. Things are very rarely right; they're usually overbought or oversold. If people were rational, markets would be fairly priced all the time, but people are not rational. They succumb to the two magic elements: fear and greed. Were it not for that, I couldn't make money.

People are just generally bad at dealing with things. Psychology is complex. Dealing with people and groups is complex. If you consider the business world, there are very few CEOs who are really good. People who have been extremely successful like Bill Gates are the standouts in the business world. There are standouts in the trading world, too. I'm sure that if Bill Gates had devoted himself to trading, he'd be an outstanding trader just because he's a brilliant person.

So, intelligence does help in trading.

Yes, especially as you apply it to other people's psychology.

Do you have to deal with your own psychology as well? Are you like a lot of people whose strongest feelings about a market move tend to be wrong?

No, I'm usually right. I'm just good at that.

So why don't you engage in improvisational trading?

I could do a lot of things. I can see a movie and predict what the grosses are going to be. I don't know why the studio heads can't.

Why do they spend a hundred million on a film I can see is only going to gross twenty million? I can see a movie that costs ten million that I know is going to gross over a hundred million. So maybe I should be a studio head. [Laughs]. There are so many things that one could do.

People are very psychologically complex. If you watch "Survivor," you'll see how incredibly difficult it is to outwit other people and to deal with psychology and your own emotions. There's a million dollars at stake, and yet they still can't resist baiting other people, succumbing to their anger, getting very emotional about it all. All you'd have to do is sit there quietly and just do your job for forty days, and you'd get a million dollars. So why are you getting into arguments with other people? How stupid can you be?

Again—human psychology: People are very emotional and unable to control themselves. If you note the people on "Survivor" who win, it's generally people who have been fairly quiet during the show. They quietly watched everybody and refrained from making a big commotion.

Human psychology is very interesting. I can go to Epcot and sit at an outdoor café and enjoy watching people for hours. I think it's important to observe people and understand the mistakes they make with all kinds of behavior. The mistakes people make on "Survivor," or getting their kids around a theme park or running billion dollar corporations are the same mistakes people make in trading. You certainly can't afford to be afraid. You can't afford to have doubts about something that you've scientifically proven to yourself. Nothing instills as much confidence in me as acting on what my research shows.

ARE TRADERS MADE OR BORN?

I'm not sure what percentage of the necessary characteristics come from nature or from nurture. I do think that by the time you're an adult, it will be determined whether or not you will be able to become a trader. It's pretty hard to convert an adult into being successful at something in which they haven't already developed the skills to be successful.

Is trading an art or a science?

I can't think of anything that is only an art or a science. You should always apply scientific principles where they can be applied, but some things are too complex to lend themselves to mathematical analysis. If you could do a scientific analysis of somebody's psychology—say you could apply it to somebody that you're in negotiations with in a meeting—that would be great, but you can't. It's too hard to quantify what's going on.

We have the ability to judge people, an ability that is built into our own neural net, but we haven't managed to reproduce that in machines yet because they're not complex enough. Computers are still maybe one millionth of the power of the human brain. We don't have that incredible neural network that could look at a person's face and determine if they're telling a lie or not.

So are there aspects of your methodology that, say, you could visually detect on a chart, but that you could not quantify into research?

No, we generally only trade that which we can quantify. There are certain circumstances where you have to be aware of what's going on and make sure that it's not something extrinsic that is not included in the model.

Aside from having your hypotheses set ahead of time and then having numbers confirm it, what else do you want your testing results to do?

We do all the normal testing procedures. We maintain skepticism throughout the process. Even a statistical approval does not guarantee that what you're looking at is real. You have to have a huge amount of skepticism and you have to be careful in how you test. You also have to be aware of the limitations of the amount of data you have.

OTHERS HAVE STATED THAT THERE'S NEVER ENOUGH DATA TO MAKE THEM FEEL REALLY SECURE.

It's more of a problem if you're developing your system from the data. If you're developing your system from a hypothesis, it's not quite as critical. If you have a few thousand cases of something working in line with a hypothesis, it means more than if you curve fit data and come up with something that works ten thousand times. That's one of the reasons that the hypothesis is so important—it's because of your data limitations. You should develop your system from a hypothesis, not from the data.

ARE YOU VARYING TRADING TIME FRAMES WITHIN YOUR PORTFOLIO?

We generally like to be flexible in the time frames. Having a fixed time frame can be another dangerous thing. When you see something happening within it, it might not mean anything. If a market phenomenon occurs across all time frames, it's much more likely to be correct...more likely to be real.

DO YOU HAVE ANY PREFERRED TIME FRAMES THOUGH?

No.

ANYTHING ALONG THE LINES OF PROFIT TARGETS?

Pretty much anything you've come across in technical trading we don't use.

SO WHAT WOULD GET YOU OUT OF A TRADE?

The fact that whatever quantitative system you're using decides that you should no longer be in the trade. We don't use stops or targets, but we have quantitative analyses that are constantly telling us how much we should be committing to each market. Today we should maybe be 50 percent long the Japanese yen and tomorrow we'll come in and it'll say we should be long 46 percent. So we reduce our position four percent. That's how we trade.

SO YOU SCALE IN AND OUT.

Scaling is a specific trading technique that we don't use. What we do looks like scaling from the outside because we're constantly adjusting position sizes, but it's not scaling. It's actually keying off independent time frames that produce independent results.

YOU'VE TACKLED SOME OF THE UPPER ECHELON PROFESSIONS, I.E. GETTING DOCTORATES IN LAW AND MEDICINE. WHY DID YOU MOVE INTO TRADING?

Well I didn't actually move. I started trading in 1973 when I was 21 years old. I started trading foreign currencies. My trades were all profitable. I was reading *The Financial Times* and *The Economist*. I formulated views on the U.S. dollar and Swiss franc, traded that and made a fair amount of money. I continued from there.

I was born and raised in England up through high school. My parents retired to the Bahamas. I went to live with them for a year. It became time to attend the university so I went back to England for a couple of weeks. It was cold and overcast and drizzly in the middle of June. After living for a year on the beach in the Bahamas, I said, "Enough of this!" I couldn't deal with it so I decided to go to the University of Miami instead. That's how I came to the States in 1972.

The bottom line is, that's when I started trading and I've been trading ever since. I took over the family office in 1976. My various degrees-computer science, physics, law, medicine—were more of a learning experience. They were never intended to be a career. They were meant to be tools.

IT'S UNUSUAL THAT SOMEONE SHOWS SUCH TRADING SAVVY FROM THE BEGINNING WITHOUT THE USUAL ARC OF GETTING BURNED AND LEARNING THOUGH MISTAKES. HOW WAS IT YOU WERE SO AWARE FROM DAY ONE OF WHAT IT TOOK TO TRADE SUCCESSFULLY?

My father had a business back in England and he had money to invest. He just basically told me, "If you make some money and you invest it and you can make money on your money, you can live off your capital. You don't have to work." That was his goal and he accomplished it.

As a teenager in high school, that was an appealing idea. [Laughs]. I don't have to work! I can just do the things that teenagers want to do and play with my money and make money on money and not ever have a job. This really lit up my brain. While everybody else was out playing at lunchtime, I'd go the school library and read *The Economist* and *The Financial Times,* two of my favorite publications. I'd be the only person there at lunchtime. I'd bring sandwiches and read my papers. They actually gave me a key to the library. I guess they thought I was crazy and I probably was. But from my mid-teens, that's where my focus was. I became very familiar with all the facets of economics. I studied for years before I actually started trading. When I did it, it worked. Things went very well.

SO DID YOU MANAGE TO AVOID JOBS YOUR WHOLE LIFE?

Yes.

CONGRATULATIONS!

Thank you. [Laughs]. Of course, it's never quite what it seems. I still work obviously, but I enjoy it so much it doesn't feel like work.

WHAT KIND OF HARDWARE AND SOFTWARE ARE YOU USING? IS ANY OF IT COMMERCIAL?

We use PCs—currently, we have 3 giga-hertz Pentium Fours. We're running Windows XP Professional. But we code in every computer language, from Assembler to Java.

We have no commercial trading or financial software at all. The only stuff we have is the Windows Operating System, Microsoft Office and the programming languages.

IS BUILDING YOUR OWN PLATFORM FROM THE GROUND UP CRUCIAL TO SUCCESS?

If you can buy it, it's probably not going to make money. If it worked, why would people sell it? There's no such thing as a free lunch.

YOU'VE HAD MUCH EXPERIENCE IN MANY PROFESSIONAL AND PERSONAL ARENAS. WHAT IS IT ABOUT TRADING YOU FIND PARTICULARLY GRATIFYING?

I think trading is very similar to most things in life. The difference is that, unlike most other endeavors, you know exactly how good you are at it. If you direct movies, how do you know how good you are? I guess you could look at your box office gross but maybe you encountered unfair critics or the movie didn't get released or promoted properly, or there wasn't enough in the budget to do it justice. Who knows why something is successful? Who knows whether you're a good director?

How do you determine whether or not you're a good writer? You know how many people buy your books, but what does that mean? It's more complex than just sales figures. Sometimes just getting the hype out will sell books. Are those beneficiaries actually better than any number of other authors with equally good books that nobody ever heard of?

You can't really judge how good you are at most things by how successful you've been. But when you're trading, you can know every day how good you are.

There are seven billion people on this planet and every one of them has some access to the markets. To one degree or another, everyone affects markets. They all have information they are processing. Think about the human processing power of seven billion people. All of them are making market decisions every day. Even if it's a farm worker in Cambodia, they are making decisions about what they will buy based on how much money they have. There's so much input into the markets. So many people have full access to all the financial information.

You are facing all those people. You are challenging them and you have to be better than them in order to, basically, take money away from them. You're proving that you can do that if, at the end of the day, you've made money. I don't have to tell anybody how much money I make. I know how good I am just because I can look at my trading results.

If at the end of the year, you've made ten million dollars, then that's not open to question. Nobody could say, "Oh well, he's not *really* a good trader." You would just laugh.

Summary 1—The Planning Stages

Don't get dazzled by good numbers alone. We can easily churn them out, given today's user-friendly software and the thousands of possibilities at our disposal. Separating the significant from the merely random is the analyst's real challenge. That comes down to a careful application of the optimization process and an understanding, going back to day one of the underlying drivers.

Although there is not an absolute science behind recognizing the predictive validity of given concepts, there are universally acknowledged reliable roadmaps. Charlie Wright perhaps best summarized them.

1. Test over multiple markets.
2. Be wary of data fields that are too narrow or peculiar to a specific market environment. Make sure you're observing the gamut of trending and trading, bull and bear, as well as inert sideways markets. Some of the interviewees acknowledged a preference for recent rather than ancient market activity, but none outright contradicted the belief that more data is always better than less.
3. Make sure that your good numbers reside in a surrounding neighborhood of similarly good numbers. As Murray Ruggiero observed, you've got a problem if you don't like the neighboring parameters because those are the ones you will likely be experiencing in actual trading.

THE AVERAGE PERSON CANNOT EXPECT TO LEVERAGE SMALL AMOUNTS OF MONEY INTO LARGE AMOUNTS. The everyday individual does not have the floor specialist's ability to take edges. Many actual floor traders can't even pull off such a feat within the intense dog-eat-dog environment. Forget the floor legend tales—they do not apply to you or me.

KNOW YOURSELF AND UNDERSTAND WHAT IT IS YOU'RE TRYING TO ACCOMPLISH. If you can create a money machine that produces a 30 percent return per year, you're near the top of the trading advisor heap. Be realistic. Take your personal wiring into account when constructing your methodology.

TRADING IS A BUSINESS. It has unique aspects, but traditional principles do apply. Develop a sound business plan. Follow it. Never initiate programs that haven't been thoroughly researched and understood. Beware of embarking with too little capital—the number one factor behind failed businesses.

DON'T TRY TO GUESS ANYTHING, INCLUDING WHEN YOUR PROFITS AND LOSSES WILL LIKELY HIT. Markets will inevitably prove that we haven't got a clue as to what is "too high", too low" or "too much."

Consider Charlie Wright's explanation about why he never wanted to scale back his funds after a big run-up. It would be a lose-lose situation because even if his de-levering impulse proved correct, Charlie would then be faced with the dicey job of explaining his actions to his investors. He wanted nothing to do the new expectations his people would subsequently acquire—that Charlie himself was as lucrative as his systems—that he'd always be able to maneuver in corresponding fashion.

Similarly, I choose not to distort someone's expectations— my own.

CONSIDER DEVOTING LESS ATTENTION TO INDIVIDUAL SYSTEMS AND HOLY GRAIL ENTRY SIGNALS. A blueprint for trader longevity has to be more all-encompassing. Diversification is key, which pretty much rules out the idea of surviving off of one system in one market over all time. Portfolio allocation and money management should command a substantial part of the serious analyst's attention.

WORK ON MITIGATING THE DANGER OF MARKET BLINDSIDES—LARGE OUTLIERS. Unfortunately, shocking events like Black Monday or 9-11 will be an eternal part of the trading equation. The challenge is maintaining as high a profitability expectation as possible while avoiding the pitfalls of over-leverage and over-correlation of systems and markets.

FINE POINTS: SOME GENERAL CONSENSUSES AMONG THE EXPERTS.
1. For the most part, profit targets diminish performance results.
2. De-levering, or finding some way to increase and decrease your positions based on the status of your account equity, is an apparent dead end. (Never say never, but so far—no good, at least on my end). Moves begin and end too quickly for an account oscillator to profitably anticipate them.
3. Momentum is the bedrock of systems. Even counter trending ideas tend to get aboard once a new direction has been established, however recently.
4. Traditional supply-demand markets best lend themselves to momentum ideas. (Particularly currencies). Indexes don't trend well.
5. Simple is best. Even those with complex programs conceded that at the core, the individual components were basic enough to incorporate easily explainable concepts.

MONEY IS A SYSTEM TRADER'S ULTIMATE ASSET. You need to be fortified to operate systems. The worst way to accomplish that is to trade on a shoestring. The ultimate objective is to have a mini-universe of systems trade in varied markets over an array of time frames.

STAY ALERT TO THE POSSIBILITY OF NEW TRADING ARENAS. I probably still wouldn't realize what a fertile field the Russell 2000 futures
had become if I hadn't gotten affirmation from my interviews, particularly Wayne Griffith's. The Russell is thinner than the NASDAQ and
S&P, but the fills are still very much in line with normal slippage-com-
mission projections. Besides, compared to the recent ratty action of
the S&P, the Russell moves in a more straightforward fashion—just
what you want for momentum trading.

The mere fact that it's a different market than my bellwether S&P's is
significant. Murray Ruggiero spoke of the surprisingly low correlation
among the various indexes, specifically the S&P and NASDAQ.
Upon re-examining the performance history of my best S&P and
NASDAQ systems, I drew the same conclusion. Consequently, I
now have a viable Russell system in my mix.

**TAKE A PAGE OUT OF THE REAL ESTATE AGENT'S BOOK. KEEP THINKING
"ROBUST, ROBUST, ROBUST!"**

MORE THEORETICAL TRADES SHOULD FORTIFY YOU BETTER THAN LESS.
The more examples you can apply to each rule you formulate, the
more confident you can be regarding probable future performance.
That rails a bit against various testing procedures such as creating
filters to weed out 'x' number of net losing trades. Within the overall
balancing act, however, more remains more.

The Ten Commandments of Mechanical System Trading

1. Thou shalt take every and all signals generated by thy program. Thou must not picketh and chooseth trades.

2. Thou shalt forsaketh the advice of thine mother, thine father, thine brothers, sisters, friends, TV commentators, the false newsletter prophets and everyone else, for only thou knowest what makes thine system truly righteous.

3. Thou shalt not fudge. Thou must not taketh thy profit a tick early nor shalt thou moveth thy stop-loss a tick up or back. Wideth is the pathway of violation, narrow and true is the path of thy research results.

4. Thou shalt not gamble. Whosoever taketh a market flyer shall fall to the earth and explode in flames.

5. Thou shalt not improvise. Maketh no exceptions for thy rules. Decideth nothing while trades are in progress. If thou likest not what thy system does in certain environments, then thou art free, in a calm, non-trading future time, to maketh thy rules more accommodating.

6. Thou shalt remain vigilant in thy continued research. Maintain eternal skepticism. Guard against too many rules, too little data, too good results.

7. Thou shalt not over-optimize.

8. Thou shalt not combine discretion with the mechanical, for verily that will beget the worst of both worlds.

9. Thou shalt not duck any scary scenarios in the false name of prudence. That which thou fearest most shall set thou free.

10. Regretteth not that thy systems are smarter than thee. Giveth thanks for thy bounty, for verily, it is the pathway to glory.

Basic Terminology of Mechanical System Trading

Drawdown—A debit amount representing a historic equity high minus the subsequent lowest level that an account reaches before moving up again and surpassing the previous high. (The ultimate amount obviously is determined after the fact). **Maximum drawdown** reflects the worst pullback in the history of the data field. A **drawdown period** is commonly thought of as extending between the previous high and the time that high is finally taken out.

Driver—Underlying market force or characteristic. It's common for mechanical traders to insist that their results conform to such understood principles as a safeguard against over-optimization.

Mechanical—As applied to trading, a methodology where all actions are determined by cut-and-dried mathematical signals. One who follows systems in pure mechanical fashion is taking all long, short and exit signals exactly as stipulated. The signals must be precise and the trader must avoid overriding or applying any kind of discretion.

Optimization—The process of massaging a trading strategy by determining which of a field of numbers produces the best historic results. Software will allow you to replace actual numerals with a variable—'x' or 'y' say, and then scroll through the different settings between a high and low parameter with increments set in between.

As an example, it is common for system traders to want to buy higher off an opening price at a certain percentage of a previous bar size. Determining the best percentage is the optimization process. You could plug in 0.1 as the lowest reading, 2.5 as the highest and then set your increment at 0.1. You will see every test result between the two numbers—in this case, 25 total tests.

Optimization will always give you some numbers that are better than others. In some cases, the differences will be significant. The challenge is in determining whether the good performers are merely the best of a random series, or something more significant.

OVER-OPTIMIZATION—is as detrimental to the analytical process as prudent optimization is vital. It can be a vexingly fine line.

OUTLIER—An extreme result, such as an abnormally large profit or loss. The occasional shocking market event, such as 9-11, Black Monday, a freeze in Brazil, etc, could have a dramatic impact on an overall data field, but what does that one isolated event ultimately mean in terms of supporting a market idea? People often remove such anomalies from their final performance results, or at least de-emphasize them. While such spikes are certainly going to continue to pop up over time, given their exclusive and special nature, their supportiveness of system concepts is questionable

RETURN-ON-ACCOUNT—The total net profit divided by the biggest historic drawdown,

SLIPPAGE AND COMMISSION—A crude way of bringing one's theoretical trades more in line with what actual trades would produce. Commission speaks for itself—every trade has that cost applied to it. Slippage refers to the nature of a pit or electronic field. Any order that is not a stipulated limit is going to be subject to the traders' edge—that is, they seek to buy at the lower bid and sell at the higher offer. To meet their demands obviously, you'll often be doing the opposite. The customary applied slippage/commission figure is a flat $100 per trade on any full sized contract.

STANDARD DEVIATION—A statistical measure indicating the general dispersion pattern of numbers within a data sample—e.g., how closely the numbers within a data set cluster around their average. Two standard deviations would have a wider dispersion pattern than one, three would be wider than two, etc

TEST (VERB)—To formulate an idea that can be expressed mechanically and then run it against actual prices in a data field. Among the many concerns to keep in mind—don't cheat. Make sure that what can't be known or implemented in actual trading isn't manifested in data either—in other words, don't let your theoretical future encroach your theoretical past.

TOTAL NET PROFIT—What a system has produced in a data field after adding all the winning trades, losing trades and slippage and commission together. An obvious gauge of system validity, but by no means the only thing you need to know.

Published by: Traders Press, Inc.®

7 Secrets Every Commodity Trader Needs to Know (Mound)
A Complete Guide to Trading Profits (Paris)
A Professional Look at S&P Day Trading (Trivette)
A Treasury of Wall Street Wisdom (Editors: Schultz & Coslow)
Ask Mr. EasyLanguage (Tennis)
Beginner's Guide to Computer Assisted Trading (Alexander)
Channels and Cycles: A Tribute to J.M. Hurst (Millard)
Chart Reading for Professional Traders (Jenkins)
Commodity Spreads: Analysis, Selection and Trading Techniques (Smith)
Comparison of Twelve Technical Trading Systems (Lukac, Brorsen, & Irwin)
Complete Stock Market Trading and Forecasting Course (Jenkins)
Cyclic Analysis (J.M. Hurst)
Dynamic Trading (Miner)
Essentials of Trading (Pesavento & Jouflas)
Exceptional Trading: The Mind Game (Roosevelt)
Fibonacci Ratios with Pattern Recognition (Pesavento)
Futures Spread Trading: The Complete Guide (Smith)
Geometry of Markets (Gilmore)
Geometry of Stock Market Profits (Jenkins)
Harmonic Vibrations (Pesavento)
How to Trade in Stocks (Livermore & Smitten)
Hurst Cycles Course (J.M. Hurst)
Investing by the Stars (Weingarten)
Investor Skills Training: Managing Emotions and Risk in the Market (Ronin)
It's Your Option (Zelkin)
Magic of Moving Averages (Lowry)
Market Rap: The Odyssey of a Still-Struggling Commodity Trader (Collins)
Overcoming 7 Deadly Sins of Trading (Roosevelt)
Planetary Harmonics of Speculative Markets (Pesavento)
Point & Figure Charting (Aby)
Point & Figure Charting: Commodity and Stock Trading Techniques (Zieg)
Private Thoughts From a Trader's Diary (Pesavento & MacKay)
Profitable Patterns for Stock Trading (Pesavento)
RoadMap to the Markets (Busby)
Short-Term Trading with Price Patterns (Harris)
Single Stock Futures: The Complete Guide (Greenberg)
Stock Patterns for Day Trading (2 volumes) (Rudd)
Stock Trading Techniques Based on Price Patterns (Harris)
Technically Speaking (Wilkinson)
Technical Trading Systems for Commodities and Stocks (Patel)
The Amazing Life of Jesse Livermore: World's Greatest Stock Trader (Smitten)
The Handbook of Global Securities Operations (O'Connell & Steiniger)
The Opening Price Principle: The Best Kept Secret on Wall Street (Pesavento & MacKay)
The Professional Commodity Trader (Kroll)
The Taylor Trading Technique (Taylor)
*The Trading Rule That Can Make You Rich** (Dobson)
Top Traders Under Fire (Collins)
Trading Secrets of the Inner Circle (Goodwin)
Trading S&P Futures and Options (Lloyd)
Twelve Habitudes of Highly Successful Traders (Roosevelt)
Understanding Bollinger Bands (Dobson)
Understanding Eminis: Trading to Win (Williams)
Understanding Fibonacci Numbers (Dobson)
RSI: The Complete Guide (Hayden)
Viewpoints of a Commodity Trader (Longstreet)
Winning Edge 4 (Toghraie)
Winning Market Systems (Appel)

**Please contact Traders Press to receive our current catalog describing these and
many other books and gifts of interest to investors and traders.**
800-927-8222 ~ 864-298-0222 ~ fax 864-298-0221
http://www.traderspress.com ~ e-mail ~ customerservice@traderspress.com

•Technical Analysis • Options • Trading Psychology & Discipline •
• Spread Trading • Elliott Wave • W.D. Gann • Intraday Trading •
• Trading Strategies •

FREE TRADERS CATALOG

• Fibonacci • Floor Trading • Money Management • Cycles •
• Short Selling/Bear Markets • Stock Index Trading • Systems & Methods •
• Videos • Trading Courses • Volatility •
• Traders Gift Shop • Many Other Topics •

Our traders catalog lists and describes hundreds of books, tapes, courses and
gifts of interest to stock, options, and futures traders.
(Regular price $10)

Get a free copy by contacting

Traders Press, Inc.®
PO Box 6206
Greenville, SC 29606
800-927-8222
864-298-0222
Fax: 864-298-0221
E-Mail ~ customerservice@traderspress.com

A copy of our catalog in PDF format
may be downloaded at
http://www.traderspress.com

Trader's Gift Shop

Market-related art available through

Traders Press, Inc.®

**Varied selections of market-related
artwork and gifts are
available exclusively through
Traders Press, Inc.®
Currently available items are pictured on
our website at
http://www.traderspress.com and in our Traders Catalog,
which is available FREE upon request**

You can contact us at:
800-927-8222 ~ 864-298-0222
Fax 864-298-0221

**Traders Press, Inc.®
PO Box 6206
Greenville, SC 29606**